JAZZ SINGING

JAZZ SINGING

A Guide to
Pedagogy and Performance

Tish Oney

ROWMAN & LITTLEFIELD
Lanham • Boulder • New York • London

Published by Rowman & Littlefield
An imprint of The Rowman & Littlefield Publishing Group, Inc.
4501 Forbes Boulevard, Suite 200, Lanham, Maryland 20706
www.rowman.com

6 Tinworth Street, London SE11 5AL, United Kingdom

British Library Cataloguing in Publication Information Available

Library of Congress Cataloging-in-Publication Data

Names: Oney, Tish, author.
Title: Jazz singing : a guide to pedagogy and performance / Tish Oney.
Description: Lanham : Rowman & Littlefield, 2021. | Includes
  bibliographical references and index. | Summary: "Tish Oney presents a
  cutting-edge guide for those teaching and singing jazz, combining jazz
  voice stylization techniques and various improvisational approaches with
  classic voice pedagogy. Legendary jazz singers' approaches and
  techniques are described to illustrate the various approaches available
  to jazz singers" —Provided by publisher.
Identifiers: LCCN 2021041963 (print) | LCCN 2021041964 (ebook) | ISBN
  9781538128442 (cloth) | ISBN 9781538128459 (paperback) | ISBN 9781538128466
  (epub)
Subjects: LCSH: Jazz vocals—Instruction and study. | Singing—Instruction
  and study.
Classification: LCC MT868 .O64 2021 (print) | LCC MT868 (ebook) | DDC
  782.42165/143—dc23
LC record available at https://lccn.loc.gov/2021041963
LC ebook record available at https://lccn.loc.gov/2021041964

∞™ The paper used in this publication meets the minimum requirements of
American National Standard for Information Sciences—Permanence of Paper
for Printed Library Materials, ANSI/NISO Z39.48-1992.

This book is dedicated to Dave Riley.
Until we meet again,
may God hold you
in the hollow of His hand.

CONTENTS

LIST OF FIGURES

ACKNOWLEDGMENTS

This book could not have been written without the input of so many outstanding teachers, musicians, and others that have supported my efforts to sing, record, write, play, arrange, analyze, produce, document, and teach jazz. I thank Dave Riley for inviting me to sing in his wonderful ensemble at Ithaca College, for teaching me the basics of jazz ornamentation and style, and for nurturing my abilities to hear and sing at an extraordinary level. I thank Dana Wilson, Steve Brown, Patrice Pastore, Randie Blooding, Deborah Montgomery, Carol McAmis, Lawrence Doebler, Joe Riposo, Ron McCurdy, Roy McCurdy, Tierney Sutton, Paul Huybrechts, Gary Glaze, Bryan Simms, Magen Solomon, Lucinda Carver, Shelly Berg, Nick Strimple, John Chiodini, Patti Thompson, William McIver, Julianna Sabol, Marge Austin, Bill Palange, Susan Crocker, Carol Bryant, and the thousands of professional musicians with whom I have worked over the years. Every one of you has taught me something (or many things) that has helped to shape the pedagogy that I have enjoyed sharing with thousands of singers and instrumentalists. I gratefully present a portion of your legacy here.

I thank the jazz masters mentioned in this book and all the wonderful musicians whose outstanding performances and recordings have inspired me to achieve greater heights in my own creative life. Many thanks to my headshot photographer, J Kay Bradford for her consistently lovely work.

I thank my editors, Michael Tan and Natalie Mandziuk, and the staff at Rowman & Littlefield for seeing this book through to publication. Mostly, I thank my husband George and our family for their support, love, and faith, and I thank God for directing my path.

INTRODUCTION

No one learns to sing by reading a book. Scores of voice lessons; live performances; excellent recordings; courses in music theory, history, and literature; concerts by masters of the art form; and many other activities and experiences contribute to a singer's education and mastery of technique. However, much can yet be learned about singing and teaching jazz from those who have performed and taught jazz for many years. I attest to having learned volumes about voice pedagogy by reading books and observing wonderful teachers of singing. In offering this to my colleagues, I set out to write a book that had not yet been written. I aim to address many of the aspects of an art form I have spent my life exploring and sharing with others.

This is not a method but a composite of experiences, observations, facts, insights, and suggestions targeted toward four distinct audiences. First, voice pedagogues steeped in the classical tradition may learn how to modify their teaching to accommodate students interested in studying jazz voice. Second, students enrolled in jazz voice curricula will find herein a textbook that lays out a practical pedagogy for learning to sing and teach jazz. Third, working jazz singers will find a trove of factual knowledge about technique, science, and other tidbits to complement their training and experiences onstage and in the studio. Fourth, instrumentalists teaching jazz singers (we know you're out there) will find information throughout the book that will explain how to more effectively train the singers in their care.

Having earned a degree in biology before garnering two advanced degrees in music, I possessed an advantage over my musical counterparts regarding my scientific understanding of the human body. During my doctoral study, while teaching a graduate-level course for jazz voice majors, I was surprised to discover that none of my students possessed any knowledge about laryngeal anatomy or function. None had even read a chapter in a book discussing the anatomy and function of their primary instrument because there was no course available in their graduate or undergraduate curricula for such instruction. I knew I had to provide them with as thorough an understanding about the science of singing as I could in the short time we worked together in my one-semester course. I strove to expand their knowledge of additional areas in which they felt they had holes in their education—bandleading skills, basic arranging, practice regimens, strategies for building voice technique, breath management, multigenre singing, and developing musicianship. I have known since then that this book needed to be written.

For decades in classical voice and opera degree programs, a working knowledge of the vocal mechanism has been a standard component of most graduate-level curricula. This indispensable material has generally been presented within the context of a voice pedagogy class. My rush to fill this gap in my jazz students' education began with one central question: How can one hope to master an instrument about which the structure and function are not understood? I would argue that understanding structure and function of the vocal mechanism ought not be reserved solely for graduate students but shared with undergraduate voice, music theatre, commercial voice, and jazz voice majors as well. Furthermore, every professional singer ought to know how the vocal mechanism works to fully understand its capabilities and vulnerabilities.

When I learned to play the French horn as an elementary, junior high, high school, and college instrumentalist, I had been given instruction at various stages along the way regarding how my instrument functioned, the purpose of its shape and intricate construction, and the physics behind the arrangement of overtones that enabled the breath, when poured correctly through the instrument, to produce various pitches. In addition to this basic understanding, my teachers added instruction regarding how to care for my horn, how to correctly align my posture while playing, how to sound a note properly, how to modify my playing to reflect changing dynamics and articulation, and how to create an embouchure that minimized mouth and jaw tension. I would not have developed the technique required on that instrument to play it in Carnegie Hall at nineteen without having thoroughly understood the horn's mechanics, assembly, and function. My years of musicianship, technique, and literature study with the instrument were built on this secure foundation. I am most thankful that my brass teachers valued the importance of presenting to me the fundamental workings of the horn before I had developed unseemly and unhealthy habits trying to make a sound.

Most undergraduates do not go on to pursue graduate degrees in the same discipline. Because voice pedagogues teach students for only a short time, the most vital information must be passed along early. I suggest that the science of singing be presented to undergraduate singers regardless of genre. All can benefit from understanding how their voices work and how to care for them. If no other avenue exists, one can always incorporate this instruction into applied voice study or studio classes. This information enhances and expands students' musical education while furthering mastery of their primary instrument.

Only after I dug into the science of singing did my own vocal technique fall into place. I then understood how my instrument worked and what physical pitfalls I personally needed to avoid. I have, therefore, endeavored to provide a thorough presentation of the anatomy and function of the vocal mechanism, anatomy of the ear, and the physics of singing in the first chapter. Graduate students, undergraduates, teachers of singing, and working jazz singers will hopefully find this chapter to be a strong resource on which to build jazz voice technique and a firm pedagogical foundation.

This book does not present a singing method but, rather, provides guidance upon which healthy singing in the jazz style may be pursued, studied, and taught. It is important to mention that there is no single correct way to teach jazz singing or to pursue jazz voice performance. Many great jazz artists lacked elements of technique that masters of other singing styles would identify as indispensable for success. Jazz and commercial singers build audiences for their art doing all sorts of unconventional things in their quest for uniqueness. My aim is to help every singer reading this to find a healthy pathway to their authentic voice and to offer suggestions for developing musicianship, tonal colors, and expressive maturity that will provide a lifetime of enjoyment singing jazz.

I have elected to frequently point to masters of the art form to illustrate aspects of technique and various singing approaches that successful singers have used. These brief comparisons are intended to increase the reader's awareness about the variety of pathways jazz artists have taken to become unique, accomplished artists. The reader is invited to listen extensively to each artist described to absorb noteworthy elements of performance practice, technique, and artistry unique to that artist. There are obviously many other outstanding jazz singers besides those I included, but this can be a starting point. Let the jazz masters teach you.

I had originally hoped to include a chapter on jazz singer's diction. However, I feel that the subject requires more than a chapter, so I address that topic from a variety of angles, including articulation, enunciation, microphone technique, overtone tweaking, brightening and darkening vowels, a vowel chart, jaw alignment, and more. Because the International Phonetic Alphabet (IPA) lies beyond the scope of this text, I strongly urge jazz singers to pursue a singer's diction course in English (and any other language in which you sing) to fill the knowledge gap. Diction study is a separate discipline that deserves a full course and textbook of its own, so I make no attempt to educate readers about IPA here but rather use phonetic spellings that English-speaking readers will understand. Although I personally use IPA every day, I realize many jazz singers do not. English diction has many rules and exceptions, so the reader is encouraged to pursue diction study separately.

Respecting the outstanding scholarship that served as resources for this book, I heartily point the reader toward the bibliography. I selected sources that every singer and singing teacher would benefit from reading. Many of the topics I touched on were much more fully explored by the authors cited, so I encourage the reader to dive deeply into that list of treasures.

Truthfully, this book is simply a taste of my thirty-five years of professional jazz singing and teaching. Being a teacher attuned to the singer in front of me (and a singer attuned to the audience in front of me), much of what I share when I teach or sing cannot be sufficiently communicated through writing alone. I adore performing, teaching master classes and ensemble workshops, and presenting one-on-one lessons that are tailored specifically to a singer's needs. I welcome further opportunities to augment the suggestions herein with demonstrations of how these principles work in the voice studio and on the stage. It has been my pleasure to learn from so many truly outstanding thinkers, performers, and pedagogues during my dual career as a performer-teacher in jazz. I look forward to continuing the journey and helping others continue theirs!

I

THE SCIENCE OF SINGING

Science and art meet as equal partners when learning and teaching singing. Although some voice pedagogues shy away from sharing technical, scientific facts about the process of singing with their students, the majority of adult singers benefit from this factual information. A singer's entire body and brain become fully engaged during the act of singing, so knowledge about what actually happens in the body during this creative process is helpful for singers to understand. A working knowledge of one's own anatomy as well as the function of different components of the singing mechanism enlarge the expertise and awareness of every professional singer. This chapter discusses anatomy of the vocal mechanism, anatomy of the breathing mechanism, anatomy of the ear, and the physics involved in singing.

For whatever reason, in jazz voice curricula, or "vocal jazz" as it has been historically called in the ensemble context, educating singers about the vocal mechanism's anatomy and function has not been standard practice. One primary objective of this book is to change that. Like any other professional voice users, jazz singers require a thorough understanding of the organ upon which their livelihood rests. Those that understand at a young age (or as early in their careers as possible) how the voice actually functions and how to preserve it are more likely to continue singing healthfully in lifelong careers than those that lack such crucial understanding. Having served for more than two decades as a professor of jazz voice, classical voice, commercial voice, opera, and music theatre, I am a proponent of requiring *all* types of voice majors to complete a course (or a series of courses) that thoroughly explains the anatomy of the vocal mechanism, principles of voice hygiene, and principles of vocal technique. Without this necessary training, commercial voice use that is every bit as taxing on the voice as opera—sometimes more so, given the added laryngeal tension required to make stylistically authentic sounds in commercial music, jazz, and music theatre—can wreak havoc on voices.

Further, I have observed that many jazz voice and commercial voice courses and ensembles today are taught, directed, or coached by instrumentalists having no singing background rather than by professional singer pedagogues. Under these nonideal circumstances, singers are taught to "play" their instruments (as if they were flutes, trombones, or trumpets) and are held to instrumental-like standards of evaluation in juries, lessons, rehearsals, and ensembles. Attention to voice "technique" (proper warm-ups, instruction in healthy, correct phonation, and vocal care during rehearsals) is often ignored because the nonsinging teacher is unaware of how to present it. Voice instructors (or vocal ensemble directors) whose primary instrument lies outside the human body must work hard to build their own understanding of healthy voice pedagogy, or vocal damage may result for the singers following their lead. Furthermore, an instrumentalist untrained in voice pedagogy will not comprehend the complex anatomical workings involved in a singer's resonance, articulation, breath management, or the vitally necessary identification and release of physical tensions over a wide array of muscles involved in singing.

A singer's instrument consists of the entire body. By contrast, an instrumentalist learns to play an external machine to release a tone. Anyone teaching singing must be thoroughly equipped and qualified through education and training to specifically train the parts of the human body that comprise a singer's instrument, to hear both healthy and unhealthy voice production and to know how to address shortcomings in technique before harmful habits form. Given this reality, I urge music programs at all levels of education to require teachers of singing (either in ensembles or one on one, for all genres) to be well educated in voice pedagogy, voice hygiene, vocal anatomy and the physics of singing, and to be strong singers themselves. Overlooking this necessary training risks causing permanent damage to young voices, potential careers, and the physical, mental, and emotional health of the singers in one's care. An important objective for this book is to raise awareness among jazz voice educators about our shared responsibility of learning from experienced voice pedagogues before attempting to teach this art form in any capacity. Resolving this education shortfall will do a great deal to bridge the bias gap that exists between teachers of classical singing and teachers of jazz singing, as well as the equally disturbing bias gap between many jazz instrumentalists and jazz singers. Voice departments and jazz studies departments will both benefit from using this book to build a bridge of collaboration, trust, and common language among musicians with different backgrounds. Healthy singing is healthy singing, regardless of style, and our students deserve the best we can give them. We owe it to them to know all we can about the structure and function of the delicate organ we guide and coax toward technical greatness.

The seriousness of this educational difference between voice and instrumental faculty may be illustrated by some personal experiences of my own. I directed the music program at a university for which I also coordinated incoming student auditions. One auditionee showed signs of voice pathology during her audition (in her case, nodules), which my trained ears could clearly detect. The other teacher assigned to adjudicate auditions was a young theory teacher having no singing background. He turned to me after the audition and blindly said, "I like her. She passes the audition in my opinion and I would love to have her admitted." Then I confidentially shared with him that I heard evidence of a potential problem with this student's voice and that I recommended she be evaluated by an otolaryngologist before her admission could be considered. He looked puzzled at first (she sounded good to his ears) but then remembered that my experiences as a veteran professor of voice may well have prepared me to make finer distinctions about voice health than he was prepared to make. I went further to explain to this inexperienced teacher that, first, I felt it was my responsibility to encourage this student to seek a physician's examination for the student's own good. Second, I explained that we (our institution) could be held liable for any voice damage the student's doctor may find several months later if we failed to detect it at the audition. I explained that we should avoid, at all costs, admitting such students without addressing audible vocal problems. Doing so could cause her greater harm due to the demanding vocal requirements for a commercial voice major at our institution. Any pathology found after her admission could be assumed by the student and possibly her physician to have been caused by the teaching we were providing. I explained that I was not willing to accept liability for a singer whose vocal problem was apparent during her audition! My fellow adjudicator realized at that moment that he was not qualified to make judgments about the health of singers and agreed that henceforth I should make all such determinations regarding questionable vocal health of prospective voice majors (we were the only two full-time professors at the institution at the time, and therefore, we were the only two faculty adjudicating auditions).

I then gently explained to the auditionee that I heard something in the audition that made me strongly encourage an immediate physician's evaluation before any voice study was pursued. Alarmed, the student's parent promptly made an appointment with an ear, nose, and throat specialist. One month later I received a call from this parent thanking me profusely for caring enough to inform a prospective student that a doctor's evaluation might be needed before undertaking any professional voice training. Nodules had indeed been found on the student's vocal folds during the examination, and the student began treatment prescribed by her doctor. The student's parent said the singer's high school music teacher had never mentioned hearing any problems, nor had any other music professionals, teachers, or institutions for whom she had sung. I maintained that she could reaudition for our commercial voice program after treatment cleared up the problem, or when her physician felt formal voice study would be appropriate following recovery.

I urge my colleagues reading this book to take similar measures when they suspect vocal problems at any stage of a student's voice training. The sooner a problem is diagnosed, the sooner healing and recovery may commence. Unfortunately, as many voice pedagogues know, too often these invisible problems lay undiagnosed until they are devastating to a singer's health, career, or future voice use.

On a separate occasion, in discussion with a world-class instrumentalist (and music department chair at a major university), I received an invitation to teach voice at a jazz camp that he directed. He openly acknowledged that he and his instrumentalist peers could not do what I do, that they lacked the expertise to teach singers in any capacity, and that if his jazz camp were to add a singing component, he would definitely hire an experienced jazz voice pedagogue (like myself) to be in charge of it rather than simply accepting singers into the program to be taught by instrumentalists. This self-aware admission of my colleague's limited ability to teach singers felt refreshing in light of the current trend at so many other institutions where singers are treated like instrumentalists, especially in jazz combos and other ensembles. Fortunately, he was wisely unwilling to entrust young singers' voices to teachers who play instruments but do not sing professionally or teach singing. My hope is that this book will help to fill in some educational gaps for instrumentalists teaching singers, and that voice teachers and jazz singers alike will appreciate a guide to help them rise to the next level of performance and pedagogy. The first step is to fully understand the voice from a structural and functional perspective.

ANATOMY OF THE LARYNX

Human laryngeal anatomy consists of bone, cartilage, muscle, nerves, and a circulating supply of blood common to all the body's organs. The larynx dangles from the **hyoid bone**, which maintains its position in the neck but floats vertically during swallowing. The hyoid bone is shaped like a horseshoe with its opening to the back. A curtain of muscle connects the hyoid bone to the larynx below. The bone provides a stable foundation for the larynx while simultaneously allowing it to move freely. The hyoid bone also provides a connection point for the tongue root and jaw muscles. The **larynx** (commonly referred to as the "voice box") functions as a valve between the trachea and the tongue. This valve not only regulates the inflow and outflow of oxygen to the lungs but also provides the human with an organ of communication through the process of phonation that its exquisite anatomy facilitates.

Cartilages of the Larynx

The human larynx includes four major cartilages: the epiglottis, the thyroid cartilage, two arytenoid cartilages (often grouped in discussions of laryngeal cartilages as if they were one), and the cricoid cartilage. The leaf-shaped **epiglottis** functions as a lid of flesh that covers the opening of the trachea (see figure 1.1). It attaches to the front (anterior) end of the thyroid cartilage. When breathing, the epiglottis is oriented upright in a vertical position to allow free movement of air down through the trachea, into the two branches called "bronchi" (into which the trachea divides), and finally into the lungs. When swallowing, the epiglottis closes (moving ninety degrees to a flat, horizontal position) and seals the lid of the trachea to prevent food or liquid from spilling into the trachea. When any substances (including saliva) enter the trachea, a coughing or choking reflex is triggered. During a cough, the vocal folds violently clap together, concomitant with a forceful burst of air from the lungs in a concerted effort to clear the airway. This violent clapping, when habitual or persistent during illness, may cause damage to the fragile vocal folds. Conscientious

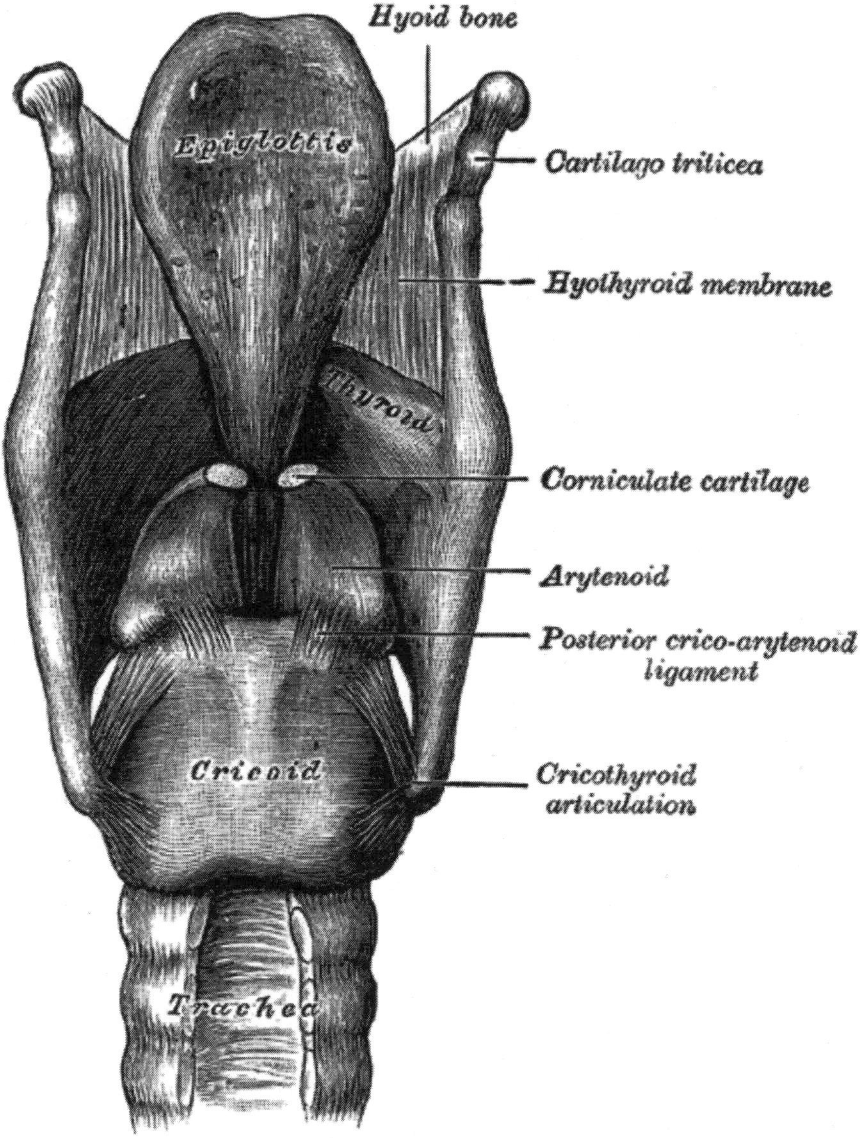

Figure 1.1. Larynx, Posterior View. Gray's Anatomy (public domain, 1918). See https://fpnotebook.com/_media/entLarynxPosteriorGrayBB952.gif

singers must endeavor to cough gently and only when absolutely necessary and not in a long series of throat-battering bursts.

Oriented below the epiglottis, the **thyroid cartilage** is shaped like a
shield with a point in the front of the neck, which we know as the Adam's
apple. It possesses two plates of cartilage joined at the anterior end, which
are angled to form a V-shape. As shown in figure 1.2, the thyroid cartilage sits atop the cricoid cartilage. The thyroid cartilage wraps around the
larynx and has upper (superior) and lower (inferior) horns at the posterior
end of the larynx. The thyroid cartilage attaches loosely to the hyoid bone
at the upper horns and to the cricoid cartilage at the lower horns via the
synovial joint. Here at the joint the thyroid cartilage can rock up and down
and slide forward and back. The Adam's apple tends to be larger and
more pronounced in men than in women, although this is not always the
case. The development of the Adam's apple in a young male voice often
occurs concurrently with the voice change appearing between puberty
and adolescence, and this rapid growth period often results in the dreaded
cracking that those voices often must endure until the growth spurt has
stabilized.

The lowest cartilage of the larynx, the **cricoid cartilage**, is shaped like
a signet ring with the broad portion in the back and a narrowing in the
front. The cricoid is situated just below the Adam's apple. This cartilage
is fixed on the topmost rings of the trachea, attaching to the first tracheal
cartilage. The thyroid and cricoid cartilages are loosely oriented together
to allow a rocking motion and a forward and back sliding action by one
or both at a time. This slight rocking or leaning forward of the larynx is
central to the production of straight-tone singing that jazz and commercial
singing require. Students need to master the delicate application of the vibratoless tone to authentically perform commercial styles including country, jazz, pop, rock, and music theatre. A healthy pedagogy addressing this
rocking motion between the cricoid and thyroid cartilages will provide
the commercial singer with an important tool for sounding authentic in a
multitude of styles.

The **arytenoid cartilages** are tiny pyramid-shaped cartilages (with the
apex of the pyramids oriented at the top) that are each located at the back
(posterior end) of the vocal folds (previously called vocal "cords"). During phonation, the arytenoid cartilages come together (adduct), causing
the vocal folds themselves to adduct. This adduction coupled with the
upward movement of air from the lungs facilitates the phenomenon of
phonation. The arytenoids attach to the synovial joint and can slide side to
side and pivot. Tiny muscles called **interarytenoids** are located between

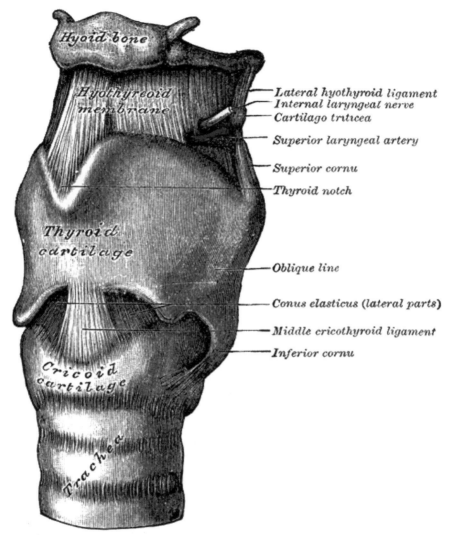

Figure 1.2. Larynx, Anterior View. Gray's Anatomy (public domain, 1918).
See https://fpnotebook.com/_media/entLarynxAnteriorGrayBB951.gif

the arytenoid cartilages and change the thickness and length of the vocal folds. These are partially responsible for closing the glottis during phonation. The **lateral crico-arytenoids** are muscles that also partially close the glottis; together, these two sets of intrinsic muscles completely close the vocal folds. **Posterior crico-arytenoids** contract to open the glottis wide, serving as abductors.

Vocal Folds

Healthy **vocal folds** are white bands of firm tissue that are stretched from the front of the larynx to the back (anterior to posterior) just above the trachea (see figure 1.3). When not phonating, the folds assume an open V-shape during which the arytenoid cartilages are fully separated (abducted), keeping the airway open and the folds at rest. In a healthy singer, when the arytenoid cartilages adduct, the folds experience complete closure over their total length, having no "chinks" or areas leaking air. Achieving a complete seal between the vocal folds without excess tension is a primary objective of correct vocal technique. The open space between the vocal folds (when one is inhaling, for instance) is known as the "glottis." The glottis becomes narrow during phonation when folds are adducted and is wide during inhalation when folds are abducted.

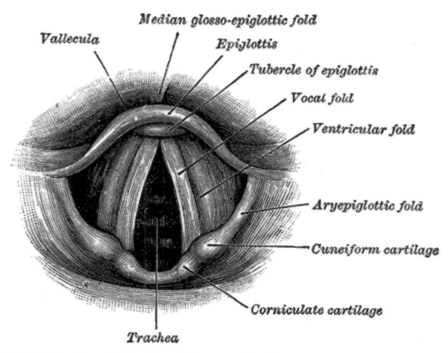

Figure 1.3.   Vocal Folds. Gray's Anatomy (public domain, 1918). See https://fpnotebook.com/_media/entLarynxSuperiorVocalCordsGrayBB956.gif

Tissues of the Larynx

The larynx is a complex organ comprised of various types of tissue. The skeletal system contributes only one bone to the larynx: the hyoid bone, which is oriented in the neck at the base of the tongue, above the laryngeal cartilages. The **mucosa** represents five layers of muscle, cartilage, and other tissue providing the larynx with a smooth surface for optimal functioning.

Proper hydration (drinking water and sometimes inhaling steam) helps to ensure that the mucosa remains moist and healthy. When the mucosa becomes dry, the body will respond by secreting the only fluid it can: mucus—a thick, slimy, stringy secretion that is a poor substitute for water. Because excess mucus on the vocal folds causes gurgling and vocal noise and inhibits clear singing, one is wise to avoid its unnecessary production by drinking plenty of filtered water (sixty-four ounces per day), especially within two days of a performance, rehearsal, or lesson, and avoiding drinks that dry the tissues (alcohol, sodas, and caffeinated beverages). When one chooses to indulge in any of these, it is wise to remember to replenish the body's hydration by adding eight ounces of water above the daily recommended sixty-four, per dehydrating beverage consumed. Singers should never consume alcohol during a performance or rehearsal because it compromises performance in at least two ways: by severely drying the tissues with which it comes into contact and by potentially inhibiting one's mental clarity.

Muscles of the Larynx

Intrinsic muscles refer to muscles inside the larynx that assist with proper phonation. **Extrinsic muscles** are muscles outside the larynx that impact phonation. Extrinsic muscles form a basket of support around and beneath the larynx. When considering a muscle's name, the first term refers to the point of origin and the second term (after the hyphen) refers to the point of insertion. The scientific name for the vocal folds is **thyro-arytenoids** because they originate at the thyroid cartilage anteriorly and insert at the arytenoid cartilages posteriorly. The **vocalis muscle (internal thyro-arytenoid)** functions as the primary flexor of the folds. When the vocalis is shortened, the folds thicken and the edges become rounded. When it lengthens, the folds stretch and become thinner. The vocalis muscle is covered by a mucous membrane that provides a smooth, moist surface for agile, healthy singing.

Intrinsic Muscles

Muscles inside the larynx include **crico-thyroids** (originating at the cricoid cartilage and inserting at the thyroid cartilage), which elongate the folds and tilt the thyroid cartilage forward. These muscle tensors are partly responsible for determining pitch. As the folds are stretched further through their action, the folds become thinner and their edges sharpen, causing the pitch frequency to increase. Both the vocalis and crico-thyroid muscles work together to refine the process of tuning the pitch. The vocalis adjusts the fine-tuning and the crico-thyroids regulate larger-scale register shifts and gross pitch movements. The fan-shaped, **posterior crico-arytenoid** muscle functions as the sole abductor (opener) of the vocal folds. It originates at the cricoid cartilage and inserts at the arytenoid cartilages. The **lateral crico-arytenoid** muscle adducts the folds to counteract the action of the posterior crico-arytenoid muscle. It provides medial compression of the folds. The **interarytenoids** form an *x* inside the larynx and pull the edges of the arytenoid cartilages together to maximize closure of the vocal folds. Each of these intrinsic muscles plays a necessary part in providing the voice with a healthy, flexible, functional mechanism.

Extrinsic Muscles

Extrinsic muscles form a basket of support around and beneath the larynx. These include **suprahyoid muscles** (located above the larynx) and **infrahyoid muscles** (below the larynx). The sizable **sterno-cleidomastoid** muscles are located on either side of the neck and represent an important pair of muscles that support the head, facilitating its free movement.

TEACHER TIP

When a singer uses what is described by voice pedagogues and physicians as a "pressed" tone, one or more intrinsic muscles may be pulling the folds too tightly together, resulting in undue tension. This could potentially cause a serious problem for the voice. Conversely, sometimes the closure of the folds is incomplete and strengthening of the adductors is required. If either phenomenon is suspected, a singer should be referred to a laryngologist who may refer the singer to a speech-language pathologist or voice therapist for exercises to resolve the situation. Often, moving the air more generously through the singer's breathing system resolves the slightly pressed tone.

ANATOMY OF THE BREATHING MECHANISM

The breathing mechanism involves sets of muscles that regulate the inspiratory phase of air exchange and sets of muscles that regulate the expiratory phase. These muscle groups are completely separate from each other, although they work in close proximity to one another. Understanding the actual muscular movements, direction of movements, function of these muscles, and their location in the body all help the singer and voice pedagogue grow a more complete understanding of how to coax the singing instrument toward its finest work.

Muscles of Inhalation

The muscles involved in inhalation include the **diaphragm** and the **external intercostal muscles**. The double-domed diaphragm (see figure 1.4) bisects the singer's body and is located as a separator between the thoracic cavity and the abdominal cavity. As air pressure within the lungs decreases at the start of inhalation, the diaphragm flexes downward toward the floor, creating a vacuum in the lungs, which draws air into the thoracic cavity. The external intercostals partner with the diaphragm to expand the thoracic cavity by lifting upward and outward in a bucket-handle motion, creating a widening of the rib cage and a spreading of the distance between the ribs. This action allows the alveoli, or air sacs inside the lungs, to more fully receive the oxygen they need to supply the blood and oxygenate the body's cells through the cooperation of the pulmonary and circulatory systems. A singer's breath thereby maximizes a body's oxygenation levels, consistently filling the lungs to a greater capacity than a nonsinger generally does.

Muscles of Exhalation

Conversely, the muscles responsible for the process of exhalation include the **abdominal muscles** (abs) and the **internal intercostal muscles** (see figure 1.5). The abs slowly move inward toward the spine during exhalation and the internal intercostals move slightly downward and inward (the bucket handle moves down). There are three main types of abdominal muscles. The **rectus abdominis** is located in a vertical orientation. It is a paired muscle running vertically along the midline of the trunk and constitutes the "six-pack" of muscles that can be seen in athletes on the outermost surface of the musculature just beneath the skin. The **transverse**

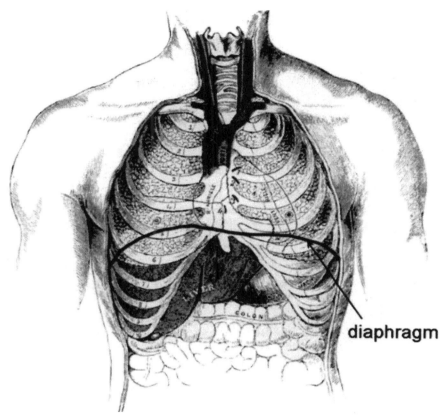

diaphragm

Figure 1.4.   Location of the Diaphragm. Courtesy of Scott McCoy. Used by Permission.

abdominis runs horizontally in the innermost layer of abdominals, just beneath the obliques. The **obliques** are two muscles that orient diagonally across the abdominal wall and support the flanks and sides of the body (see figure 1.6). When singing or exhalation begins, these abdominal muscles support the inward movement of the epigastrium (outer surface of the abdominal region that one can touch from outside the body) toward the spine. This gradual inward motion counters the sense of resistance, or **appoggio**, that Italian masters taught singers. Appoggio refers to a leaning of the air from inside the lungs on the chest wall, which maintains a broad stretch through the thoracic cavity even during the controlled exhalation of singing a long phrase. To maintain a sense of resistance or appoggio, the singer must cultivate "singing on the gesture of inhalation," which

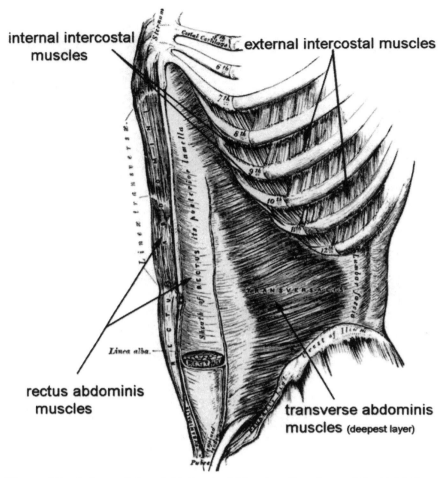

internal intercostal muscles

external intercostal muscles

rectus abdominis muscles

transverse abdominis muscles (deepest layer)

Figure 1.5. Intercostal and Abdominal Muscles. Courtesy of Scott McCoy. Used by Permission.

translates into a long, well-controlled struggle between inhalation and exhalation muscles. When singers can phonate for several seconds without suffering the collapse of the rib cage, they have learned to sing on the gesture of inhalation, as if they were still inhaling. This technique requires a good deal of practice with a seasoned voice instructor to make sure the singer is not holding the breath, blowing air out with the tone, creating tension in the breathing mechanism, or causing undue pressure upon the vocal folds. Singers are encouraged to seek teachers who understand the

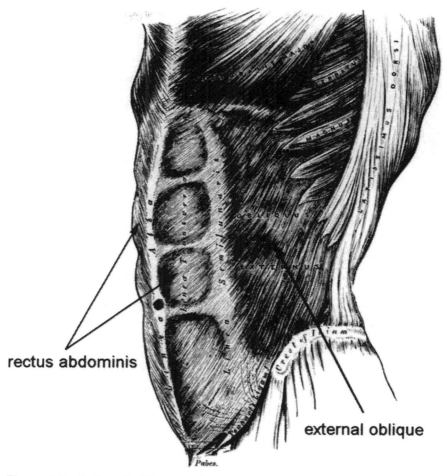

Figure 1.6. External oblique and rectus abdominis muscles. Courtesy of Scott McCoy. Used by Permission.

physics and function of the body's organs to gain the greatest mastery of these concepts and to build a foundation of excellent breathing technique.

ANATOMY OF THE EAR AND HEARING PROTECTION

Equally important as understanding the anatomy of the vocal mechanism and the anatomy of the breathing mechanism, understanding the anatomy and function of the human ear is an indispensable, if overlooked, aspect of every well-equipped singer's working knowledge.

On a general level, the human ear consists of three distinct regions: the outer ear, the middle ear, and the inner ear, as shown in figure 1.7. The outer ear consists of the **pinna**, a fleshy appendage attached to the head at the top of the ear, visible from the outside and the **auricular lobule** (earlobe) at the bottom of the external appendage. The ear canal (also called the **external auditory canal**) is a part of the outer ear where wax buildup can occur. This canal connects the pinna to the middle ear where the anatomy becomes more intricate and vulnerable to damage. The external auditory canal meets a fragile veil at the **tympanic membrane** (eardrum), which acts as a rather weak boundary between the outer and the middle ear. This membrane serves as a receiver of sonic vibrations from outside the body. The middle ear consists of the space between the tympanic membrane and the **oval window**. Inside the middle ear lie the eardrum and three tiny bones: the **malleus** (known in layman's terms as the "hammer"), the **incus** ("anvil"), and **stapes** ("stirrup"). When the eardrum vibrates, these three bones pass the vibrations along one to the next until the stapes passes the message to the oval window at the border of the inner ear. Fluid inside the snail-shell-shaped **cochlea** (inside the inner ear) is disturbed, continuing the vibrations toward tiny hairs whose sensors transmit messages to the **auditory nerve**. These are translated into our

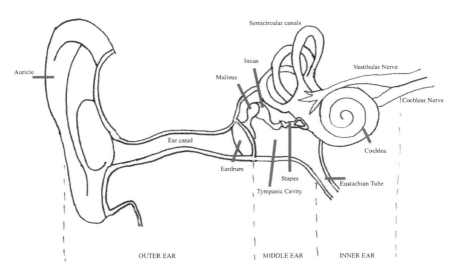

Figure 1.7.   Anatomy of the Ear. Courtesy of Author

perception of sound in the brain. The **vestibular nerve** and the **cochlear nerve** innervate the inner ear mechanism to pass along information to the brain. Three **semicircular canals**, located behind and slightly above the cochlea as part of the same tissue, aid with the body's balance, sending messages to the brain via the vestibular nerve.

The external auditory canal becomes the **tympanic cavity** just beyond the tympanic membrane (in the middle ear). The canal continues into the inner ear, extending downward, becoming the **Eustachian tube**. This wide tube extends toward the back of the throat, opens to the nasopharynx, and remains vulnerable to infection when upper respiratory or throat infections rage.

The tiny hair cells inside the inner ear and tympanic membrane represent some of the most vulnerable parts of the human body. When these delicate structures sustain damage (through age, medication, injury, or noise), little can be done to cure the hearing loss that may result. It therefore behooves each singer to take their hearing seriously and adopt habits that protect these vulnerable organs.

Hearing Loss: The Musician's Bane

Singers who use electronic amplification (microphones) are particularly susceptible to damage of the ultrasensitive ears on which they depend as much for successful singing as on their larynges. Therefore, jazz and commercial singers, even more than opera and classical singers, must be thoroughly informed about the fragility of their delicate hearing organs, particularly because once hearing is lost, it is usually and permanently gone. Although hearing aids may assist those whose hearing has suffered over the years, there is no cure for hearing loss, and many times it is an irreversible, slippery slope one must continue down once the journey has begun. Worse yet, otolaryngologists report that hearing loss may accelerate in many people after it begins. Occupational hearing loss remains the single largest physical risk faced by the professional musician. Orchestral musicians, big band musicians, singers in large choirs, musicians in rock, heavy metal, or pop bands, and all musicians who are routinely exposed to loud music run the risk of losing the most important of the five senses on which their livelihood rests.

Singers take heed: prevention is by far the best medicine to preserve hearing. No matter how phenomenal a vocal instrument may be, if a singer's hearing is damaged, (s)he will most likely not be able to maintain a professional singing career. Specific frequencies that healthy ears can discern are lost in varying degrees by those experiencing hearing loss, making intonation a greater and greater challenge. Any singer with slight or moderate hearing loss has experienced the frustrations of not hearing stage instructions from conductors, fellow band members, stage managers, or technical directors. Even subtle changes in hearing can result in a singer not receiving a callback for a return engagement or in a singer having an embarrassing moment in front of an audience. Also, the perception of one's own singing is skewed when specific frequencies begin to decline. Sopranos often lose the frequencies they most need to stay in perfect tune. Higher frequency hearing, sabotaged by amplified feedback accidents during sound checks and problematic stage performances, is necessary for any treble singer's good intonation. On the lower end of the sound spectrum, bass frequencies may be lost when electric bassists, deejays, or technical directors allow the extreme "chest-vibrating bass" to be turned up beyond decibel levels that are universally safe. Singers, instrumentalists, and music patrons are strongly encouraged to wear hearing protection when around concert stages where decibel levels get out of control.

Furthermore, singers are strongly encouraged to visit an audiologist at various times during their lives to better understand their unique hearing spectrum and to obtain a baseline test early in their careers. The audiologist can help a singer manage any lost frequencies within the hearing spectrum, obtain fitted ear protection designed especially for musicians, and gain helpful strategies for protecting the hearing that remains. A good audiologist can come alongside a hearing-impaired singer and offer assistance while suggesting ways to protect the singer from further hearing damage.

When hearing loss is underway, it is impossible to reverse and often accelerates as one ages. Wearing musician-grade earplugs tailor-made to fit one's external auditory canals is highly recommended for every musician who is subjected to loud rehearsals and performances. These include orchestral musicians, big band musicians, rock musicians, singers in large choirs, and particularly singers who use microphones, PA systems, and onstage or in-ear monitors. Musicians' ear protection (available from an audiologist) filters out the loudest decibels and allows the wearer to still hear spoken words, music, and other sounds at a lower volume.

Protecting one's hearing is a necessary but too often ignored part of the professional musician's lifestyle. Music faculty are wise to take precautions against subjecting themselves and students to decibel levels that exceed safety guidelines whenever they rehearse or perform. Phone apps are available that measure decibels in the room and show warnings when safe decibel levels are exceeded.

Sound Checks and Tech Rehearsals

Singers are wise to always wear musician's earplugs to sound checks and tech rehearsals when electronic feedback (high-pitched, loud, piercing power surges) is most common and likely. Hopefully by the time the performance arrives, safe volume levels for amplified instruments and microphones have been firmly set, but that is not always the case. Knowing how to talk frankly and honestly about tech needs with those operating the mixing board and mic levels (even establishing signals to use during a performance) is an absolute must. Singers need never be afraid to verbalize what they need with tech directors before and during performances. Well-prepared singers set levels during the sound check and communicate with the tech director before the performance to establish discreet signals that will be used to communicate sound needs during the performance. Tech riders, which describe an artist's stage plot and equipment needs in writing weeks or months ahead of a concert, are highly recommended whenever possible. Tech directors are there to help musicians sound their best and not to damage their ears.

Although hearing aids have come a long way in recent years, they are still not ideal for instrumentalists or singers on a practical basis. Some aids cause high pitched ringing and audible interference. Others may slightly change the pitch singers hear in their inner ear, so singing with hearing aids is not recommended. **Tinnitus** (perpetual ringing in the ears) is a condition that can be caused by hearing damage or as side effects of certain medications. Sound accidents sometimes happen in public concert settings (through no fault or negligence of the musicians on the stage), and these stage occurrences unfortunately may hurt every unprotected ear in the room. College bandleaders and music faculty are wise to educate all music students about the importance of hearing protection and to encourage musicians to take active precautions starting as early as possible.

THE PHYSICS OF SINGING

In my thirty-five years of singing professionally I can honestly say that the more I learned about the science behind singing, the better I sang. After several years of applied voice lessons, I augmented the effectiveness of that training by adding to my own knowledge of voice science. As my love for teaching grew, I vowed that I would never withhold knowledge from my students but would, instead, share all I knew, especially in regard to the anatomy of the singing voice and the science of phonation. Strategically timing that knowledge-sharing is necessary, of course, to avoid information overload and filling up lesson time with more material than can be assimilated in one session.

A few terms from high school physics would be helpful to refresh. **Frequency** refers to pitch. Raising the frequency yields a higher perceived pitch. The upper notes on a piano illustrate this best; the further one moves to the right of center on the keyboard, the higher the pitches sound. Each key played represents the fundamental frequency of that particular note. A440 refers to the A played on the piano just below middle C. The number 440 refers to the frequency of that pitch in Hertz (units of measuring frequency). This means that the full sine wave of oscillating sound vibration occurs 440 times per second when that specific pitch is sung or played by any instrument. Octaves are related to the fundamental frequency by doubling when moving to an octave higher and by halving in the case of moving down an octave. The fundamental frequency of the first A above middle A is 880 (440 × 2), whereas the fundamental frequency of the bottom-space A on the bass clef is 220 (440/2) and so on. Understanding this principle of doubling the frequency for ascending octaves helps the singer better understand how to sing precisely in tune. Just a few "cents" low or high (437 or 443 instead of 440) can cause a pitch to sound flat or sharp, especially through a microphone. For this reason, jazz singers need to be reminded to sing precisely in the center of the pitch. If vibrato is employed, it must not obscure the pitch.

Amplitude refers to volume. When the volume knob is turned up on a car radio or mixing board, the increase of amplitude (or height above and below neutral in the sound wave's sinuous shape) causes increased loudness. When a singer performs a crescendo, the amplitude of the wave begins at a lower height on the wave's graph (quieter) than at the end of the crescendo where the amplitude is at its full height (louder). A trained singer's technique should be able to adjust frequency and amplitude (pitch and volume) seamlessly and smoothly, regardless of genre or style. Any intentional "breaks," bumps, or yodels can be learned as may be stylistically appropriate but should not characterize a singer's baseline, neutral voice. Singers should learn, through microphone technique, how to modify the volume of their voices without involving a volume knob on a mixing board. This mindful approach to volume is apparent in all great jazz singers' voices and influences phrase shaping, breath management, and nuance.

The Myoelastic-Aerodynamic Theory of Phonation

For several decades, voice pedagogues and scientists have been intrigued by the action of the singing voice. Only in the twentieth century did technology finally exist to assist scientists in explaining the physics involved in singing. In the late 1950s Van den Berg proposed the Myoelastic-Aerodynamic Theory of Phonation (MEAD), which offered an early explanation that has since been refined and further explained.

The production of sound through the vocal folds begins with inhalation. Inhalation is initiated when the vocal folds abduct (separate), the diaphragm contracts downward, and the external intercostal muscles contract, lifting and opening the rib cage. The drop of the diaphragm creates a vacuum in the thoracic cavity. The lungs experience this vacuum by filling with air as the higher air pressure outside the body equalizes the lower pressure inside. Antagonism between the inspiratory muscles and the expiratory muscles is created.

MEAD proposed the following phenomenon: Vocal folds adduct (come together) and air pressure builds beneath them, causing them to burst open. The movement of air between the folds causes a decrease in pressure beneath the folds according to the Bernoulli effect (a principle of physics by which air in motion is less dense, causing "lift" as under an airplane's wings). This decrease in pressure creates a vacuum that sucks the vocal folds together, essentially "chopping" the airstream. This chop produces a sound wave. Almost instantaneously after the folds adduct, the pressure beneath increases again, bursting them open and starting a new cycle. The entire cycle is repeated hundreds or thousands of times per second at the rate of the fundamental frequency (if A440 is sung, the entire cycle is repeated 440 times for each second that A is sung).

Beyond the MEAD Theory

This theory represented a major step forward in our understanding of the physics of singing. Since MEAD was first proposed, however, measurements of subglottal pressure inside the human body during phonation have shown that at low fundamental frequencies, a maximum pressure value occurs at the onset of phonation followed by dampened oscillations, unlike what was proposed in the initial theory. These oscillations can be thought of as transient acoustic resonance phenomena that occur during singing in both the subglottal region (which I call "tracheal resonance") and the vocal tract (Svec, Schutte, Chen, and Titze, 2021). Further study revealed that a mucosal wave—the sinuous movement of the outer layer of the vocal fold mucosa over an inner layer of the folds—plays a primary role in phonation rather than a chopping action of glottal closures as were previously thought. As scientists continue to study the process of singing, further discoveries will surely add to our current understanding of singing science.

According to voice pedagogue Dr. Paul Huybrechts, singers should focus on the fact that air comes *through* the folds, and not *to* the folds. Knowing a bit about mucosal waves and the gentle flexion of muscles that produces a tone may help singers to cease phonating with undue pressure or force formerly assumed to be necessary to sing well. With this added knowledge, singers become free to experience the pleasurable sensations of singing without added tension or pressed phonation, opening themselves to a world of new color choices, healthy sensations, and sonic textures.

Jazz singers are encouraged to become equipped with expertise about their bodies' anatomy and function so they can use the vocal organ in a healthy manner that works toward its fullest potential. Being professional voice users with distinctive needs and vulnerabilities, jazz singers owe it to themselves to become masters of this material, as do their counterparts in every style of singing. As singers' knowledge and mastery of the science of singing expand, they become better equipped to fill in educational gaps and solve some of their own problems. This greater scientific awareness sets the stage for a healthy, efficient technical education and a lifetime of musical discovery and enjoyment.

2

VOCAL HEALTH AND HYGIENE

Paying attention to vocal health and hygiene is integral to the longevity of every jazz singer's career. Certain habits must be nurtured to grow and sustain a healthy vocal instrument for decades-long enjoyment of singing. Adequate hydration, nutrition, and sleep remain paramount priorities for every professional singer. Developing a daily vocal workout routine will keep the voice healthy, strong, and primed for impending vocal use. Avoiding vocal abuse at all costs is an area particularly important for the preservation of the singing voice.

HABITS TO CULTIVATE FOR A HEALTHY VOICE

Best practices of vocal health and hygiene begin with focusing attention on a singer's overall physical health. The crucial importance of the entire body's health cannot be overstated. Because the human voice represents an instrument in itself, the container in which it is permanently housed must be protected from harm, preserved from excess strain, and cared for when ill. Singers who are injured in other areas of their body or who are experiencing illness, chronic disease, or pain have a difficult time singing well, even if the voice itself is healthy and in good shape. This fact presents another difference between singers and instrumentalists. A violinist may carry a Stradivarius violin in a broken, beaten up case and still play beautifully—the condition of the case does not necessarily affect the condition of the instrument (although if one plays a Stradivarius, one is wise to obtain a suitable case in which to protect this priceless violin). But in the case of the singer, a painful broken limb, a headache, an earache, a toothache, a bad mood, hormonal fluctuations, or myriad other types of physical changes or minor ailments can greatly affect one's ability to deliver a polished performance. Herein lie two responsibilities for each professional singer. Protecting and maintaining one's health and well-being must rise to a high priority if one is to be serious about pursuing singing as a career. Furthermore, singers must train themselves to sing well despite many physical, emotional, and environmental fluctuations or nonideal circumstances that arise every day. Lifelong professional singers know there is always something that can distract. Superior vocal technique and mental toughness (see chapter 13) are necessary for every singer to grant mental focus and power to the music at hand rather than to one's personal or circumstantial challenges.

The Athleticism of Singing

Singers have often been described as athletes because more muscles throughout the body are engaged during the process of singing than when running, swimming, mountain climbing, or playing aerobic sports. Like any athlete, the singer must remember that to excel requires a diligent commitment to training, workouts, rest, nutrition, self-care, discipline, concentration, and study. Like pursuing professional athletics, becoming a professional singer is akin to accepting the disciplined life of a nun or priest. Certain activities that are potentially harmful to one's health or one's voice must be consistently avoided to protect the delicate instrument that resides within the singer's body.

Good habits that keep the singing instrument healthy, regardless of the genres one sings, must be understood and maintained for optimal vocal health. A heightened awareness of one's day-to-day habits (both healthy and unhealthy) greatly benefits the professional voice user. Aspiring professional singers will maximize their voice's potential by adopting healthy habits at a young age.

Physical Exercise

Regular physical exercise is no longer a mere suggestion for the professional singer. For the instrument to function properly and for the singer to be poised for the demands a professional career requires, the entire body needs routine physical conditioning. Although many obese singers can sing beautifully, it is well-known that maintaining a healthy body weight enhances a singer's life in several ways. Formerly overweight opera stars have confessed that their energy levels and stamina for long rehearsals and performances improved after they attained a healthier body weight. Their confidence both on and off the stage also increased as a result of this positive life change. Breath management improved because the aerobic conditioning of the heart and lungs became healthier. Their stagecraft and deportment developed more strength, balance, grace, and agility. Singers are encouraged to pursue a healthy lifestyle to build strong, durable bodies that will help them deliver strong performances.

Physical exercise is also recommended for singers who maintain a healthy weight despite not exercising. Aerobic exercise, flexibility training, and strength training each week will do wonders for adding energy to one's daily round, not to mention improving mental clarity and improved emotional health, and immunity. Exercise lowers blood pressure and pulse while strengthening the heart and lungs. As always, singers are advised to check with their physician about which exercise programs are appropriate to their specific needs and interests. Many singers engage in walking, jogging, cycling, swimming (but watch out for swimmer's ear), yoga, Pilates, tennis, weight training (but be careful about power lifting, which may put pressure on the vocal folds), and hiking. Incorporating some kind of physical movement work is generally vital to the optimal performance of the voice.

Hydration

Hydration is an area of vocal hygiene that singers often forget to address. By the time thirst is detected in the mouth, the vocal instrument has likely been dehydrated for some time. Sipping water every few minutes during a practice session or rehearsal is standard procedure for most professional singers. Mindfully hydrating the body for a full seventy-two hours before a performance (particularly when singing in a dry environment like an outdoor venue or in an air-conditioned space) greatly improves one's chances of maintaining good hydration during the rehearsal, sound check, and performance.

Having a room-temperature bottle of water at my fingertips during practice and rehearsals is a necessary part of my performance routine, and whenever I travel in the car, I bring filtered water. Essentially, water is in my bag whenever I go anywhere so that I can sip every few minutes, and I instruct my students to do the same. During concerts I also make sure there is adequate water offstage or even onstage (for extended performance sets). Audiences have become accustomed to seeing jazz singers drink water between songs or at discreet places during a performance. Given the extreme drying action of fans, air conditioners, and forced-air heating units used in concert halls, universities, schools, auditoriums, and theaters, planning ahead to keep the voice hydrated before, during, and after performances in these venues remains a high priority for the professional singer.

When possible, singers must try to avoid taking medications that dry the larynx and throat tissues near performance time. This pertains to many over-the-counter cold and allergy remedies that can make a singer's tone sound brittle and prone to cracking. The folds and their surrounding tissues function maximally when they are properly hydrated, so antihistamines and other drying medications should be used sparingly whenever possible.

The temperature of a singer's drinking water should be neutral (room temperature) during singing activities to keep the voice warm. Ice-cold water slows circulation in all the tissues it touches, so if a voice has recently completed a "warm-up," only warm or room-temperature water should touch the delicate swallowing tissues. Nothing kills the effects of a freshly warmed voice faster than a shot of cold water. Warm water can be used offstage during the winter season to help urge the voice toward a healthy, warm, hydrated condition.

Nutrition

Eating healthfully represents yet another area of discipline in the serious singer's toolbox. Because no two singers are alike, singers' diet should be ideally tailored to their specific needs. Feeding one's body fuel via a balanced diet of protein, carbohydrates, vegetables, fruits, healthy fats, vitamins, minerals, and pure filtered water, while limiting empty-calorie foods, including fast food, sugary foods and fatty, high-cholesterol foods, becomes an increasingly vital necessity as a singer advances in age. Creating the requisite nutritional discipline early in one's career helps a singer maintain physical health through all sorts of challenging times.

Avoiding Vocal Abuse

Conscientious singers must increase their awareness of their voice use and become keen toward listening to their body's feedback. Vocal abuse takes many forms including yelling, screaming, talking over the din of a loud room (simply having a conversation at a cocktail party or inside a busy restaurant), singing while sick, habitual coughing or throat clearing, using the voice for too long, singing or speaking beyond the onset of pain, and singing with poor technique. Drinking alcohol while singing, engaging in illegal drugs, inhaling harmful substances, smoking, or vaping all constitute forms of vocal abuse. Singers should recall how tiny and fragile their vocal folds are before engaging in any activities that might compromise those vulnerable tissues. Because the vocal folds' fragility makes them prone to injury, the professional singer becomes increasingly protective of them, avoiding breathing extremely cold air, keeping the body at a comfortable temperature, wearing scarves or turtlenecks in cool weather, avoiding too-hot or too-cold beverages, and protecting the pharyngeal and esophageal tissues surrounding the larynx from acidic foods and drinks.

Night Club Gigs

Because jazz is intimate music, the night club constitutes a primary performance venue for jazz. However, night clubs often harbor a slew of challenging situations for the singing artist. Jazz musicians tend to have long performances, often playing up to thirty or more songs in one show. Inferior sound amplification systems, balance issues among band members, excessive background noise in restaurant or club environments, marathon sets, and singing in smoky surroundings all constitute potential hazards for the jazz vocalist. Pacing oneself, taking breaks, and making sure songs are transposed to comfortable keys will help to ensure a successful, healthy singing performance. Avoiding the mid- or postperformance meet-and-greet is also recommended because vocal stamina may be spent visiting with guests instead of making music.

Pre-performance Voice Preservation

The mindful singer takes measures to protect and preserve the singing instrument for days in advance of a concert and for the entire performance day. Singers whose schedules include daily performances (like Broadway singers) take great care to limit all speaking on the day of a show.

Pop singer Celine Dion has shared that she routinely avoids all spoken communication on days of concerts, only first phonating during her pre-performance warm-up. This restful practice ensures that she saves her vocal freshness for the performance. The inherent value of such watch-fulness becomes apparent when one listens to Dion even several decades after the start of her career. To the date of this writing, her clarity and strength of tone have not waned, thanks to her diligence in protecting and preserving her instrument. Dion has also remained committed to singing with an outstanding mix.

DAILY CHECK-IN AND WARM-UP

The daily warm-up and gentle practice session prepare every singer for a lifetime of good vocal habits. Having a daily check-in with the voice pro-vides each singer with an opportunity to assess the day's challenges and strengths. The human body (both female and male) changes in miniscule amounts every day. The body's hormones, stress level, degree of hydra-tion, and changes related to food intake, alcohol, caffeine, medicines, and supplements can cause unexpected voice changes. So can illness, air qual-ity, temperature of the hall, humidity, and sleep quality and quantity. The warm-up and daily check-in help the mind take inventory of systems that are working well and systems that are having difficulty on a given day. A morning warm-up routine gently prepares the voice for the day's speaking and singing requirements. Morning reminders about breath management, clear phonation, coordinated onsets in speech, and speaking on the breath prepare singers for healthy vocal habits that last all day. On a performance day, singers may choose to rest the voice until they arrive early to the performance hall to begin a slow, relaxed warm-up routine.

Suggested Daily Regimen

A suggested regimen for the daily check-in includes:

- Physical stretches
- Breathing exercises
- Descending glides on pure vowels
- Staccato exercises
- Legato exercises that move at rapid tempi (e.g., runs, scales, arpeg-gio, and melismas)

- Targeted exercises that focus on building one aspect of vocal technique, unique to the day's needs
- Messa di voce < > exercises (crescendo and decrescendo on one note and one pure vowel). I generally use a slow, eight-beat pattern with four beats for the crescendo and four for the decrescendo, aiming to match tiered dynamics on both sides of the dynamic arc (beats one and eight are *piano*, two and seven are *mezzo piano*, and so forth). These should begin in the middle of the singer's range on a comfortable pitch and ascend by semitone through the comfortable top of the voice. Beginning again at the midpoint of the range and descending by semitone will bring this important skill into the low range. This exercise covers a multitude of technical strengthening issues and is a favorite of advanced professional singers.

The vocal check-in is a singing workout that precedes daily repertoire study, whereas the warm-up is a shortened version that prepares the singer for performance, rehearsal, or a voice lesson. Because cold muscles should never be stretched or worked out, it is crucial to maintain a consistent warm-up before every rehearsal, performance, or recording. The order of exercise types is important whenever preparing the voice to sing. The voice responds more consistently when a routine of exercise types—not necessarily the same exercises every day—remains constant. To accomplish this, singing teachers may create a large compendium of favorite legato exercises, for example, and teach or sing different ones on different days, depending on the needs of the voice. I prefer to vary warm-up and check-in exercises daily to keep my brain fully engaged rather than on autopilot. Following the list of exercise types ensures that the voice is warmed gently, even though the exact exercises may differ each day.

The Singer's Warm-Up

Singers must never attempt to sing without completing at least a few minutes of gentle warm-ups for the same reason a professional athlete would never begin a track and field event without taking several minutes to completely stretch and warm up the entire body. Injury can easily happen to a voice that is not warm before it is forced to deliver performance-level phonation. Even if the music is "easy," the human voice benefits from a slow, thorough warm-up routine that is neither rushed nor stressed. Voices are temperamental, so a singer's stress level is often evident in the resultant vocal quality. Therefore, it is vital that a singer spends time centering the mind and calmly massaging the voice into a pleasant state before every singing appearance. Singers must consider this both a physical and mental exercise.

Journaling for Vocal Health

Journaling to track one's daily sensory feedback can be a helpful tool throughout a singer's life because it can help identify problems and patterns. Those notes can provide doctors (otolaryngologists, ear, nose, and throat specialists; general practitioners; speech-language pathologists; voice therapists; and other medical professionals on one's health care team) with valuable information that is dated and tracked over time. Journaling helps a singer document the frequency and length of practice sessions and performances, as well as the material sung and any advancements or insights achieved each day. Practice journals are useful for keeping track of music to be learned, documenting changes in the voice, setting goals, and noting milestones, discoveries, and tips that have aided technique and performance. Singers can quickly recall recent improvements and start where they left off the day prior simply because they recorded a new discovery or gained an inch of technical development that was immediately documented in their journals. This discipline coupled with a daily check-in creates a helpful set of ongoing data that records a singer's progress and journey throughout their career.

THE HEALTHY SPEAKING VOICE

When the speaking voice is habitually breathy, noisy, overly nasal, or not spoken on an optimal pitch level for the range in which one sings, a voice therapist, speech-language pathologist, voice teacher, or physician may offer guidelines to help the singer speak on the breath with proper resonance and pitch. This will help ensure that the vocal folds are not taxed harmfully during normal speech. Often the speaking voice needs adjusting when student singers find they experience problems with the singing voice.

Optimal Pitch

Learning to speak on one's optimal pitch is step one in developing healthy speech habits for singers. To ascertain one's optimal speaking pitch, speak the word "ping." This onomatopoetic word tends to naturally locate the speaking voice's optimum pitch without conscious thought. When the pitch of that spoken word is determined (listen carefully and play it on the keyboard), it is wise and healthy to work on adjusting the speaking voice to approximate that pitch level.

Supported Speaking

In addition, a well-supported spoken voice requires as much breath preparation as singing a long, sustained phrase. Singers must learn to take a supportive low breath before launching into any kind of speech or spoken communication, including phone calls, virtual conversations and face-to-face discussions. Habitually remembering to breathe well before each sentence requires mindful practice and diligent self-observation.

Speaking of Mix . . .

Allowing the voice to speak in a mix of chest and head qualities (instead of one or the other) represents the third aspect of a healthy speaking voice. Each spoken word should have at least a small amount of both light and heavy ("head" and "chest") mechanism involvement, a blend that pedagogues refer to as a "mix." The varying proportions of that mix are dealt with in chapter 5. The healthy spoken voice sounds as clear, smooth, well-supported, beautiful, and strong as a healthy singing voice.

SLEEP HYGIENE

An adequate amount of quality sleep is a worthy goal that is critical for singers to achieve on a consistent basis. According to Dr. Robert Sataloff's *Vocal Health and Pedagogy* (2017, 541), sleep deprivation may inhibit speech, respiratory function, and among singers, intonation and articulation. Without adequate sleep, performers lose alertness and stamina and experience increases in fatigue and listlessness. Such conditions are obviously not conducive to performing well. Because stress raises the body's level of cortisol, which increases anxiety and inhibits restfulness, seeking ways to reduce stress to ensure healthy sleep must become a high priority for every singer.

Many strategies may be used to encourage healthy sleep patterns. Rising at the same time every day and going to bed at the same time every night both assist the body in developing a routine that helps to keep sleep cycles predictable and regular. Most adults require seven to nine hours of restful sleep each night to function properly each day. Avoiding caffeine (including caffeine-containing foods like chocolate), alcohol, and acidic foods helps the body power down instead of ramp up as the evening hours ensue. Finishing dinner three to four hours before bedtime and eliminating late-night snacking help singers achieve restful sleep. Dimming lights in the home after sunset prepares the body for a restful pre-bedtime routine. Avoiding blue light from electronic devices by ending screen time on phones, tablets, and computers at least two hours before bedtime also helps the brain decrease its elevated level of stimulation in time to sleep soundly. Finally, providing oneself with thirty to sixty minutes of daily exercise is one of the best ways to ensure that one's body is ready to rest by the time bedtime approaches. These sleep-inducing routines are helpful in disciplining the body, mind, and voice for a lifetime of successful singing.

THE VOICE CARE TEAM

Professional singers are wise to assemble a voice care team to address needs that arise at various times during their career. These professionals include physicians, voice therapists, a voice teacher, and other specialists that a physician or teacher may recommend for specific purposes. Today more and more physicians and teachers are working in tandem with voice care teams to better support professional voice users like singers, actors, orators, and radio personnel. Jazz singers need never feel they are alone in traversing the challenges of a lifelong singing career. Leaning on members of the voice care team as the voice changes and as health ebbs and flows gives singers a safety net. These valuable experts come alongside singers to offer assistance as needed.

Otolaryngologist

Finding an otolaryngologist that works with professional singers ought to be one of the young singer's first priorities. Some voice programs in higher education require all incoming voice majors to receive a baseline laryngeal evaluation by an otolaryngologist upon entering the institution for voice study. This evaluation serves two purposes. First, it provides a (hopefully asymptomatic and healthy) reference point for any future vocal concerns against which later issues may be compared. Second, it confirms that the vocal instrument is, indeed, healthy when the student first enters the institution. Unknown vocal pathologies may be detected even before symptoms begin. Early is obviously the best time to detect any vocal problems, so all aspiring professional singers are advised to have an evaluation by a physician at the start of their careers. After the baseline evaluation has been completed, regular checkups by the physician are recommended as are visits addressing any problems that arise. Singers are wise to do the homework of finding a voice doctor they love before they need one so that the doctor is only a phone call away when an urgent matter presents itself.

Voice Therapist

The physician may sometimes recommend a voice therapist when the voice requires specific exercises or treatments that do not require surgery. The voice therapist is a member of the voice care team much like a physical therapist. The therapist's job is to provide training, vocal exercises, and instruction in voice care so that singers gain knowledge and supervised practice doing activities that will build and strengthen healthy vocalism. The voice therapist is also an excellent resource to help singers learn to speak healthfully.

Speech-Language Pathologist

The speech-language pathologist may also be recommended by the physician as a member of the voice care team. This professional can examine the vocal folds and laryngeal tissues using video stroboscopy and other technology. This voice professional identifies problems and pathologies and can refer the patient to a physician if necessary. A speech-language pathologist may be called on to provide medical advice and specific education about caring for the challenged voice.

Audiologist

An audiologist may be consulted in cases when hearing is an issue. Because singers are often in hearing-compromising situations (especially singers whose ears are exposed to loud electronic noise onstage), the hearing organs must be protected whenever possible. Singers are encouraged to wear musician's earplugs (available from an audiologist and tailor-made to fit the ear canals) or other ear protection whenever they report for sound checks; run a lawnmower, hair dryer, vacuum cleaner, or loud equipment; or are otherwise exposed to loud noise or music. In addition to losing certain frequencies in the hearing spectrum, singers may develop a decreased tolerance for normal loud noises. **Tinnitus**, or permanent ringing in the ears, is a type of hearing damage that leaves a lasting mark. Hearing loss is a major problem for many singers of every style and genre, regardless of age. The more a young singer takes measures to care for the delicate hearing organs they possess, the longer they will enjoy healthy ears and the more they will benefit in later years when age-related hearing loss becomes more likely. Detrimental effects on the hearing organs tend to worsen as time progresses, so singers' best strategy is to fiercely protect their hearing from loud noises, beginning at a young age.

HEARING PROTECTION

Just as a singer should use a microphone to protect one's vocal instrument when speaking to an audience in large rooms, a singer should also habitually carry earplugs or hearing protection to concerts and all public outings in case the unexpected jackhammer, train, or jet airplane suddenly appears. Another great tool is a decibel application on a mobile phone, which instantly informs users of the noise level in their environment. This app will instantly show whether current background noise or music exceeds a healthy level. It is also an indispensable tool in the band rehearsal room to make sure singers and instrumentalists are not playing music at potentially harmful levels.

Singing teachers relegated to teach in practice rooms or other small rooms may sustain substantial hearing damage when teaching students having large (naturally loud, projective) voices. Ideally, teaching should take place in large enough spaces in which performances can occur (never practice rooms or tiny offices) so that the voice can be free to explore the larger dynamic range singers should develop without harming their own ears or a teacher's ears. Singing in small rooms has caused not only hearing loss for many teachers (particularly adjunct instructors in higher education) but also anxiety for singers who are self-conscious about being overheard by others during practice sessions or lessons. These students sing while holding back the voice, singing cautiously instead of with freedom and confidence, sometimes causing undue laryngeal tension. Furthermore, singers who are constantly reined in during lessons and practice sessions rarely, if ever, experience the correct sensations and auditory feedback needed for learning what the voice can do in a large performance space. This sets students up for failure when juries, recitals, or concerts occur in large concert halls, on opera stages, or in auditoriums. A singer's education should ensure that such unfortunate small-room-syndrome situations do not become the norm in the university or conservatory setting.

ENVIRONMENTAL CONSIDERATIONS

Air quality, although sometimes ignored by voice professionals, greatly affects one's health and ability to sing well. A room's humidity, dust content, scents, allergens, pollutants, particulates, and toxins in the air change from day to day, so it is important for the singer to try to keep the air clean in the home, car, workplace, and practice space. Filtering all one's breathing spaces with a high-quality filtration system will help maintain a clean breathing environment for the lungs and delicate, vulnerable tissues in the nasopharynx, throat, and larynx. Sometimes pollutants, fumes, asbestos, insulation, pollen, or fragrances cause sore throats, pharyngeal irritation, congestion, mucosal secretion, or edema (swelling), so maintaining a clean, pure working environment is absolutely necessary for every serious singer. It is commonly known that smoking, vaping, and inhaling secondhand smoke cause severe vocal health problems, so singers must do everything in their power to avoid smoky environments.

Smoking has been linked to a wide variety of serious health concerns including lung cancer, which took the life of jazz great Nat "King" Cole at the young age of forty. A chain smoker, Cole unknowingly nursed a habit that ultimately ended his life and livelihood long before his musical ideas and genius were exhausted. Unlike Cole's generation, modern singers have received fair warning and plenty of education about the ravages of cigarette, cigar, and pipe smoke on the lungs, throat, and vocal mechanism. Smoking marijuana and vaping have also been shown to be harmful to lung health and pharyngeal tissues. Singers are wise to avoid contact with all airborne contaminants and large particulates of pollution and to conscientiously avoid being in environments where they have to inhale any kind of smoke or other toxic substances.

Masks for Vocal Health

Singers must consider using either disposable or washable face masks (as appropriate) whenever they come into contact with known breathing aggravators like fiberglass, strong fumes, household cleaning chemicals, insecticides, herbicidal chemicals, pollen, mown grass, sawdust, industrial dust, paint dust, hay, mold spores, and many other potential hazards in the air. Singers living within twenty to fifty miles of seasonal forest fires (as in various cities in California) must take precautions to avoid inhaling large particulates including ash and thick smoke when they venture outside during the wildfire season.

Since the COVID-19 pandemic, many singers have become much more aware of the need to protect their lungs and other breathing tissues (as well as other people's) from potentially harmful aerosols that emerge from normal human exhalations. People who appear healthy may infect others with a variety of airborne pathogens that live each day in lungs, throats, or nasal passages. Even when one's immune system is healthy, viruses or bacteria residing in the lungs or sinuses may be exhaled onto a person having a weak immune system, and that pathogen can proliferate in the new host's body. This phenomenon is not new, and accounts for much of the spreading of the flu, staphylococcal infections, and colds every year. SARS-CoV-2 has claimed millions of lives worldwide and has been shown to be especially dangerous in large gatherings of unvaccinated people. Singers are known super-spreaders because of the force with which they project aerosol from the lungs and the length of time they spend in the exhalation phase of the breathing cycle. This is why it is crucial to avoid singing in public when sick with any contagious, upper respiratory illness. Furthermore, singers can contract more serious cases of upper respiratory illnesses because of how deeply they breathe and the large amount of air inhaled when singing. The close proximity of singers in choral groups and small teaching studios amplifies this risk of transmission. Face masks became an everyday part of the prepared singer's standard hygiene toolbox during the COVID-19 pandemic. Stocking masks and hand sanitizer in the car, office, and at home helps singers protect their vulnerable singing organs, overall health, and the health of others when around a person who is ill or when traveling.

Allergies and Singing

Many singers exhibit allergy symptoms around known aggravators like pollen, dust, smoke, animal dander, and mold spores, resulting in asthma-like complications, throat itching, postnasal drip, runny nose, hives, and vocal fold edema. Sometimes the singer exhibits a slight sensitivity to such aggravators; at other times, allergens may set off a cytokine storm resulting in a full-blown allergic reaction or strong histamine response warranting medical intervention. Singers are advised to consult a physician for advice about how to manage allergy symptoms and to avoid exposure to known allergens. Seasonal allergies may wreak havoc for a singer performing an outdoor concert during the spring or fall allergy seasons. Singers battling seasonal allergies are wise to request that outdoor events be scheduled during off-season months when a severe allergic response is less likely to occur. Face masks may be worn outdoors, especially during exercise, at outdoor rehearsals, or sound checks to minimize exposure to known seasonal allergens.

VOICE PROBLEMS AND PATHOLOGIES

Understanding the repercussions that certain vocal abuses may cause represents a crucial component of a jazz singer's education. We are responsible for caring for our instrument, and it is therefore incumbent on each of us to know how best to care for our own voice. When signs of a vocal problem arise, singers are strongly advised to consult a physician who specializes in working with professional singers—either an otolaryngologist, a laryngologist, or an ear, nose, and throat (ENT) specialist. It is good to learn what is your doctor's specific area of expertise. Some are primarily ear surgeons; others deal mostly with sinus infections for the general population. Not all ENT specialists are specialized to work with high-level professional singers, so I recommend asking other professional voice users whom they recommend for singer-specific medical advice. Singers need to know what types of vocal problems or pathologies can affect the singing instrument, so several will be described here.

Acid Reflux Disorders

Acid reflux is a condition that unfortunately affects one in four singers. Some physicians have proposed that this high percentage comes from the repetitious, inward-moving lower abdominal action that singing requires, essentially forcing stomach acid back up into the esophagus through abdominal muscle flexion. **Gastroesophageal reflux (GER)** occurs when stomach acid travels in the wrong direction—up into the esophagus. **Laryngopharyngeal reflux (LPR)** is caused by stomach acid traveling up the esophagus all the way to the laryngeal and pharyngeal areas. Because the delicate esophageal lining as well as the larynx and pharynx cannot withstand the burning damage caused by regular exposure to the stomach's hydrochloric acid, reflux disorders represent serious health ailments with the potential for causing permanent, irreversible damage to fragile tissues, so a physician should be consulted for proper diagnosis, treatment, prevention, and guidance. Both GER and LPR can cause excessive phlegm, burning sensations in the chest, sore throat, laryngeal swelling, or esophageal damage. Singers who suspect they may have GER or LPR are advised to see a physician for a proper diagnosis and help managing the condition. In many cases, doctors recommend dietary changes (a low-acid diet), elevating the head of one's mattress, and avoiding eating late in the evening. Although many doctors may prescribe medication to treat acid reflux, long-term concerns have been raised about taking proton-pump inhibitors over many years, so nonmedicinal solutions may be preferable whenever possible, except in severe cases or when used for short-term symptom resolution.

Food Sensitivities

Many singers find that dairy products pose a problem of excessive phlegm production, which should be avoided before performances. Other singers find that dairy or gluten sensitivity may cause abdominal bloating or even swelling of the laryngeal tissues. Singers are advised to pay close attention to the information their bodies communicate. Take notes in a journal and work toward maintaining equilibrium so that the body remains as consistently well cared-for and comfortable as possible each day. This will help to ensure consistently strong performances. If singers' health becomes compromised by insomnia due to caffeine, late-night binges, or indigestion due to unhealthy food choices, singers must learn to respond kindly to the messages their body sends. If singers suspect they are having an allergic reaction or sensitivity to environmental or food sources, seeing a doctor is strongly urged before the situation worsens.

Voice Trauma

According to the American Speech-Language-Hearing Association, when a singer develops something clinically troublesome on the surface of the vocal folds it most often occurs as a result of vocal misuse leading to trauma. "A voice disorder occurs when voice quality, pitch, and loudness differ or are inappropriate for an individual's age, gender, cultural background, or geographic location."[1] According to Dr. Robert Sataloff, **or-**

ganic voice disorders may be described as physiological and categorized as either **structural** (resulting from physical changes in the mechanism like edema or nodules) or **neurogenic** (resulting from neurological causes like spasmodic dysphonia or vocal fold paralysis). **Psychogenic voice disorders** are caused by psychological stressors leading to maladaptive dysphonia (problematic phonation that sounds hoarse, strained, or weak) or aphonia (inability to phonate). **Functional voice disorders** are preventable but caused by vocal abuse or improper or inefficient use of the voice. In an effort to facilitate prevention and self-aware protection, these disorders will be the main areas discussed here.

Nodules

Nodules (also called "nodes") are calluses that develop on the surface of one or both vocal folds as a result of repeated, violent striking of the folds together (common in shouting, screaming, chronic coughing or throat clearing, vocal abuse, and habitual use of explosive glottal onsets). Symptoms of nodules include a breathy, noisy, or hoarse voice caused by the inability of the vocal folds to adduct completely. The raised nodule prevents complete fold closure. Treatment for nodules generally involves extended vocal rest to allow the callus to heal. Vocal rest means avoiding throat clearing, coughing, whispering, talking, singing, humming, and whistling. Although this may sound like a terrible sentence for a professional singer, resting the voice as the doctor orders will generally yield a full recovery. If, after a period of prescribed vocal rest, the nodule has not resolved, a physician may recommend surgery. Singers may wish to seek a second opinion and consultation with an additional otolaryngologist who specializes in working with professional singers before consenting to any type of surgery affecting the voice.

Polyps

Polyps are blood-filled, benign growths on the surface of the vocal folds caused by acute, chronic trauma to the folds, including hyperfunctional glottal phonation (as in screaming forcefully) leading to bleeding in the superficial lamina propria (SLP), a thin layer on the surface of the folds. Treatment of hemorrhagic polyps includes surgical amputation, which results in improvement of mucosal wave propagation and improved glottal closure.[2]

Cysts

Cysts are common in some people in various organs of the body. Those who are prone to cysts in one area of the body (breasts, skin, etc.) may be susceptible to developing cysts in other areas, including the vocal folds. Cysts are commonly aspirated (drained of fluid using a fine needle) but often recur unless the lining of the cyst is surgically removed. Cysts on the vocal folds may cause breathy production due to the imperfect glottal closure caused by the cyst's raised presence on the surface of the fold. A cyst on the vocal fold's surface prevents complete adduction when the arytenoid cartilages draw the folds together, and depending on the precise location of the cyst, the voice may be slightly or severely affected. Singers with cysts on the surface of the vocal folds may have breathy, noisy, or raspy voices, and they may be unable to produce a clear tone. Cysts are generally removable only by surgical intervention.

Bowed Vocal Folds

Bowed vocal folds occur when the folds themselves are shaped in a manner that prevents complete glottal closure. Bowed folds, like bowed legs, meet at the top and bottom but not in the middle. This "chink" or space along the midline of normal glottal closure creates breathy, weak production, which exhausts the singer after only a few minutes of singing. Because complete closure is impossible with bowed folds, the singer's attempts to use more air to power the voice, result in blowing even more air through the bowed folds and tiring the voice quickly. Bowing is caused by the atrophying of the thyroarytenoid muscle. It sometimes occurs in singers of an advanced age. It can also occur when one vocal fold is paralyzed. Singers with bowed folds must consult a laryngologist for guidance and may be treated with voice therapy or surgery.

Vocal Fold Paralysis and Paresis

Paralysis and **paresis** of the vocal folds occur when nerve input to the laryngeal muscles becomes disrupted. In paralysis, vocal fold movement ceases altogether because the nerve impulse is completely interrupted. In paresis, vocal fold movement is unusual or weak due to a partial interruption of the nerve impulse. Paralysis of one vocal fold causes difficulty swallowing and voice problems because the folds cannot adduct properly.

When both folds are paralyzed, breathing may be seriously threatened. Certain surgeries and resultant injury to the recurrent laryngeal nerve sometimes cause vocal fold paralysis and paresis. Tumors along the nerve, viral infections, and trauma may also cause these pathologies. Voice therapy and surgery are treatments a physician may recommend to resolve these conditions.

Voice Teachers as First Responders

When a teacher encounters a singer who cannot sing for more than ten minutes without feeling winded and exhausted, bowed vocal folds or another vocal pathology might be the problem. Singing teachers must know when to refer a student out to a physician and when a problem can be safely addressed by attending to technique in lessons. Training the ear to detect warning signs of nodules, polyps, cysts, or other pathological problems on the folds (excessive breathiness, hoarseness, inability to phonate in sections or single pitches of a singer's range, metallic rattling sounds in the voice, or other vocal noise) is a necessary piece of every voice teacher's education.

Young pedagogues are wise to suggest a laryngologist's examination whenever they are not sure if a singer sounds healthy. As one's experience and expertise with pedagogy grow, those questions become easier to answer. Teachers are urged never to suggest a diagnosis to a student singer. Instead, refrain from offering an opinion until a physician's examination has occurred and their instructions and a written report are received. With a student's authorization, most physicians are glad to share information with a voice teacher, particularly if the student needs rehabilitation or specific guidance in voice training. I have traditionally refused to teach any student demonstrating questionable vocal health until a physician has examined him or her, and I always ask the student for permission to see a written physician's report of any findings. Building trust is, of course, paramount here. Students do not want to share personal information with a professor unless they are confident of that professor's sincere concern for their vocal health. Nowadays, a professional voice team requires cooperation among a voice teacher, laryngologist, voice therapist, speech-language pathologist, and vocal coach. Most students will greatly appreciate anything a voice teacher does to discreetly seek professional healing for their vocal and overall health.

VOICE PRESERVATION

Many voice-related activities are harmful to the singing voice. Taking care of the voice requires daily discipline and a commitment to avoiding certain everyday situations. To preserve the voice, teachers should use a microphone when speaking in large rooms or conducting choral rehearsals in concert halls. Jazz singers should never attempt to sing over a band or in a large room without a microphone, even during rehearsals.

Attending sporting events during which shouting or cheering are tempting (cheerleaders beware!) is fine but learn to blow a whistle or clap hands instead of joining the crowd in using your vocal instrument to add to the yells of a stadium audience. Bringing a mechanical noisemaker is a great solution to the dilemma of the singer-sports fan—a good noisemaker creates more decibels of sound than a single voice can produce anyway (but remember to wear ear protection!). Singers must be mindful that they walk around with their instrument encased inside them and participate in various types of communication and emotive release throughout each day. The vocal instrument's preservation depends on important daily choices involving how the voice will and will not be used.

Oversinging in the Choral Ensemble

Oversinging is a problem in choral situations when a director asks for more volume from a section that is already giving its maximum healthy volume. Instead the director must learn to ask the other sections to reduce their volume to match the lightest voices. This point cannot be stressed too much! Some choral directors fail to understand the damage they cause their singers (who are usually trying their best to please the conductor, often to the point of hurting themselves) by asking them to sing louder and louder. Proper choral blend and musicality cannot be maintained when a singer is pushing the voice, nor can vocal health. Voices can almost always reduce a dynamic level, but after a certain maximum, they can no longer increase their volume. Choral directors must always be mindful about the fact that vocal pain is a problem in many choirs, and the directors have the power to minimize or eliminate it altogether by simply teaching choirs to balance throughout all the parts of the ensemble. All singers must listen to the other parts around them and blend/match vowels to the *lightest* voices in each section. Choir directors are charged to take care of all the voices in the ensemble. Singers in possession of enormous voices take notice: to be a successful chorister one must never strive to be the loudest voice. Choral singing is not a competition rewarding whomever can be heard above the rest. It is the responsibility of every choral director to be ever mindful of how beautiful and musical the voices sound. If the volume is louder than can be sung beautifully, with good balance and blend throughout the ensemble (can you hear *every* member of your choir?), then the volume is too loud. A too-loud choir is an environment in which vocal abuse runs rampant. Choral directors of all genres (jazz, classical, opera, show choir, community choir, men's choir, women's choir, church choir, etc.) owe it to their trusting members to rethink every directive that might result in vocal harm.

The Emotional Binge

Excessive crying is another human activity that the professional singer must seek to avoid whenever possible. Crying causes swelling of the vocal folds, which can lead to swelling of the entire larynx. Obviously, life happens, so it is natural for everyone to cry sometimes, but for people with depression, severe anxiety, or who have suffered a recent loss that has caused an extended period of grief, the voice bears the brunt of sometimes severe physical damage. The voice suffers when crying and sobbing get out of control over a prolonged period, so a doctor's (or trained professional counselor's) intervention is strongly recommended when singers need help reining in their emotional meltdowns.

Taking care of the vocal instrument is a complex process and a series of daily choices. How we practice, care for the voice, strengthen and nurture the entire body, and manage environmental, nutritional, vocal, emotional, and mental health considerations will ultimately determine how well our voice is maintained over the long haul of a lifetime of singing.

NOTES

1. A. E. Aronson and D. M. Bless, *Clinical Voice Disorders* (New York: Thieme Medical Publishers, 2009); D. R. Boone, S. C. McFarlane, S. L. Von Berg, and R. I. Zraik, *The Voice and Voice Therapy* (Boston: Allyn & Bacon, 2010); L. Lee, J. C. Stemple, L. Glaze, and L. N. Kelchner, "Quick Screen for Voice and Supplementary Documents for Identifying Pediatric Voice Disorders," *Language Speech, and Hearing Services in Schools*, 35(2004): 308–19.

2. I. I. Hochman and S. M. Zeitels, "Phonomicrosurgical Management of Vocal Fold Polyps: The Subepithelial Microflap Resection Technique," *Journal of Voice*, 14, no. 1 (March 2000): 112–18. Available at: https://www.sciencedirect.com/science/article/abs/pii/S0892199700801010. Accessed September 3, 2020.

3

POSTURE AND ALIGNMENT

A singer's command of proper body alignment represents the starting point for good vocalism, breath management, and performance practice. Regardless of style performed, the singer's instrument is the entire body—not just the larynx and surrounding tissues, bone, cartilage and muscles that comprise what is known as the "vocal mechanism." Professional actors, orators, teachers, singers, and anyone that routinely uses the voice in public set themselves up for greater success by understanding how to align the body for optimum vocal performance. Furthermore, it is well-known that not only professional voice users but also everyone can benefit from optimizing one's body alignment. This optimization results not only in more efficient breathing, support of the voice, orientation of all body parts for the greatest ease, strength, and potential for good singing or speaking effectiveness but also in walking, standing, sitting, lying down, eating, exercising, and a host of other human activities. Proper alignment supports the back and prevents injury. It projects confidence and conserves the body's collective energy. It allows for proper function of all the various interior workings of the body from the circulatory system to the respiratory system, the nervous system, and the muscles and skeleton and supports optimum organ health. Indeed, a simple activity like standing upright or walking with good alignment can re-energize a fatigued body, reset a pinched nerve, and release tensions, built-up toxins, and gases that cause pain.

Generally, great singers consistently possess body alignment that signals confidence and health to their audiences. When renowned opera or jazz stars take the stage in a recital or in front of an orchestra, the first thing an audience sees is how they walk and hold their body. A singer that does not feel well can rise above their physical sensation of illness and send a message of overall health and well-being simply by choosing to elevate the sternum and walk with a buoyant lift elongating the spine. These habits are worth cultivating because the visual picture of a singer hunching over or exhibiting physical compression has ousted more than a few student, preprofessional, and even professional singers from awards consideration during an otherwise excellent audition. The visual picture of confidence is every bit as important to hone and craft as the actual state of mental toughness required to consistently perform well. Audiences and adjudicators alike strongly prefer an upright, energized, elongated physical stature when watching singing, acting, or oration. Practicing outstanding alignment helps a singer make a compelling entrance and puts the audience at ease. A strong, well-aligned entrance sets the stage for an exciting, positive, polished performance.

Jazz singers are wise to heed this advice. Great jazz singers show excellent body alignment, an energized spirit, and a picture of health every bit as much as great classical singers do—because their objectives are the same. A jazz performance need not be shabby nor so lackadaisical and overly "casual" that the audience feels awkward. A singer's attention to posture can remarkably and instantly telegraph a high level of professionalism, confidence, and readiness to the audience.

BALANCE POINTS IN THE SKELETON

The human body may be mapped to designate five key balance points at major joints. These include ankles, knees, hips, shoulders, and the atlanto-occipital joint. To maintain good alignment throughout the body, each joint must be free from undue tension and properly aligned with each of the other joint systems. Singers may visualize each joint (or pair) dangling freely above the ones below in a long, flexible line. Singers are encouraged to identify, gently move, and mindfully align each of these points of balance at the start of each lesson or before practice sessions, rehearsals, and performances. Proper alignment can be achieved by starting at the bottom joints and working upward.

The Ankle

The first balance point is found at the ankle joints. A singer's full body weight, when standing upright, should be balanced evenly on both feet, oriented shoulder-width apart. Some people feel more stable with one foot slightly in front of the other, but either way, weight distribution should feel equal. Leaning one's weight over to one side or to the front or back leg will not allow the body to maintain proper alignment. The weight should be on the balls of the feet, or in the forward dimension of the foot's structure where the toes join to the foot bones. Ankles are easily turned or sprained from stumbling or falling when balance is poor, so singers are advised to engage in yoga, balance work, aerobic exercise, or gentle physical stretches to enhance the strength, flexibility, and health of these important joints. Sensible, supportive footwear for the stage is integral to firmly establishing secure alignment and strength for these important joints.

The Knee

The next pair of balance points, the knees, should align vertically above the ankle joints in a comfortable line to provide the singer with proper body balance, symmetry, supportive strength, and flexibility during the process of singing. The knees should remain slightly bent, never locked, to provide the stability and strength necessary to meet the demands of supporting the body's weight for long periods. For the body's abdominal and thoracic core to do the breath management work required in singing, the lower body must be supple, strong, and equipped with stamina. Channeling the tension toward the quadriceps—among the largest muscle groups in the body—rather than letting the tiny vocal muscles bear the brunt of long-duration phonation is excellent advice and a useful image for a singer to remember. But only proper alignment can accomplish this task. Singers' knee flexibility is important to cultivate and maintain as well as strength, so full leg exercise and stretching remain important activities to enhance alignment, joint health, and balance throughout their careers and lives.

EXERCISE

One excellent exercise (which was suggested to me by pedagogue Dale Moore) to help the singer find their body's axis and to keep the spinal column in balanced alignment is to stand firmly on one foot while swinging the other leg forward and back bending only the knee. This creates the need for other areas of the body to achieve balance by becoming aligned to prevent a fall. This balance and alignment exercise helps singers isolate their postural axis. The spine nearly instantly compensates by elongating and assuming a properly aligned orientation at each flexible curve. Once the exercise is relatively simple to accomplish on one foot, move to the other foot and repeat the exercise, continuously swinging the other leg forward and back moving only at the knee. Singers may find that one leg is more successful at sustaining this exercise indefinitely than the other. As long as balance can be retained while actively swinging the leg, the axis is in alignment and the body is awakened to a state of extreme balance. Singing can be practiced while either leg is swinging to feel the sensation of singing while the axis is engaged. When both feet are firmly planted shoulder-width apart following this exercise, the singer should feel quite well-aligned, energized, and keenly balanced.

The Hip

The hip joints represent the next higher balance points in this model. These are optimally oriented roughly above the knee joints, with a freedom of "micro-motion" continually available to these joints, as alluded to in Feldenkrais movement study. The hips should maintain a degree of freedom and flexibility to prevent the misalignment of the pelvis, which creates problems for back posture, shoulders, and even neck and head alignment. Tucking the pelvis slightly under and forward creates a comfortable line for most singers. Allowing the tailbone to venture backward creates a "C" shape in the lower spine and impedes correct posture. Tucking the pelvis under while slightly bending the knees helps singers to find the appropriate balance in their lower systems of joints as they teach their bodies to optimize good alignment. It also helps to free the diaphragm to fully lower itself on inhalation, maximizing the interior breathing space and optimizing the diaphragmatic muscle function available to a singer.

The Shoulder

The shoulders are the next balance points. Aligning the shoulder joints according to the same continuum established by the lower points of balance helps to orient the spinal column, the chest, and the arms in a manner that greatly impacts the process of singing. In master classes, voice pedagogue Dale Moore advised singers to bring their shoulder blades as close together as possible in a parallel but relaxed orientation with one another. This causes the sternum to stay elevated so that the chest cannot easily collapse. Gaining a sense of comfort in this orientation requires practice. Chest-opening exercises (squeezing shoulder blades together and releasing) can do a great deal to provide the requisite comfort.

The singer must take care to watch how reorienting the shoulder blades affects the lower balance points. In many singers' bodies, bringing the shoulder blades more together causes the hips to lose their downward tuck, so finding a sense of body awareness that allows both the shoulders and the hips to maintain alignment while remaining as free as possible, continues to be an ongoing objective for most singers throughout their lives. As bodies age and change, a singer's orientation awareness of each balance point represents the key to finding solutions to new physical challenges. Attention paid toward establishing excellent alignment and posture at as early an age as possible will ensure that singers are well on their way toward a lifetime of physical and mental awareness that will help solve new technical problems as they arise.

The Atlanto-Occipital Joint

The final balance point is the atlanto-occipital articulation in the neck. This structure, comprised of two synovial joints, connects the occipital bone in the skull to the first cervical vertebra. The weight of the skull sits on this important joint. This joint is roughly situated between the ears inside the back of the neck. To properly align the head, singers are wise to consider the four pillars of muscle that support the neck—two on either side in the front and two on either side in the back. Practicing the release of these muscles and engaging in neck massage and self-massage of the neck, face, and jaw can do wonders in achieving freedom of this joint's function. When muscles contract in the back of the neck, the chin lifts (e.g., singing to the balcony). When those muscles are elongated, the head drops down toward the chest, stretching the muscles in the back of the neck. Singers must strive to keep the head evenly balanced among all four pillars.

> **EXERCISE**
>
> Regularly engaging in a "bobble-head" doll exercise serves to increase the awareness of where the head most comfortably sits while freeing the neck muscles from holding overt tension. Doing this exercise in a mirror helps the singer gauge which, if any, muscles need to release more and where the ideal head position is.

In proper head alignment the chin should be parallel to the floor, never lifted up. Starting with a slightly tucked (downward-sloping) head posture may be advisable for those singers who are inclined (pun intended) to lift the chin and tip the head back when they sing. Backward-tipping of the head shortens the vocal tract, causing the voice to strain during phonation. Singers should be able to sing all their repertoire with a slightly downward-pointing face, indicating that the muscles in the back of the neck are not exerting too much force by pulling the head to an upward-pointing stature.

One principle to keep in mind is that the head should be vertically free (to move up or down) during inhalation and horizontally free (to move right, left, or center) during phonation. This guide (suggested by multi-genre singing star Nathan Gunn) helps singers remember not to lift the head while they are singing, and it also reinforces the need for absolute horizontal freedom to be maintained during the act of singing.

When balance points operate in proper alignment throughout the body, the singer's instrument is free to perform at its maximum capacity and potential. Breath management and technique are enabled and enhanced by the instrument's "tube" being in a straight line. Alignment also impacts the concept of body tensions that plague many singers. Shoulder tension, hip tension, locked knees, neck and jaw tension, and even tongue tension can stem from problems with physical alignment. Correcting alignment issues often corrects areas of tension that interfere with ideal voice function.

COORDINATING BODY ALIGNMENT

Proper body alignment through attention to upright posture contributes
to breath work by allowing the chest to remain open (rather than closed
when shoulders slouch or the spine collapses). The rib muscles that aid
in respiration function optimally when they are not compressed by a
hunched-over posture. Similarly, the abdominal muscles and diaphragm
function properly when the body is fully open and well-aligned. Excellent posture contributes toward a performer's confidence and attractive,
assured appearance onstage. Proper head, neck, and jaw alignment allow
the larynx to function optimally, too. The neck should not pitch forward
or back but support the head in a comfortably vertical orientation, well-
aligned with the spine.

Jaw Alignment

The jaw, when it releases open, should pivot downward and backward
from the temporomandibular joint (TMJ) hinge. When pushed forward,
even slightly, the lower jaw is considered to be out of alignment in most
people. Singers must work on speaking and singing with mindful jaw
alignment if jutting the jaw forward occurs habitually. Singing (and
speaking) while looking in a mirror is important for growing singers'
awareness of their actual practice. When the jaw is properly aligned, the
molars are vertically oriented so that the top teeth are directly over the
bottom or slightly in front of the bottom molars when the jaw is swinging
downward and back. Some pedagogues find success describing the down
and back jaw motion as a "glide" to coax their students toward a gentle
rather than forceful motion of release. The jaw should never be forced
backward but should tend down and back in a subtle, general sense. Forcing the jaw backward, downward, or in any direction is never advisable,
so singers must take great care and time to get to know how their bodies
are naturally oriented to find the best alignment while pursuing ways to
release tension.

   It is important to point out that jazz and contemporary commercial music singers need not contort their faces, jut or force their lower jaws, lock
or press the tongue, or otherwise sing with overt muscle tension to create
a sound (or even a visual effect) they feel is desirable. There are always
healthy, technically efficient ways to achieve a stylistically desirable
sound, as this teacher who has taught professional rock singers how to
"scream" onstage without pain well knows. Effort must be spent by both

teacher and student to develop authenticity in jazz style without creating or maintaining poor technical habits.

Alignment When Holding Microphones

Jazz singers are unique among professional vocalists in that they often must hold a microphone in their hands (or play an instrument like piano or guitar) while standing or sitting as they simultaneously sing. This creates an entirely different class of tension challenges. Singers must first conquer the tension challenges that are present when they simply stand and sing if they are to be successful managing the tensions compounded by holding a guitar or a microphone. Jazz singers are advised to first work on singing while standing behind a mic supported by a microphone stand, without tensions added by holding a mic or sitting down. Only after a singer is relatively successful at minimizing the tensions inherent in singing while properly aligned in a standing position can singing be attempted while sitting down, playing a piano, or holding a microphone or guitar. After singing without holding a microphone yields physical freedom among all the skeletal balance points plus the jaw and tongue, a singer may work on holding a microphone gently with all the fingertips, a flexible wrist, elbow, shoulder, and an elongated, relaxed neck and spinal column. Moving the mic from one hand to the other periodically during performances can give the arms and shoulders a rest. When holding a microphone, singers must also be mindful of maintaining a healthy head position with the chin parallel to the floor and not tipped backward.

Too often jazz singers build on the tensions they bring to the craft by constantly practicing while holding a mic or self-accompanying instrument but never spend time correcting their inherent tensions. I have taught several instrumentalists who desired vocal instruction but never had previously attempted singing without holding (or hiding behind!) their instrument. Singing without accompanying oneself must be a high priority when training the singer-instrumentalist to establish good voice technique and body awareness. Tension issues must be worked out one variable at a time (releasing each individual point of balance) to set up a singer for maximum success. Additionally, the added instrument complicates the process of performance and distracts the singer from concentrating wholly on singing. All instrumentalists seeking voice instruction of any kind are strongly encouraged to put down their mechanical instrument whenever concentrating on voice technique to focus fully on maximizing the efficiency, alignment, and relaxed function of the vocal instrument within their bodies.

Alignment When Seated

When sitting on a stool or chair during a performance, the alignment of the singer's breathing and vocal mechanisms must be maintained. Sitting on the edge of a chair or stool (rather than sinking down and back into it) while lifting the sternum keeps the spine and tucked-under pelvis in proper alignment. Singers sit onstage for various reasons. One objective of sitting is to stay on the same vertical plane as the seated guitarist, pianist, and drummer rather than towering above them. Another purpose of remaining seated is to demonstrate the desire to create a casual, relaxed, intimate rapport with the audience. A jazz singer's stool is often employed to momentarily take the audience's focus off the singer when other band members are playing solo material. During extended instrumental solos singers may use a stool or chair, especially to conserve energy to prevent fatigue during long sets. Learning to sit using proper physical alignment is important both from a singing perspective (knowing how to sing well in a seated orientation) as well as a visual perspective (to continue projecting confidence and professionalism to the audience).

SINGER-INSTRUMENTALISTS

Singers playing instruments while singing have unique alignment challenges. After some initial instruction geared toward establishing a good foundational technique and excellent standing posture, the singer-instrumentalist must explore ways to maintain good alignment while playing the external instrument during singing.

Singer-Pianists

An important consideration for pianists and keyboardists is the shape of the lower spine. In a seated orientation, singers must sit on the edge of a bench to tilt the pelvis down enough so that the spine and breathing system stay in line. As previously stated, a curved *C* in the lower spine (due to the arching of the back or protrusion of the buttocks) throws the breathing tube out of line, so finding a supportive chair or stool that allows the pianist-singer to stay aligned is crucial. Also challenging for the pianist-singer is the position of the arms and its influence on one's posture. Pianists who crouch or hover in a "hunchback" fashion over their keyboards set themselves up for spinal problems and endurance issues as they age. If they sing, the problem becomes even more seriously compromising to their ongoing career. The arm and shoulder position must be as relaxed and comfortable as possible while keeping the sternum lifted and the pelvis tucked during playing. Performing artists are advised to experiment with a variety of moveable postures through disciplines such as Feldenkrais, Dalcroze, or Alexander Technique to find an alignment system that keeps the body physically free.

The head position is also important for singer-instrumentalists to keep in check. Singers who play the piano must remember to keep their breathing tube in proper alignment while seated with hands extended in front. Positioning the microphone on a boom stand so that the head and neck postures remain healthy while playing the piano is an important way to guide the body toward proper alignment. Too often I have noticed seated singers tipping the head upward into a microphone when more proper positioning of the mic could easily remedy that problematic postural habit. If, for instance, a singer tends to "sing to the balcony," an easy adjustment would be to keep the mic low enough to encourage an elongated back of the neck and a slightly downward tip of the chin. This posture lengthens the vocal tract and elongates the spinal column, allowing for maximum freedom of both intrinsic and extrinsic muscles, while ensuring that the various postures affecting the voice, back, and neck are optimally maintained.

Pianists whose eyesight requires bifocal glasses can sometimes develop neck problems in their singing and playing due to the need to tilt the head upward to see the music in the lower half of their glasses. For this reason, singer-pianists may wish to ask their eye doctor or eyeglass manufacturer to raise the dividing line for the lower bifocal lens so that more of the lens (50 percent rather than just a small percentage of the bottom of the lens) accommodates reading. New contact lens technology now allows multifocal vision (both distant and close ranges), which accommodate the pianist's vision needs. Professional singer-pianists require eyewear that facilitates reading music without tilting their heads backward. I have found that communicating this need to an eyeglass manufacturer or optometrist may yield exactly the right solution.

Singer-Guitarists

Singer-guitarists have a completely different set of challenges. They often must perform while seated, supporting the guitar on one leg. At other times, the guitar may be held by a strap that presses into one shoulder. Compounding all this, both hands and arms are completely occupied and held in different, non-parallel orientations, flexing and relaxing in quick succession scores of muscles to execute the intricate technique the instrument requires. Because playing the guitar requires so much coordination and concentration (which can also be said for playing the piano, bass, or drum set while singing), it is imperative for the singer to take breaks now and then during practice and simply sing to first establish good vocal habits. Singing each song in a standing position without self-accompanying is an excellent way for singer-instrumentalists of all types to learn a new song. This decreases the complexity of the task and helps the artist first establish a vocally sound approach to each new song. After the vocal considerations have been addressed and vocal challenges worked through, adding the accompanying instrument becomes an easier task, and the artist has a greater potential for successfully navigating both. Before attempting to perform both instruments simultaneously, the singer-guitarist must master each instrument's part independently without the interference of the other instrument, so singer-guitarists are encouraged to practice voice and guitar separately before bringing them together. One may think this point is obvious, but aspiring voice pedagogues may be surprised to find that many instrumentalists who wish to learn to sing have never tried to sing without playing their guitars or keyboard instruments! Dividing this performance load (as one divides the load of playing a piano nocturne by practicing one hand at a time) yields much more efficient, productive practice time, which leads more directly toward the attainment of performance goals.

Singer-Bassists

Singer-bassists (acoustic) have an advantage over pianists and many guitarists of orienting themselves in a standing position, so spinal health can be maintained by trying to align the first three points of balance (ankles, knees, and hips) while standing. However, the arm, hand, and shoulder positions necessary to perform music on this instrument require an ongoing commitment to maintaining freedom and relaxation while playing.

Singer-bassists also face the challenge of perfectly aligning the micro-phone in such a way that prevents having to lean toward it. As a matter of fact, mic placement for all singer-instrumentalists is a crucially important facet of good posture.

Singer-Drummers

Singer-drummers may have an advantage over all the rest of their singer-instrumentalist counterparts in that the only additional issue becomes placing a microphone correctly to capture the singing voice. All drum-mers at a drum kit are seated with legs akimbo—a position that lends itself well to properly aligning the vocal instrument, provided that the pelvis is slightly tucked under. As long as arms, shoulders, and core muscles are continually allowed to play in a fluid and relaxed manner, adding the voice to the quadrupedal performance style is more an issue of coordina-tion of yet another musical layer for the brain to process than an additional postural challenge. The mic should be placed on a boom stand positioned below singers' mouths to make sure they are not tilting the head backward to sing into it. The singer should always sing with the chin parallel to the floor or slightly downward toward the microphone for optimal neck alignment and spinal and vocal tract elongation, irrespective of what other instrument is being played simultaneously. The singer-drummer has the advantage of being able to maintain constant motion of the body, which can prevent undue tensions from creeping in, although one must concen-trate to allow the back, arms, and legs to frequently relax. Some drummers play in a constant state of muscle tension throughout the body and, there-fore, must be taught proper technique to release built-up tension as they play. As for any instrument, mastery of good technique must be achieved before a second instrument (the voice) may be successfully added for simultaneous performance. Good technique ensures that an instrument is played as healthfully and energy-efficiently as possible.

Singer-Wind Instrumentalists

Singers that play brass or woodwind instruments are faced with the chal-lenge of jaw alignment issues and tongue or throat tension when moving from singing to playing or vice versa. Brass and wind players have dif-ferent challenges depending on the way their instrument is played. Brass players may get accustomed to pursing the lips tightly to elicit a tone. Wind players may lock the jaw around the mouthpiece. Oboists may contort and pinch the pharynx and press the tongue to create a tiny aperture for the air to pass through. Each requires an understanding teacher well acquainted with tension-reducing strategies for that instrument to assist with letting go of unproductive, excessive tension in their playing. A teacher once recommended that a student singer cease playing the French horn because she noticed the student seemed to be singing "with embouchure," meaning that playing the horn may have been causing excess lip, jaw, or tongue tension in the student's singing. Rather than force singers to make a difficult choice, encourage them to seek help adopting better instrumental and vocal technique (and discuss how reducing lip, tongue, and jaw tension in one may enhance the other). This compassionate logic may allow students to pursue both disciplines. Helping students solve their own problems by providing excellent technique must be a primary goal for every music pedagogue.

Singer-trumpeter Chet Baker (early in his career) represented a good example of the relaxed sound a singer can achieve even right after playing a brass instrument requiring a powerful breath stream and some lip tension. Baker's relaxed singing mirrored his relaxed horn tone quality and showed that his laid-back, easygoing, gentle approach to singing could quickly modify into an efficient trumpet embouchure without producing any pinched or forced tone in either the horn or the voice. Another good idea to reduce lip and jaw tension experienced by a singer-brass instrumentalist is to "play" a mouth trumpet (imitating the sound a trumpet makes by using only the mouth). This exercise requires a relaxed pair of lips that easily blow apart when air is passed through them in the manner of a kazoo or semioccluded vocal tract exercise. Teaching singers to reduce their real-world tension in physical ways that are specifically pertinent to them and relevant to the instruments they play is an area of music pedagogy long overdue.

Singer-instrumentalists reading sheet music or tablets from music stands must consider positioning the stand at an optimum height to prevent leaning over and creating spinal curvature. As much as singing technique in the rehearsal and practice room requires attention to good posture and alignment, one mindlessly placed music stand or mic stand can ruin an otherwise well-prepared public performance. Singers are wise to make sure these ancillary tools are positioned to enhance their best singing posture and not sabotage it. Such details that can make or break not only the delivery of a singer's breath but also the audience's visual image of a confident performer must be routinely considered to be vital aspects of every performance.

University performance faculty would be wise to hold classes for singer-instrumentalists to specifically address the challenges inherent in playing instruments while singing. Releasing tension, maintaining good alignment, and executing other performance skills like breath management, diction, mic technique, and phrasing all require extreme coordination, which fluctuates on a case-by-case, student-by-student basis. Wise are the voice pedagogues who occasionally ask singer-instrumentalists to bring their instruments into the studio (or to demonstrate self-accompanying at the piano) to specifically work on the coordination of singing with instrumental playing and the reduction of resulting muscle tension. Such teachers constructively respond to the practical needs of their students.

BENEFITS OF EXCELLENT POSTURE

Optimal singing posture and alignment provide the pathway for the jazz singer (and all other types of singers, both professional and avocational) to achieve their fullest potential in areas of breath management, tone production, diction and enunciation, resonance, physical freedom, stage deportment, and expression. The manner in which one holds the body telegraphs a variety of issues to an audience. Audiences, by reading body language, can ascertain a performer's anxiety level, mental focus, ease (or lack of it) with which the performer approaches a performance, and overall confidence. Audiences want to be put at ease about these issues. No audience wishes to feel uncomfortable or anxious because of a performer's telegraphed anxiety. The gracious, confident manner with which a singer takes the stage and leaves the stage is important to practice. Singers that have rehearsed bows and entrances know precisely the path they have to travel and time the entrance or exit strategically with applause or proper deportment will be welcomed by the audience as appearing more "professional" than those performers who stumble to their starting places on the stage, walk with a slouch, or exhibit nervousness.

Improved Movement Onstage

Attention to excellent body alignment creates body awareness, good balance, and graceful stage deportment. Wearing comfortable shoes that support the feet and legs represents an essential part of supporting good alignment. Footwear that maximizes comfort and foot health (rather than four-inch spike heels that distract the audience and prevent the singer from walking normally with good posture) can add a measure of confidence and poise to a performance. Shoes with heels that place the singer "on their toes" contort the contour of the spine in extremely disadvantageous ways, compromising a singer's alignment. Watching singers precariously balance on too-high-heeled shoes can set an audience on edge. Singers respect their audiences by wearing clothing that puts the viewer at ease and exudes professionalism. Singers must carefully consider not only the appropriateness of their concert attire for each public performance but also the practical value of foot comfort and spinal alignment during a long show. Pinched toes and tight shoes may create a serious distraction from the art a singer intends to create onstage. Choosing sensible footwear for the challenging performance at hand is not just a matter of aesthetic but of heightening one's performance potential and practicing self-care.

Improved Everyday Health

Postural work facilitates freer movement of blood and lymph throughout the body and prepares it for any strenuous activity. It lengthens tight muscles, frees stiff joints, and provides a respite from habits that cause body fatigue, stiffness, and pain. Singers may notice improved attention and stamina throughout their workday from spending time practicing better postural habits.

To the surprise of many singers, poor posture may actually cause vocal fold pathologies, including nodules and polyps. The body's ongoing struggle for good posture involves the skeletal system's long bones, skull, pelvis, and spine. Constant muscular give and take, or push and pull, when poor posture and alignment are allowed to win the struggle, cause these major bones to be oriented suboptimally during the course of life. As explained elsewhere in this book, the larynx dangles from the hyoid bone through a complex network of muscles, ligaments, and attachments to the prevertebral fascia. It also is attached above to the basicranium and below to the trachea. Any undue pulling on this interconnected system by poor orientation of the skeleton can eventually wreak havoc on the carefully balanced equilibrium a person's postural system strives to maintain. Obviously, other body systems, including the vocal mechanism, may suffer damage or long-term harm if postural malalignment is allowed to habitually continue. With this knowledge, any singer is wise to place the cultivation of excellent postural habits among the highest priorities for vocal and overall health.

To create healthy habits, proper posture and alignment must be attended to during other activities of the singer's everyday existence—not only during singing. Checking one's posture periodically throughout the day is a great way to cultivate greater awareness of one's postural habits and alignment challenges. I suggest checking posture while driving a car, typing at a desk, walking the dog, standing in line, and so on. The advantages of standing well and keeping the vocal instrument as properly aligned as possible while singing, walking, standing, and doing countless daily activities cannot be overstated. The proof of the value of this heightened awareness will be shown by increased quality and consistency of vocal performances, the visual enjoyment of the audience, and the physical freedom and comfort of the performer.

Methods for Enhancing Posture and Body Awareness

Several approaches to enhancing spinal and postural health are available to the performing artist. These approaches remind the artist of the four natural curves a healthy spine possesses: the sacral and thoracic curves are concave while the lumbar and cervical curves are convex (see figure 3.1). Caring for one's spine involves practicing the sensation of lengthening when compression is sensed. Becoming adept at using various yoga stretches and poses helps to keep the spine healthy by extending distances between vertebrae and strengthening various muscles throughout the body—particularly core muscles in the abdominal and back regions. Yoga can safely be practiced daily by those with normal spinal health, although checking with one's physician is always advisable before undertaking any exercise routine.

Studies in Alexander Technique or Feldenkrais become extremely relevant when adopting measures to improve postural health for both singers and nonsingers. Both disciplines greatly increase one's personal awareness of postural habits. Both Alexander Technique and Feldenkrais educate performing artists about how to maximize their own abilities to release posture-related tensions and to adopt a new lifestyle of healthy alignment.

POSTURE LESSONS FROM THE MASTERS

Films and photographs of Peggy Lee's posture during live performances clearly showed a broad, open chest, a head in good alignment with the spine and the rest of the body (neither tipped backward nor tucked downward, but right in the "sweet spot" to maximize laryngeal efficiency and

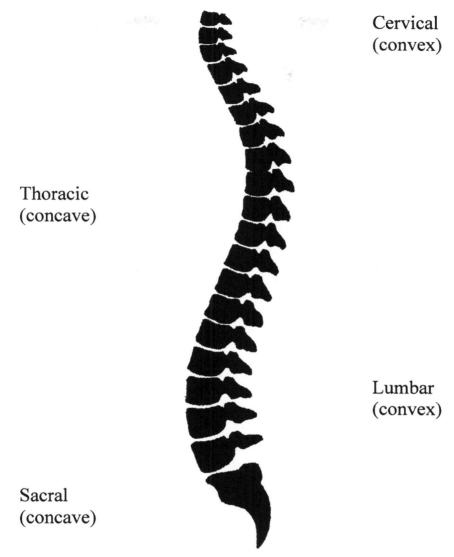

Cervical
(convex)

Thoracic
(concave)

Lumbar
(convex)

Sacral
(concave)

Figure 3.1. Curves of the Spine. Courtesy of Author

length), and an upright, relaxed body orientation, which commanded attention and provided strength, confidence, and stamina for her performances. Even when seated for duets with Frank Sinatra or Judy Garland, the camera showed Lee's posture clearly maintaining proper alignment, setting her up for successful singing. Part of Lee's ability to hold an audience in the palm of her hand came from her elegance and self-assurance conveyed by correct body alignment.

Nat "King" Cole was a highly accomplished jazz pianist who could play and sing effortlessly. His posture as shown in televised performances reflected alignment that did not interfere with good vocalism or absolute freedom of his piano playing. He even sometimes stood up and walked away from the piano while still playing the last lick of a solo in a manner that maintained his spinal alignment as he moved from a seated position to standing. Sarah Vaughan also played piano professionally and even started her career not as a singer but as a backup pianist. Vaughan was able to sit and sing with posture that kept her vocal instrument properly aligned with arms and shoulders relaxed as she played. Developing the advanced coordination required to self-accompany requires diligent practice as well as keen body awareness. Singer-instrumentalists must learn to pique their awareness of tense areas before they develop serious problems that interfere with best performance practice.

Because excellent posture and alignment facilitate the best performance results regardless of genre, one might expect that most of the finest jazz singers in history possessed exemplary posture. This is the case and not only because proper posture enhanced singing excellence but also because the best singers looked their best *and* sounded their best. Professional singers were and still are expected to look as professional as they sound. Ella Fitzgerald, Frank Sinatra, Sarah Vaughan, Nancy Wilson, and scores of other outstanding jazz voice artists were known not only for the outstanding voices and style they possessed but also for their excellent stage presence, a major component of which is proper alignment. This "total package" rendered these artists consistently inspiring on their recordings, in their live performances, on television, and in film.

A well-aligned singing instrument provides optimal tone production, breath management, stamina, physical freedom, stage deportment, and overall health for the professional and avocational vocal artist, regardless of the style or genre of music performed. Given the various ways in which poor alignment or posture can hinder or even harm the voice, contrasted with the myriad ways fine posture provides the greatest potential for musical success, the task of moving toward a lifestyle of optimizing one's own posture is well worth pursuing. Finely tuning one's alignment, and not only of the singing mechanism but of the points of balance and all areas of the skeleton and its network of connections, can only enhance and increase physical strength, balance, flexibility, functionality and general health.

4

MANAGING THE BREATH

A singer's airflow provides the energy through which all singing occurs. The quality of a singer's tone depends largely on the extent to which the sung phrase is adequately energized and supported by air. The airstream must be highly energized without being forced through the aperture made by the adducting vocal folds. All professional and student jazz singers are behooved to possess some working knowledge of efficient breath management as well as exercises that will enhance their developing breathing technique. As singers learn coordination of the breathing muscles along with the expressive delivery of a song, they learn that the craft of breath management is an aspect of singing to be diligently and patiently honed and exercised as much as any other aspect of singing technique. In many respects, to breathe well is to sing well.

THE PROCESS OF BREATHING

The **diaphragm** is a double-domed muscle that separates the abdominal cavity from the thoracic cavity. It flexes downward toward the floor during inhalation and relaxes upward toward the head during exhalation. This important respiratory muscle is the muscle most responsible for the process of inhalation. The diaphragm cannot be touched from the outside of the body—a fact that often causes confusion for those told to "sing from the diaphragm." Often those offering such advice have compounded the confusion by placing hands on the abdomen, as if that were the location of the diaphragm. In truth, the **epigastrium**, and not the diaphragm, is the abdominal area that can be touched from the outside. During exhalation, the epigastrium moves gradually inward toward the spine through the action of the lower abdominal muscles, which are the primary muscles responsible for exhalation. The coordinated action of both the diaphragm and the abdominal muscles creates the process of healthy respiration. The degree of inward movement of the abdominal muscles varies from teacher to teacher. Some prefer a lot of movement, and others hardly any. I have discovered that being flexible is the most important aspect here, and that because every singer's body is different, the body's needs and comfort level should be allowed to play a part in determining how far the abdominals actually travel toward the spine during each exhalation. No matter how far the epigastrium travels, it remains imperative that the sternum never drops to a lower, collapsed position and that the sense of intercostal support is maintained throughout each phrase, until the end of the phrase is released.

Release and the Singing Cycle

Experienced singers learn to energize their release (the final sound at the end of the phrase that ceases at the moment inhalation begins) as much as their onset is energized. There is never a part of the singing cycle that involves "holding" of either muscle or breath. Inhaling is followed by singing, which is followed again by inhaling, and so on. Professional singers do not exhale after releasing their phrases. They teach their bodies to spend all the breath on singing the phrase at hand, regardless of its length, without collapsing the chest cavity. Then singers gently replenish the air that was spent during the next inhalation. Likewise, singers do not pause and wait (to hold or to count) after a release or before or after an inhalation. This commitment to the singing cycle, singing—breathing—singing—breathing, requires disciplined practice because when we speak we often hold our breaths or hold muscle tension. Singers teach the body that we cease singing because we have already begun to inhale and that we inhale until the moment we begin to sing, with no hesitation, suspension of time, or hovering of breath in between.

Appoggio

In singers the "struggle" or oppositional forces at work between the diaphragm and the abdominal muscles constitute the concept of **appoggio**, the Italian singing term describing the leaning of air against the rib cage from the inside. A strong appoggio technique gives the singer long, consistent lines, evenness of tone, stamina for extended phrases, dynamic control, and energy to maintain breath support for as long as the phrase endures. Regardless of style and genre sung, every professional singer would benefit from learning the fine skill of appoggio breathing technique in the manner of the Italian bel canto opera masters.

Intercostal Muscles

Muscles between the ribs, called "**intercostal muscles**," also play an important role in the process of respiration, as anyone who has broken a rib can testify. Broken ribs create severe pain during even the calmest and shallowest breathing, showing how instrumental they are in the body's process of air exchange. External intercostals, located outside the ribs, work together with the diaphragm to regulate the inspiratory phase of respiration. Internal intercostals, located inside the rib cage, work with the abdominal muscles to regulate the expiratory phase of respiration. The rib cage lifts in an upward and outward pattern during inhalation, in what some pedagogues refer to as "bucket-handle motion" to vividly paint a picture describing the movement they perform. By contrast, when the rib cage lowers during exhalation, the "bucket handles" move downward and inward, effectively decreasing the chest's volume of air.

The Gesture of Inhalation

The singer's objective is sometimes described as singing on the gesture of inhalation. This means the singer must work on allowing the rib cage to occupy an open, stretched position for as long as possible during every sung phrase, as though the singing were happening during the inspiratory process. In reality, of course this is not so, but helping the brain and body enjoy the sensations associated with fullness in the rib cage and buoyancy of the newly replenished lungs *for as long as the phrase endures* creates the potential for the singer to sustain longer phrases with greater supportive energy as one's breathing technique grows. Singing on the gesture of inhalation helps the singer keep the throat open and the thoracic cavity wide and fully expanded instead of allowing the rib cage to collapse as singing occurs. Many inexperienced singers literally blow out their air along with the tone, causing the thoracic cavity to implode somewhat as the air leaves the body. The gesture of inhalation assists singers in addressing this tendency and gives them an alternate action to perform during singing. Instead of allowing the body to collapse, the spine is extended, the rib cage remains open, and the outward stretching of the ribs must feel as though it continues through and beyond the release of the phrase. To accomplish this, a singer must work mentally to convince the body that continuing the motion of stretching the ribs outward acts as buoyant support for the tone (which it absolutely does). Singers' appoggios should not result in a holding of tension in the rib cage or elsewhere but rather an outward directional lean and expansion as they sing. Gently singing a variety of exercises (legato, staccato, onsets, melismas, and messa di voce) while this process is practiced will yield a greater awareness about the intercostal and abdominal actions present in the singer's breath. These exercises strengthen the body's management of its respiratory muscle systems as the airstream is regulated.

APPLYING THE SINGER'S BREATH TO JAZZ

Many jazz singers have not been adequately trained in the art of breathing well. Broken sentences, unfinished thoughts, noisy breaths, phrases cut too short, and even words interrupted by a breath happen all too often in contemporary commercial and jazz singing. This is not artistic, nor worthy of emulation. All of the greatest interpreters of jazz and Great American Songbook standards placed the importance of expressing the lyrics through a well-supported tone among their highest performance priorities. Sarah Vaughan, Ella Fitzgerald, Betty Carter, Carmen McRae, and many other jazz greats knew how to spin long, alluring lines, breathing only where the spoken phrases demanded a breath. The microphone does not help a singer breathe well, but it certainly amplifies poor breath management for the entire audience to observe at close scrutiny. Singers are wise to cultivate breathing technique that spurs compliments from audience members, and not for singing marathon phrases through commas and periods, but for the purpose of possessing a well-trained instrument that breathes only at punctuation marks and natural speech pauses. Singers must train the body to obey the mind's directive to sustain a phrase with excellent support and expression until a natural speech pause arrives. Cultivating sound breathing technique takes aerobic strength and years of work. It also requires daily practice to fend off muscle atrophy of the abdominal muscles and intercostal muscles.

The singer's breath represents the power and stamina beneath every beautiful tone. Regardless of style or genre, artistic singers work to cultivate a responsive breath management system and muscle coordination that can be relied on and trusted not to hold excess tension. Finding this balance is not always easy nor straightforward. Developing a sound breathing technique or modifying one that needs adjustment represents one of the primary objectives of every good voice teacher. Singers dealing with breath management challenges are encouraged to seek an experienced teacher who can address this shortfall because it is difficult to teach oneself to breathe correctly. A second set of ears and eyes is often required to adequately ascertain the source or cause of a breathing or alignment issue troubling a singer.

HELPFUL BREATHING EXERCISES

Every voice pedagogue needs a handful of breathing exercises that help students become aware of the action of their breathing muscles. Some exercises create this awareness, while others deepen strength and flexibility in the muscles involved in breathing. Many of the exercises that help opera and classical singers also greatly assist jazz singers as they work to develop sound breath management. Teaching breathing technique involves both resolving inefficient or unhealthy vocal habits as well as teaching new healthy habits. The experienced teacher keeps an eye (and ear) on detecting poor habits while commencing instruction of healthy breath management.

Resolving the Noisy Breath

The singer's breath must not only support each phrase of text and music but also be commenced and released in a manner that does not draw undue attention to itself. The most effective breaths are silent, owing to a fully open trachea and oropharynx. The resistance supplied by a partially closed breathing passage can create more and more resistance (and noise) as time progresses. Resolving the resistance causing an overtly noisy breath must be a high priority for the voice pedagogue. True, jazz singers may sometimes choose to inhale with sound (as in a sigh or other effect) but they must not be forced by default to always inhale with excess noise.

The noisy breath is a habit worth resolving to open the trachea and the oropharynx as fully as possible and allow the singer fuller access to air.

Often, exercises that increase singers' awareness of the height of their soft palate can help to open a too-closed airway. The letter *k*, when made with a relaxed jaw and tongue, can facilitate some exercise for the soft palate.

EXERCISE: THE "K-BREATH"

Breathe in a [k] by inhaling at the precise moment that the back of the tongue lightly and briefly touches the roof of the back of the mouth (the soft palate). Then exhale the *k* as a whisper, with no phonation, using the same light, brief tongue-touch to the roof of the mouth. Repeat several times, breathing in and out, increasing your awareness of the soft palate's ability to elevate on demand. This "k-breath" causes the soft palate to lift, opening the back of the throat. When doing this be sure the jaw rocks down and back to open (never tightening or jutting forward) and simply dangles there. Allow the front of the tongue to lie gently on the bottom lip or touch the back of the bottom teeth.

EXERCISE

Sing [ku ku - ku ku - ku ku - ku ku - ku] on the following scale degrees in a key starting in the middle of the singer's range: | 5 5 5 5 | 5 4 3 2 | 1— |. Use an eighth note rhythm for every syllable until the final tone, which will be a whole note. Modulate upward through the middle-high range and descend again to the bottom-middle of the singer's range. This gives the soft palate and tongue a workout and teaches the mind that, when healthy, it can some-what control the position of the tongue, soft palate, and jaw. The jaw should be in its well-aligned place rocked downward and back, just hanging loosely open (not chewing or jawing in time with the *k* enunciations). The back of the tongue does all the movement in this exercise and the jaw should rest. The front tip of the tongue should lie in its "parking space" atop the bottom teeth, touching the back of the bottom lip. This prevents the root of the tongue from pulling backward or locking. A relaxed throat, tongue, and jaw are necessary for all singers to use at will, as part of their baseline, natural technique of breathing and singing.

A Lesson from the Italian School

For several generations, the Italian bel canto method of singing has taught that to train the body to breathe well for singing, one should mindfully work on it all throughout the day's activities, whether actively singing or not. One can do this while doing other things by breathing four slow counts in, suspending the air inside the lungs with a wide intercostal stretch for four counts with the glottis open, and exhaling for four slow counts, working to maintain the outward stretch even during the exhalation phase of the cycle. Repeating this three-part cycle for several minutes throughout the day helps to engage the low, wide breath whenever a singer remembers to do it. This mindful breath cycle forms a sound basis for a singer's breath as long as the middle stage of the cycle (the suspension stage) allows the chest to remain open and relaxed (practicing the outward appoggio lean) rather than tight or pressed.

Breath of Fire

Various aspects of yoga lend themselves to developing an efficient breathing technique for singing. The following exercise illustrates the "breath of fire," which represents an excellent approach to expanding strength and flexibility in the breathing muscles. I learned this in a voice pedagogy course taught by Dr. Paul Huybrechts at the University of Southern California as a technique that assists singers in developing the abdominal, diaphragmatic, and intercostal muscles while calming the body and mind.

EXERCISE

Be seated on the floor in a cross-legged position, lotus pose, or half-lotus pose maintaining a long, stretched spinal column and a relaxed neck and shoulders. Rest the hands open with palms upward on the knees. Begin to pant like a dog with the jaw gently hanging open. The lower abdominal muscles should gently flutter in and out in keeping with the pattern of exhaling (moving the abs inward toward the spine) and inhaling (releasing the abs which pops them back outward to starting position). At no point is it necessary to push the abdominal muscles outward or to suck air inward—simply letting go of the abdominal muscles' flexion after drawing them inward toward the spine creates enough vacuum (decreased pressure) inside the lungs to automatically bring air back into the lungs. Try this slowly until the pattern becomes natural and then increase the speed of the pant. Beginners will need to stop and breathe every minute or so. As you become more advanced, you can regulate your oxygen intake as you pant over several minutes (adjusting how much or how little air is invited in) as needed for maximum comfort of the breath, without ever having to stop the exercise to breathe deeply.

The next step in this "breath of fire" exercise is to continue to pant but close the mouth and forcefully exhale through the nose for each exhalation (abs moving inward toward spine), and fully release (let go of) the abdominal muscles to complete the inhalation stage of every breath cycle. The forceful exhalation should emit a sound as the air rushes past the nose, but the inhalation should stay silent. As comfort with this exercise increases, speed of the pant cycle may also increase. Although physically challenging at first, this exercise will eventually build flexibility, strength, and superior control by the mind over the body's breathing technique.

EXERCISE

Another breathing exercise that has been circulated through many pedagogues' studios over the years in various iterations is what I call the "four-part breathing exercise." It consists of inhaling slowly and deeply, and then rapidly executing sixteen unvoiced consonants or consonant clusters while taking a quick "sip" of breath in between each one (much like the panting exercises just discussed). The pattern goes thus: [s]-[s]-[s]-[s]-[sh]-[sh]-[sh]-[sh]-[ft]-[ft]-[ft]-ft]-[wht]-[wht]-[wht]-[wht]. Each sound is given rhythmic equivalence and the entire sixteen-part cycle is repeated without pause four times. If desired, the final four [wht] syllables may be slowed down to half-time feel to facilitate a chance to breathe and fully release the abdominal muscles between each one at the end of this strenuous exercise.

In each of these breathing exercises, it is important to remember that "pulling" air into the lungs is unnecessary. Air rushes in automatically when the abdominal muscles are correctly released, and they return (spring forward) on their own, back to the starting position. When exhaling, if the abs move gently toward the spine (neither violently nor with a great dramatic motion), a complete abdominal release pops the epigastrium forward, lowers the diaphragm, and triggers the inhalation phase, which is easy to notice. Singers are often astonished to discover they no longer need to intentionally pull air into the lungs to sing! The energy conserved by allowing inhalations to be relaxation responses in the body rather than laborious work often transforms a singer's technique and mindset. Correct singing and nimble breath management technique naturally imbue pleasant sensations as one sings with both phenomena employed.

Singers whose vocal instruments are inherently breathy may initially have difficulty with these exercises, but they may find that cultivating good breathing technique actually clears up the noise in the voice. Inefficiency of the breath is often the main culprit for the chronically breathy voice that cannot sustain a complete phrase without breathing in the middle of it. Jazz and commercial singers who prefer using a breathy tone still benefit a great deal when their breath efficiency grows. The air can be used more mindfully and doled out accordingly as the singer pleases when breath management improves, rather than in random ways that sabotage a line of music or a meaningful phrase of lyrics. No longer should a "breathy" singer need to breathe every couple of words! With improved breath flexibility and management, one can use a breathy quality in the manner of Anita O'Day without dicing up phrases into much-too-small components that distract audiences from the meaning of the text. A singer who cannot make it through a phrase sounds less of a musician than one who can, with or without a breathy quality in the tone.

Semioccluded Vocal Tract Exercises

A class of exercises that assists in developing efficient breath management is the semioccluded vocal tract (SOVT) group of exercises. As documented by voice scientist Ingo Titze in the *Journal of Singing* (2018), these exercises are often used for vocal rehabilitation, developing mixed registration, and stretching the vocal folds while strengthening the vocal ligament for improved performance of high tones.

Voiced Consonants

SOVT exercises come in various types. Singing scales, arpeggios, or melismas on the z consonant sound (as in "zebra") represents a good introduction to this class of exercise. Modifying this consonant slightly toward "zh" (as in "pleasure") creates another variation that can be used successfully. To maintain the semioccluded quality, singing should be done while sustaining only the voiced consonant—not merely starting with an initial "z" or "zh" and then opening to a vowel. Sustaining the "z" or "zh" through a run or slide allows the voice to phonate on pitch with less pressure on the folds and less volume needed to sing high pitches. It also facilitates legato singing throughout the entire compass of the voice, with easier access to high tones than a singer can achieve using open vowels. This is a wonderful approach for helping singers learn to mix the head-dominant sound with the chest-dominant sound to arrive at a healthy blended mix.

Another SOVT exercise is simply to sing through exercises or song passages while sustaining either the voiced "th" (the first sound in the word "this") or "v." Singing scales and other pitch patterns on these voiced consonants engages the breath powerfully while encouraging efficient and healthy vocalism.

Straw Phonation

One SOVT exercise popular with voice pedagogues and made well-known by Dr. Titze involves the use of a straw. Buzzing one's scales, arpeggios, exercises, and song melodies through a straw (I prefer the coffee-stirrer size) enables the singer's breathing mechanism to self-regulate the amount of air pressure needed to cleanly execute the assignments. With lowered phonation threshold pressure provided by SOVT exercises, singers can phonate softly and gently with less pressure exerted on the folds, while building their vocal mix.

Singers and teachers must make every effort to minimize the tension that buzzing through a straw may add. Some students press the lips too firmly together or tighten the jaw, tongue, facial, or neck muscles in an effort to successfully perform this exercise. Careful monitoring in the mirror and by the teacher should help eliminate unwanted, added tensions. One suggested way of using straw technique is to perform every other phrase of an exercise or song with the straw and singing the alternate phrases. This may help enhance singers' awareness of the differences they feel when phonating the passage in two very different ways.

Breathing Pedagogy in the Real World

Teachers need to be mindful of teaching the student in the room. That means addressing whatever specific technical needs the student presents on a given day. Although challenging, this requires teachers to keep their ears and eyes open for clues about what technical areas warrant practice and immediate attention. Great teachers always use their eyes and ears (and physical sensations if they are highly sensitive to a student's tension) to address and remedy issues that directly pertain to that student on a given day. This personalized approach tends to work better than a unit by unit pedagogy given to every student the same way every day. Voices and individuals are so unique that a tailored education is absolutely necessary when teaching any branch of voice—whether jazz, music theatre, pop, rock, opera, or any other genre. Instrumentalists must take this to heart when teaching singers. There are no "one-size-fits-all" exercises to coax the best breath management technique from every student because people complicate healthy breathing technique in their own unique ways. Teachers must think on their feet and carefully notice what their students' habits reveal. Unhealthy habits or tendencies must first be addressed and resolved before a student can sing to the next level of their potential. The mix of exercises must therefore be flexible and malleable toward each student's needs. Although many students may start at the same point when they learn basic posture and breathing technique (as in a voice class forum), individuals will show their own particular habits or unique approaches to singing. It is most important, then, that teachers begin recognizing and documenting at the first lesson or class what a student's strengths and weaknesses are. Through the regularly instituted discipline of documenting lessons, young teachers will discover how important lesson journaling (by the teacher for each student's lessons) can be for their own pedagogical development (see chapter 15). Additional breathing exercises (with dual objectives of cultivating both breath management and mindfulness) are suggested in chapter 13.

Assessing Breath Management Problems

A crucial consideration in all voice pedagogy is the requirement for the teacher to specifically address any problems, challenges, or knowledge gaps pertaining to each student. I emphasize this point because many young pedagogues (and even experienced ones) start on a path of teaching certain units to their singers in the same order, using the same repertoire, the same exercises, and the same approaches for every student. This practice reflects neither how the human body nor the mind works. Often, getting to the root of a student's problem is the first order of business for the voice teacher. A student's breathing habits may provide the first clue to any inherent problems with phonation, so teachers must pay close attention to how a singer breathes and phonates at the first audition or lesson.

For instance, for a student whose abdominal muscles never completely release, a teacher may find the breath of fire exercise helpful. Anyone working with singers—whether voice teachers, choral directors, vocal coaches or small ensemble directors—must learn what correct breathing technique looks like visually (and what the result should be aurally) as well as how to regularly incorporate exercises or warm-ups that teach singers the invaluable skills of breath management. With ample knowledge and observation, corrections can be made before poor habits become further ingrained and possibly injurious to a singer's voice or career.

Breathing Technique Exemplified by Jazz Greats

Legendary jazz singers found ways to support their voices with outstanding breath management. Even today the most compelling performers are those whose bodies do not collapse when expected to sing long, lush lines of text or improvised solos. Examining the breathing techniques of jazz greats is an area of pedagogy most interesting and worthy of exploration.

Peggy Lee

Early in her career Peggy Lee recorded a stunningly beautiful rendition of Richard Rodgers' and Lorenz Hart's "Where or When" from the 1937 musical *Babes in Arms*. Her recording fabulously illustrated the principle of appoggio applied to jazz and commercial singing. Lee managed to consistently sustain breath energy evenly and seamlessly through the long, slow, final ascending scale in the last bars of the piece. She skillfully kept her timbre, pitch, and vibrato steady through that legato passage, using a lovely mix. Throughout the first three decades of her career, Lee exemplified the advanced ability to reveal different levels of breathiness in her tone depending on the song, tempo, style, and mood. In "Hallelujah, I Love Him So," Lee used a clear, exuberant tone quality, almost a belt, while in the melancholic ballad "Johnny Guitar," she poured on the pathos through a rush of air coming into the microphone along with her tone. Throughout the *Black Coffee* album from 1953, Lee used varying degrees of clarity in her tone, yielding great contrast in timbre and mood among the songs. For the title track, her overtly breathy style suggested a sultry, tired affect, whereas in "My Heart Belongs to Daddy," her belted tones in the refrain reflected an entirely different attitude. This profound control over her tone quality helped to make Lee the chameleonic artist that she became—always willing to let the song dictate how she should sing it while honoring the composer with her thoughtful rendition.

Years later Lee abandoned most head voice singing, partly due to breathing problems brought on by decades of smoking and a later bout of pneumonia. Although continuing to sing professionally after losing much of her upper range, she focused on other aspects of her craft, which were particularly outstanding (rhythm, timing, phrasing, and expression) because her breath management was compromised to the extreme extent of needing oxygen backstage to get through her performances. Singers would be wise to consider the decline of Lee's breathing capacity and severely compromised lung health when deciding how best to take care of their lungs and overall health for their own sake as well as for career longevity.

Tony Bennett

Tony Bennett by contrast, ninety-four at the time of this writing, sang long, energized phrases with impressive power and outstanding upper range even well into his nineties. His consistently strong breath management proves that it is possible for a professional singer to continue singing into their older years when care is taken to protect and preserve the instrument and overall health. Bennett also gave his voice regular workouts, never ceasing to perform, but allotting himself proper rest when necessary. Bennett's example can be a lesson for us all—take care of the voice and it will take care of you.

Bennett's various live and studio recordings of "The Best Is Yet to Come" illustrated several facets of outstanding breath management. The song's long phrases, having intricately leaping chromatic melodies, were consistently sung in tune with even support. His key changes sounded effortless in part because of his finely honed system of energized breath. He also possessed remarkable power in his upper register, which rarely sounded forced or unstable—all owing to his ability to sustain the breath consistently through each phrase as well as any well-trained operatic tenor.

Nancy Wilson

Singers are wise to remember that a breathy quality should be reserved for specific purposes—not used in every song or simply by default. Healthy voices are able to create various mixes of focused tone, yielding a much greater timbral palette of aural choices for the expressive jazz, pop, or blues singer. Nancy Wilson's singing exemplified this breathing mastery—on many occasions her tones practically sighed into the microphone with a great rush of air, lending a sensuous quality to her voice. On other occasions, she sang with pure tonal clarity that enabled her to use a variety of colors and volume levels. Wilson was not forced by poor technique to sing with excess air on every tone; she chose to sing in a breathy way sometimes, for effect.

Tonal clarity must be a goal for every professional singer because it tends to be indicative of vocal health and longevity, and it greatly increases a singer's compass of sound possibilities. A healthy voice can sound breathy when the singer chooses that timbre, but an unhealthy voice cannot always phonate with clarity.

Sarah Vaughan

Sarah Vaughan provided another excellent example of a singer in full command of her breathing technique. Throughout her career she consistently demonstrated how to spin a lush, exquisitely beautiful tone that connected all her notes throughout her broad range. Her ability to crescendo and decrescendo at will afforded her an artist's palette supplied with a variety of colors and options for changing moods and intentions. All this interpretive and musical power came from her commanding breath management skills. Vaughan's outstanding breathing technique was demonstrated on "Tenderly," which she recorded with stunning soft dynamics and delicious portamenti—connective ornaments as exquisite as those performed by professional opera singers. Vaughan achieved a dazzling mix of light and dark colors as she leapt from the lowest pitch point of the song to the highest nearly two octaves away. The very qualities that made "Tenderly" a song many singers avoided (a broad range and sophisticated breathing requirements) became the points at which Vaughan excelled, drawing clear distinctions between herself and her contemporaries.

Addressing the complex process of developing an efficient breathing technique involves creating familiarity with breathing muscles and their function, exploring various exercises that strengthen the coordinated breath, and listening to singers whose impressive breathing techniques are apparent in live performances and recordings. The jazz singer's achievement of the efficient singer's breath is a goal richly rewarded by a vastly improved tone quality, potential for masterful phrasing, a greater ability to create nuances and stylistic distinctions, and improved coordination of the singer's energy source. All this leads to much greater command of vocal technique, increased confidence on the stage, and a heightened value of musicianship in the eyes of both the band and the audience.

5

PHONATION, ARTICULATION, AND RESONANCE

Jazz singers possess a wide range of approaches to phonation, articulation, and resonance. Some singers have gravelly voices, and the jazz world has been quick to welcome them. Other artists are more speakers or poets than singers. Unlike in classical music, the jazz industry has judged singers less by the tone quality, clarity, and technical mastery of their voices than by the originality and authenticity of their music. Imitators are less apt to be embraced than those whose emulation of others plays directly into their own interpretive style.

As jazz voice pedagogues, our job with singers is to help them sing as healthfully as possible first. Assisting a singer with knowledge about how singing and breathing occur in their own bodies represents a good starting point. Helping singers access the vocal sounds they like is often a tricky job when the sounds (in the teacher's opinion) may not be the healthiest. However, as singer-pedagogue Nathan Gunn told me in an interview, "you can do a lot with your voice that's healthy even though it sounds 'on the edge.'"[1]

PHONATION

Phonation occurs when the vocal folds adduct (come together) as the lungs exhale a stream of air, producing a tone. Phonation takes many forms. Speaking, singing, grunting, wailing, screaming, laughing, whining, and vocal fry represent various manifestations of this natural human phenomenon. Not strictly a human activity, phonation is practiced regularly by many animals, as anyone who has experience around them knows. The dog's bark or whine, a cat's meow, a pig's grunt, a cow's moo, a lion's roar, and countless other animals' vocalized sounds are possible because mammals share the trait of a pair of vocal folds within a laryngeal structure fixed at the top of the trachea. This organ serves as a valve facilitating respiration, communication, and prevention of choking (via the epiglottis) during the act of swallowing food or drink.

The Onset

The precise moment a phonated vowel begins is termed the **onset**. Onsets may occur in three basic ways: **breathy**, **glottal**, or **coordinated**. Only the coordinated onset is considered correct in healthy singing.

The Breathy Onset

The breathy onset (sometimes called "breathy attack") occurs when the air begins moving through the vocal folds from the lungs out of the body before the folds adduct. This type of onset mingles pure tone with an audible stream of air, and it can lead to a consistently "breathy" tone production in some cases (although at times it may only be the onset that sounds breathy). The breathy tone can be quite an alluring addition to the jazz singer's toolbox when such a color is warranted, but for healthy lifelong singing, it should be stressed that a breathy tone is simply one of many colors we use to paint our aural works of art. Using it all the time yields unhealthy vocal production, poor phonatory habits, and a somewhat limited palette of vocal color.

The Glottal Pop

The glottal or hard onset occurs when the folds adduct prior to the start of airflow. The resultant tone begins with a popping sound (a "glottal pop") during which the folds literally slap together. This type of onset, when done to extremes or habitually, can cause stress on the folds, which may lead to vocal fold pathology. When performed to excess it is considered a form of vocal abuse. Nodules (calluses that develop on the surface of the vocal folds) may result from habitual glottal onsets, so it is incumbent on every singer to learn the proper way to begin a tone that starts with a vowel sound. On occasion in jazz, a glottal pop or a breathy onset may yield a temporary desired effect, but I stress that these are choices a knowledgeable singer makes and not habits that singers should pursue as their default "style." Because self-care is an important consideration for a singer's longevity, every singer must learn to properly coordinate the onset, thereby maximizing healthy phonation habits.

The Coordinated Onset

The coordinated onset has for many generations of professional singers delineated a crucial starting point for healthy singing because it determines how the rest of the phrase will be sung. This type of onset occurs when the folds adduct at precisely the same moment airflow begins, providing a cushion of air that protects the folds from slapping together forcefully, while at the same time avoiding an overt outflow of air preceding the tone. This onset may be accomplished by practicing the imaginary *h* at the onset of each tone that begins with a vowel sound. In his revered pedagogy textbook, *The Structure of Singing* (1986), Richard Miller describes the hard onset as a "grunt" and the breathy onset as a "whisper," neither of which represents an ideal onset that singers should habitually pursue. The imaginary *h* at the start of a sung vowel requires the correct engagement of the abdominal muscles with a slight inward movement of the lower abdominals in concert with the phonated onset. Practicing staccato passages with a gentle coordinated onset is part of many professional singers' daily workout because it coordinates the low breath, engages lower abdominal muscles, and adducts the vocal folds simultaneously. Few concentrated exercises are more valuable to both the beginner and the seasoned professional singer.

EXERCISE

Sing "ah" five times slowly on quarter notes on the same pitch in the middle of the range, with quarter rests between each syllable. Release the abdominal muscles fully to inhale during each rest. Sing each syllable with a gentle glottal pop (a hard attack) at the onset of the tone. Then repeat the exercise replacing glottal pops with breathy onsets (sing "hah" on each syllable). Finally, subtract the initial *h* for each (but imagine that the *h* remains) to sing with an imaginary *h* at the onset. This is the basis for the correctly sung coordinated onset. Each type of onset may be instructive depending on how pressed or loose the student's glottal closure may be. The thoughtful teacher can use a combination of these onset exercises to help a student find ideal vocal fold closure.

The Natural Baseline Voice

In jazz singing, a variety of onset types can provide several distinct colors for the artist's palette. Grunts, pops, vocal fry, breathy whispers, and coordinated onsets can all be valid choices for approaching the first tone of a phrase, depending on the song, mood, genre, and theme. First and foremost, however, all singers (regardless of genre) must discover and nurture their "baseline" voice. This "natural," "neutral," or "baseline" voice refers to the free, healthy, well-supported tone that is not influenced by any particular genre or style. The singer's baseline voice exhibits balanced resonance with a mix of both head and chest-dominant qualities. This healthy mix should be used whenever vocalizing, warming up, learning a new piece, coaxing the voice back from the margins after having sung a character role, or recovering from illness or vocal rest. All singers should work hard to cultivate a healthy, vibrant, energized natural voice that "walks the center line" away from overt nasality, breathiness, huskiness, breaking, cracking, or other sounds singers add on occasion. Consider these alternate timbres to be different colors but not the primary starting point. The natural voice is akin to a paintbrush which never changes. Shades of musical color represent the paint. Different amounts of air mixed with tone (breathiness or huskiness), vocal noise (gravel, harshness, or vocal fry), or nasality may be added to the healthy, natural voice to reflect style or mood, and to add color appropriate to the given song. To first establish one's healthy center line represents the single most important priority for singers and singing teachers in contemporary commercial music (CCM). If that neutral baseline voice is unhealthy, there is little a singer can do to add beauty or to improve a tone. Slightly tweaking a healthy, well-supported natural voice to be stylistically correct across a multitude of styles (music theatre, jazz, pop, country, rock, metal, folk, and even baroque music and opera) remains the task of successful contemporary singers. Once the healthy, well-supported baseline or natural voice (without added colors, affects, or stylistic tweaks) becomes firmly established as the singer's go-to for their most natural, healthy tone, there is no end to the colors and nuances that can be added or modified to create authenticity within a given style.

What is this "natural," "baseline," or "neutral" voice? The healthy baseline creates fully supported, pure vowels that are tension-free and resonance-balanced. It is based on solid technique, proper body alignment, mindful awareness, healthy breath management, vowel purity, and whole-body singing. This point has sadly been lost on many modern singers. Too often a contemporary singer breaks and cracks the voice to fill the audience's ears with interesting vocal noises but cannot sing an uninterrupted legato vowel line to convey vocal beauty in a ballad. Singers' career longevity depends on their ability to find the natural, healthy voice at a moment's notice and always return to that foundational baseline before adding vocal color of any kind. Successful singers stretch and work out the baseline, healthy voice each morning or at the start of the warm-up before every performance. Ideally, the neutral baseline is the voice with which a singer speaks as well as sings. Speaking resonantly with air supporting each spoken word is the first step toward cultivating a healthy vocal instrument.

Lessons from the Masters

Historically, outstanding jazz singers have created tone in a wide variety of ways (some healthy and some unhealthy). Somehow, even those without pristine technique were able to keep audiences returning to hear them perform over and over again. Jazz aficionados collected recordings by singers whose artistry consistently shined. What were these artists really doing in terms of phonation? Students and teachers alike benefit from observing specific aspects of technique possessed and displayed by the jazz masters of yesteryear. We can also learn how to take better care of our voices by understanding healthier ways to achieve a desired sound.

Nat "King" Cole

Nat "King" Cole's voice may be described as essentially clear and well supported in his earliest years of recording vocals, with a slight edge of huskiness developing as he continued smoking on a daily basis through his two decades of professional singing. Not to be tempted to chain smoke as Cole did, singers would be wise to remember that he died from lung cancer at age forty! It is far better for singers to learn to add a breathy quality using good CCM technique rather than to depend on vocal abuse through smoking to accomplish the same end. Still, Cole managed to maintain clean articulation via careful attention to diction and balanced resonance using a beautiful mix, outstanding phrasing, and dynamic contrast to his distinct advantage.

Peggy Lee

Peggy Lee's voice traveled a similar route, starting with absolute clarity in her late teens and early twenties, as heard in her earliest recordings with the Benny Goodman Band. Listen to "Where or When" for a lesson in seamless ascending scales! Her voice became progressively huskier and breathier as she worked through six decades of professional singing. By the end of her career (exacerbated by years of smoking and a bout with pneumonia), Lee's lung health had greatly deteriorated, so she was limited in her compass of vocal beauty. Her clarity had all but disappeared, although she retained the ability to shape phrases, swing hard, and express texts with uncanny skill. Her clean articulation, rhythmic timing, and artful phrasing helped to balance the losses in her clarity and lush vocalism. Lee's two late-career Grammy nominations spoke volumes about how a true artist could make the most of what she still had amid severe physical obstacles.

Billie Holiday

Billie Holiday's early recordings included a bit of organic noise coloring her natural, sunny sound, which grew more and more breathy, gravelly, dark, and raspy as she aged. Illegal drugs and alcohol abuse (brought on by significant trauma) played significant roles in her obvious vocal changes toward the end of her forty-four-year life. But the decline of Holiday's vocal beauty never obscured her growth in musicianship, phrasing, and masterful expression. Had she possessed a healthy "baseline" voice, however, an even greater depth of expressive potential and a wider range of tonal choices may have been hers. The tragedy of Holiday's demise can speak to every jazz singer that follows. It has been well documented that smoking, alcohol, and drug use wreak havoc on the professional singer's instrument. Breathy production is easy to teach as an add-on choice for effect or coloring. It is not necessary for a jazz singer to actually smoke (or otherwise harm the voice) to create the requisite breathy, "smoky," or edgy quality desired for a particular sound, style, or song. Singers succeed far better without the liabilities of substance abuse damaging their voices and overall health.

Nancy Wilson

Nancy Wilson's unique use of breathy production deserves mention. She masterfully used coordinated onsets and could consistently produce a tone properly balanced on the breath with clarity and purity of tone. However, as both a color choice and an extremely expressive device, Wilson would sometimes blow excess air right down the middle of a vowel sound to create a breathless quality in her words. Few other singers in jazz history have regularly employed this type of effect, making Wilson's voice quite recognizable. Consider her televised performance of "The Very Thought of You" at the Hollywood Palace. In the opening phrase of the introductory verse, Wilson sings what sounds like "I don't need your photogra-(h)-ph." By inserting a bit of exhaled air within a vowel, she deftly paints an aural picture of intimacy and breathlessness. She continues to use this technique frequently throughout the piece, constantly reminding the audience that this is a nearly whispered song. Her tone quality itself is not what voice teachers would characterize as breathy (tone accompanied by a steady stream of air, creating a husky or disconnected sound quality). Instead, she exhales individual streams of air periodically amid purely phonated vowels. The final effect yields excellent vocalism occasionally interrupted by a technique of blowing air to create a breathy, whisper-like tone. Although mastering this technique takes practice and great coordination, in this teacher's opinion it is a far healthier method of creating a breathless sound than incorporating a culture of breathy tone production all the time or even all the way through a song. Wilson's technique proves that breathy production can be achieved without sacrificing good phonatory technique. Further, her approach creates powerfully persuasive picture of intimacy—much more than simply breathy tone creates.

Frank Sinatra

Frank Sinatra's voice exhibited consistently coordinated onsets, vocal clarity, and tonal purity for most of his career. His boyish, energized tone refreshed his audience. He used a great deal of breath energy in the same manner as would a classical singer, as evidenced by a strong, consistent, narrow vibrato that sometimes rode slightly above the pitch center. That quality aided Sinatra's reception by classical music audiences as well as popular audiences because the inherent sound was somewhat classic in nature. The vowel purity with which he sang; the open-throated, resonant tone; the tonal clarity, the vitality of breath energy; and the relaxed, confident delivery marked him as a unique storyteller whose voice represented a strong natural baseline most of the time. He did not depend on gimmicky tricks, colors, or vocal weaknesses to stylize his singing. Instead he maximized his natural color and presented an honest voice, replete with its own authentic beauty. Sinatra set an excellent example of the baseline, natural male voice at its best, with little to no added tweaking to the tone.

Ella Fitzgerald

Ella Fitzgerald possessed a pure, youthful tone that remained consistent through most of her singing years. Her technique of employing clear, co-ordinated onsets and tone production had presented itself early in her career and was therefore easier to maintain throughout her remaining years via a lifestyle that avoided vocal abuse. By taking great care of her vocal instrument during her career she maintained vocal clarity and healthy phonation that preserved her youthful tone. As a result, she enjoyed a long recording career many others singers would find enviable, even though her voice had begun to waver with a wider vibrato than she had used in her younger years (heard in her excellent, late-career duet recordings with Joe Pass). Fitzgerald was able to add a bit of "gravel" or raspy noise to her voice as a chosen color, frequently imitating the gravelly voice of Louis Armstrong. Her ability to add and subtract Armstrong's vocal quality while always returning to her healthy baseline voice makes Fitzgerald an excellent role model for jazz singers today.

The Aging Voice

A widening vibrato remains a common trait among older singers, but according to Dr. Robert Sataloff in his various writings and conference presentations on the aging voice, it does not have to happen to everyone. Singers are urged to stay committed to daily workouts to keep their voices in good condition and ready for the demands of professional performances for as long as they can, and for many, there is no reason to abandon plans to continue singing simply because one has passed their "prime." Dr. Sataloff maintains that it may be more challenging to keep one's voice in shape the older one gets, but the same is true for physical conditioning of

the entire body. He urges aging singers to keep with it, do their due diligence, and continue showing up to a daily practice session for maximum
results in maintaining vocal agility, breath management, and tone quality.

ARTICULATION

William Vennard, in his important voice pedagogy treatise *Singing: The
Mechanism and the Technic* (1967), eloquently explains the role of articulation in the phenomenon of singing:

> Singing involves two distinct polarities, the use of the vocal mechanism as a
> musical instrument, and its use a means of verbal communication. The one
> implies establishing optimum conditions for the production of musical tone,
> essentially regular and maintained constantly. The other implies the making
> of a rapid series of symbolic sounds, essentially noisy and in continual flux.
> Such is the singer's dilemma; he is trying to do two contradictory things at
> once.[2]

Here Vennard beautifully outlines the challenge inherent in all artistic
singing—that to communicate words clearly often creates less-than-
ideal musical moments, and if the music is given preference above the
words, textual meanings may be ultimately sacrificed, misunderstood,
or improperly expressed. Vennard also makes the case that singing represents the necessary struggle between "noise" (consonant sounds) and
"tone" (vowel sounds). The two together create "sonance," a feat that all
singers are charged with producing while walking an ever-varying line
of combining consonant noise with vowel tone. This represents a formi-
dable challenge that no instrumentalist faces. Add to that challenge the
additional conundrum of communicating actual *language* while making
music, and the singer's responsibility is doubled. Instrumentalists would
be wise to remember this increased level of difficulty singers face before
perpetuating untruths that a singer's job is somehow easier than playing
an instrument, requires less knowledge to do well, and that anyone who
can match pitch should be able to do it.

In jazz, as in other genres, the singer must learn to convey song lyrics in
a manner that reflects the beauty, drama, tragedy, and the affect of the music. The beautiful truth about jazz is that this art form allows many types
of voices to take a turn expressing a text with unique musical style. A jazz
singer with a gospel-singing background may interpret "At Last" with a
heavy vibrato, a good deal of volume, and a richness that matches the

quality of singing heard Sunday mornings in churches where gospel music is the norm. By contrast, a lighter-voiced singer steeped in the sounds and gentle singing quality of Chet Baker, might approach the same piece with a completely different weight in the vocal instrument, straighter tone, and gentle directness that breathes new, unexpected life into this well-worn song. Both approaches are valid in jazz. Both approaches beg the singer to articulate words cleanly, paying attention to the dynamic nuances prevalent in each phrase's language, so that music can be made while the lyrics are explored and shared with integrity. Jazz thus allows many more correct interpretations of its repertoire than does opera or classical music. Jazz is everyman's (or everywoman's) means of musical expression, with or without a large, amply trained operatic vocal instrument.

This truth, however, does not excuse the prevalence of poor vocalism practiced by some professional jazz singers, nor does it excuse poor teaching of jazz singers. Always seeking greater mastery of artistic expression, singers must expect themselves and their students to move forward musically, onward and upward, never backward or sideways. Moving forward inherently means cultivating more tools to use in performance, growing better and better technique, improving the coordination between the vocal instrument and the music and text it is called on to interpret, and opening the mind to the challenge of learning.

The greatest lyricists and composers of vocal music create words and music that work well together, functioning as a team to express the composite message between the two. In the hands of a masterful interpreter both artistic elements (words and music) may be delivered effectively. A challenge singers face is to deliver both text and melody without jeopardizing the integrity of one over the other. This conundrum has a lot to do with why singing well is a lifelong undertaking, and not something that can be mastered once for all. It is rather a continuum we travel on moving forward one step, one piece, and one performance at a time throughout our lives.

Articulators

Articulators of the voice include the lips, teeth, tongue, soft palate, and hard palate. Each of these plays a role in changing the shape of the vocal tract or otherwise altering its acoustic properties. Singers are taught to articulate consonants on the front tip of the tongue, teeth, and lips to maximize the audience's ability to understand the text. The dexterity of a singer's tongue, lips, and soft palate can be developed using exercises that practice enunciating consonants in rapid-fire succession, in repetition, and in mixed fashion among many different consonant sounds (e.g., "la-me-ni-po-tu," and other variations of this popular exercise on one note). Such practice creates flexibility and readiness for the variety of sounds and shapes singers regularly encounter.

Stretching Facial Muscles

Another recommendation for strengthening and warming up articulators is to stretch them at the start of the practice or warm-up session before a rehearsal or performance. Actors are taught to warm up facial muscles (including lips) by moving those muscles around, massaging the face in small circles with the hands, and readying the face to create a wide range of expressive facial gestures.

EXERCISE

Stretch several facial muscles simultaneously on command: "big face" opens the mouth, eyes, and nostrils wide; "small face" pinches the lips, eyes, and nostrils to a closed position toward the center of the face. Alternating between these two extremes and holding each for a couple of seconds prepares the facial muscles for a host of different expressions they may be called on to perform during a concert or rehearsal. This is a particularly useful exercise for performers accustomed to monotone singing or lacking facial expressivity. Practicing these faces in front of a mirror prepares singers for the work of cultivating a wide range of expressions they can use as they articulate texts.

Tongue Articulation Exercises

The tongue trill builds an important articulator of the vocal mechanism by coordinating the release of a narrow stream of air with the vibration of the tongue against the hard palate. Elusive for some singers, this exercise is worth pursuing because it trains the tongue tip to stay relaxed and in contact with the hard palate while also training the breath mechanism to empower the tone with a strong stream of air. I also recommend a series of tongue stretches to train this articulator. Extending the tongue out as far as it will go and holding it out for a few seconds is a way to release tension held at the root of the tongue. I also like to ask students to write their names in the air with their tongue. This activity usually inspires laughter, especially in choral situations, but it always elicits a release of tongue tension. Singers must feel the difference between holding the tongue inside the mouth, retracting it, and releasing it forward in a stretch. Singers whose tongues are consistently retracted and continue to retract during speech and singing feel a powerful release during tongue stretches. It is vital for a singer to associate the stretched, forward tongue sensation with relaxation so that retraction does not result in pulling at the larynx or jaw. So often laryngeal or jaw tensions that create major problems for singers can be traced back to tongue tension and unhealthy retraction of the tongue. Singers that create mindful awareness about their tongue activity during speech and singing will experience great benefits in a more relaxed, aware singing voice whose tongue articulator has been freed at last.

Lip Articulation Exercises

The lips create a pair of articulators that are vitally important for the jazz singer to discipline to use effectively and artistically. Popped consonants in a microphone almost always point to *p* and *b* consonants having too much air accompanying them, resulting in the sound of a popping balloon. Pop, R&B, and jazz singers all benefit from mindfully training the lip articulators so that consonants remain crisp and clear but well controlled so that sung lines are not disrupted by explosions of unwanted, noisy air. Lip trills (vocalizing tones, scales, and arpeggios while buzzing the lips—blowing a focused stream of air between them so they vibrate in the manner of a "raspberry") create lip flexibility, coordination, relaxation, and an engaged airstream which energizes tone production. The lip trill remains one of the most widely used, productive exercises in voice pedagogy. Singing a lip trill into a microphone is a wonderful exercise to train the lips to modify their air expulsion on *p* and *b*. This exercise teaches the breathing mechanism to adjust the airstream to accommodate the microphone while it teaches the lips to minimize wasted air.

The Hard Palate as Articulator

The hard palate is the bony inside roof of the mouth to which upper incisors (front teeth) are attached to the skeleton. Because the bone of the hard palate is part of the skull (and sometimes called the "upper jaw"), we cannot adjust or move it. The tongue articulates consonants against the hard palate. The manner in which this action occurs yields important ramifications for intelligibility in both speech and singing. Voice pedagogues often teach students to articulate the *l* using the front tip of the tongue touching the forward ridge of the hard palate, just behind the front top teeth. Keeping consonants on the front of the tongue, teeth, and lips generally yields better enunciation and diction, adding to the comprehensibility of the text. These considerations are especially important during microphone use. An ugly or sloppy consonant sound will be amplified by a microphone, so jazz singers with clean diction and good mic technique always fare better. Good articulation is paramount in jazz because the text and music must come through clearly, without distracting the audience.

The Soft Palate as Articulator

The soft palate can be a troublesome articulator for singers. Located in the posterior roof of the mouth, this squishy, fleshy, soft tissue behind the hard palate can rise and fall during speech, singing, and breathing. The yawn opens the airway more completely than any other human activity and initiates a high arch of the soft palate. Practicing the yawn and feeling the sensations it yields constitutes good "awareness" practice for this articulator. Singing teachers sometimes speak of approaching a high sung pitch starting with a vowel from the perspective of simulating the start of a yawn as one inhales and begins to sing. This "start of a yawn," as clearly shown in a mirror while doing this exercise, causes the soft palate to stretch upward, allowing the throat to open. This throat opening can be useful in creating space for vowels and may yield a more open-sounding tone to the singing voice. The soft palate, however, is tricky to control, and many singers have trouble discovering how to use its movements to their advantage.

The moveable articulators can be strengthened one at a time—tongue, lips, and soft palate—with what I call "targeted exercises" (having a specific technical end in mind). The soft palate can be strengthened and stretched using exercises employing the consonant *k*. Exercises beginning with *k* are useful for creating crisper consonants, an obedient tongue, and greater soft palate flexibility.

The way an artist articulates text can make or break a musical performance. Articulation represents an aspect of singing that singers of all styles are behooved to practice and master in conjunction with expressive nuance and artistic stylization. Without crystal clear articulation audiences cannot comprehend a song's words. When words are indiscernible, an audience feels alienated and frustrated. Listeners then experience a disconnect from the artist's communication instead of connection. Good articulation invites the audience into the performance. By carefully crafting one's articulative style, a singer literally creates a person-to-person bridge with every listener in the room and intimacy is given an opportunity to thrive. A singer cannot create intimacy or trust through music alone—the delivery of the language is a crucial element of this coveted connection. At the same time, an exquisitely enunciated text in the midst of poor musicianship or inappropriate style cannot create intimacy or trust between an artist and the audience. A dynamic melding of both music and text must be sought and maintained to make a vocal performance great.

Articulation Enables Communication

Jazz singers whose articulation stood above the rest were uncoincidentally the finest musical communicators of their time: Frank Sinatra, Tony Bennett, Peggy Lee, Doris Day, Rosemary Clooney, and Ella Fitzgerald, among others. Each of these artists paid great attention to clear, correct enunciation and thoughtful articulation of words. Their efforts allowed them to become known for their outstanding abilities to communicate texts, shape phrases, and appropriate the inherent musical qualities of language to their advantage. Conscientious singers pay attention to the sounds they produce and work to deliver lyrics clearly with good projection. It is often nuanced, finely shaped articulation that sets one singer high above another as a superior interpreter of jazz music. Teachers and students alike would do well to pay more attention to this oft-ignored aspect of singing. Because mic technique is strongly connected to this element of jazz singing, more about this will be covered in chapter 9.

RESONANCE

Resonance may be defined as the frequency synchronization of two vibrating bodies. In this case, the resonating bodies consist of the oropharynx (vocal tract) and the vibrating vocal folds. Resonance advantageous to sound carriage is created when a vowel shape in the oropharynx (also called a "formant"—the pitch of the air in the vocal tract) synchronizes with a frequency (harmonic) produced by the vocal folds during the process of phonation. Sometimes singers may desire this additional power—and other times they may wish to dampen it. Jazz singing allows these choices, but the informed, educated singer has a wider palette of possibilities when resonance is understood and the ability to maximize it correctly is cultivated.

The only resonator involved in the process of singing is the vocal tract because it possesses both an opening (the mouth) and a resonating cavity (the oropharynx). Although we talk about chest resonance, the chest cavity has no opening to the outside so it does not constitute an actual resonator. Also, the head has no cavity space for resonating, so it is not a resonator either. The nasal passage, while having an opening, has far less space available than the vocal tract, and its influence usually dampens sound waves rather than boosting them. What were previously called chest, head, and nasal resonance are now understood to be sympathetic vibrations of bones in or near these areas that give a singer certain types of sensory feedback when resonance is being achieved.

When might a jazz singer need additional resonance? I have spent several years as both a jazz singer in intimate settings (often described as ideal for the jazz style) and a jazz pops soloist with symphony orchestras in large auditoriums indoors (seating three thousand) and enormous outdoor arenas with more than ten thousand patrons in attendance. Like it or not, the singer who accepts the latter engagements had better be extremely well versed in the ability to resonate over an orchestra, even with a microphone. Knowledge about vowel shaping and resonance balancing is a huge help when going through an orchestral score and noticing the places I will need some added power beyond what I would do vocally in a small venue with a jazz combo. If jazz singers want to branch out into orchestral or big band work, they must have some understanding of how to naturally and safely amplify (and dampen) their voice without constant external help from a technical director. Directed attention toward breath management, resonance balancing, vowel shaping, and microphone technique are required for this advanced large ensemble work.

Resonance Balancing

Great singers from every genre learn to create resonant, pure vowels in their "baseline" voices. Knowing how to make a vowel taller, deeper, darker, or brighter constitutes a set of necessary skills every singer must study, preferably under the tutelage of a skilled teacher. Rosemary Clooney and Bing Crosby represented excellent examples of singers who used their natural, baseline voices to sing predominantly pure vowels. The purity of the vowel and its formant-reflecting shape add beauty to the voice. The purer the vowels, the more resonant the voice sounds to the audience. Jazz singers need to know how to isolate pure vowel shapes in their voices so that when they make conscious choices to seek out other sounds or to return to the pure, resonant vowel, they know precisely how. Increasing one's command over resonance gives contemporary jazz singers the power to modify their voices at will to grow their musicianship, vocal beauty, and breath efficiency.

Part of understanding resonance balancing is knowing when the various dominant qualities we talk about as singers (head dominant production, chest dominant production, and nasality) are out of balance. Singers must learn to be technically adept enough to restore and modify resonance balancing at will. Nasality (sometimes formerly and mistakenly called nasal resonance) is often used as a jazz singer's tool to maximize pitch precision when singing with a microphone. Singers must take care not to let this quality be overdone. Much research has been done (including filling the nasal cavities with cotton, yielding no change in the singing voice) to show that the nasal passages and sinuses do not actually function as a resonator. However, the sensations a singer feels in the body through sympathetic vibrations of facial bones, sternum, ribs, and so on are important feedback signals that help a singer remember and learn how it feels to sing a tone with balanced resonance. Those sensations, through guided work with an experienced voice teacher, are important to point out, isolate, memorize, and replicate so that when the passage comes around again, the singer remembers how it felt to sing it with proper resonance balancing that suits the note, word, piece, passage, key, and style.

Teachers and singers alike would be wise to remember that nasality is a tool that can be used to add a slightly forward-sounding brightness to the tone. Adding a touch of nasality also allows the singer to maintain greater control over pitch precision and intonation, which is why many great singers sound slightly nasal when scatting a bebop line. Fast-moving passages like bebop scat lines require great pitch accuracy and nasality or a sensation of buzzing at the hard palate can help. Particularly when singing with a microphone, slightly increasing nasality tends to provide a greater degree of "point" to the tone, which allows singers to better hear their own voices and, therefore, tune the pitch. Modern singer Michael Bublé sometimes adds a touch of nasality to his baseline tone, enhancing his pitch precision and forward projection. He tastefully illustrates how this added quality can be employed to create his signature resonance mix in his jazz and pop work.

Nasality is also important to remember when teaching a voice that is excessively breathy and underenergized. The added projection provided by a touch of nasality, coupled with greater breath energy empowering the singing from below, often corrects the flattening (of pitch or timbre) inherent in a breathy tone better than simply asking a student to "use more breath." This correction may be applied to assist the underpitch singing of students performing any other style (opera, music theatre, pop, etc.) but is especially effective in jazz because the improvisatory nature of the art form allows for changes in timbre more readily than other genres do. If a jazz singer's voice suddenly becomes a bit more nasal, for instance, listeners may interpret that as a distinct color choice to provide variation in the timbral spectrum for expressive purposes, but during an operatic aria, the introduction of nasality requires more discretion and consistent blending of colors to achieve a seamless line. Resonance balancing must be undertaken for every voice to attain its ideal beauty and that requires understanding a bit about formants and a healthy mix.

Formants

A vowel formant is a frequency peak at a point of resonance in the spectrum of the human voice. Singers are taught to shape their vocal tract in certain ways to cause the oropharynx to resonate with the column of air traveling through the singer's instrument. When a vowel formant in the vocal tract resonates with a harmonic produced by the vocal folds, they share a frequency that leads to a local maximum or greater amplitude (volume) than either vibrating body would achieve alone. Resonance maximizes vowel volume by acoustical properties without the help of amplifying electronics (microphones). Maximizing resonance is a necessary goal in classical singing and opera, which traditionally relied on the singer to project over an orchestra without external amplification. In the case of jazz singing, the mic represents half the instrument (the half that is responsible for volume and filtering out fewer desirable frequencies while boosting others). However, jazz singers can still benefit from a firm foundation in understanding how resonance and vowel formants enhance their vocal options.

The vocal tract produces several formants to amplify speech and singing. The first two (F1 and F2) create vowels. Formants higher than these help differentiate various idiosyncrasies and individual qualities that make voices unique. The formants most relevant to jazz singers are the first vowel formants (F1). The first vowel formants for primary vowels occur at fixed frequencies. These will be illustrated using the International Phonetic Alphabet (IPA) to identify the main vowels concerned. The first vowel formants outline a C major chord in first inversion, open position starting with E4: [i] (rhymes with "bee") and [u] (rhymes with "too") have formants at E4. The next formant higher occurs for [e] (rhymes with the first syllable in "favor") and [o] (rhymes with "bolt") at C5. The highest vowel formant occurs for the [a] vowel (rhymes with "la") at G5. Singing these vowels on their formant pitches yields a bloom in the sound due to resonance between the sung tone and the formant located on the same pitch. Singing these five vowels on their respective formants in the order from bright to dark, [i-e-a-o-u], follows the pattern E4-C5-G5-C5-E4. This shows the parallel relationship between the bright and dark vowel series, the gradual movement of the tongue from bright to dark vowels (which moves the back of the tongue from high to low position) and the continuum of colors available when singing among vowel formants. Understanding formants helps the jazz singer use and play with amplitude variations and overtone colors available in the vowels they sing.

DR. ONEY'S MIX CONTINUUM

Early in my teaching career I created a tool that helped my voice students gain better control over their resonance balancing choices. This tool also provided a wider palette of possible colors for every singer in my studio. Some singers possessed voices with a distinctly nasal quality. Some came in singing very dark, somewhat swallowed tones. Others sang with larynges positioned high in the neck, sporting super-bright vowels. Each of these benefited from my Mix Continuum in that it assisted with not only resonance balancing but also with decisions about where in a singer's range mixing can occur for music theatre, commercial, and jazz styles. In my studio we termed pitches at which more head- or chest-mix could be added "crossover pitches" because they represented the sensory experience involved when singers "crossed over" from what they considered "chest-dominant" quality to "head-dominant" (or vice versa on descending passages). These crossover points vary depending on the genre, the song, and even the phrase.

Nowadays many experienced pedagogues acknowledge the principle that all healthy singing is a mix. In healthy singing, there is rare use of

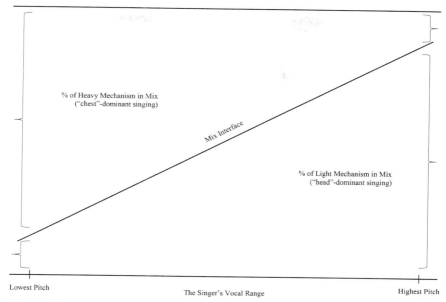

Figure 5.1. Dr. Oney's Mix Continuum. Courtesy of Author

either pure head or raw chest voice. Because healthy singing is the goal for every teacher, professional singer, and student singer (regardless of style), we proceed assuming that a healthy baseline voice is the common starting point.

The Mix Continuum consists of a chart (see figure 5.1) in which the horizontal dimension extends through the full compass of the singer's range from the lowest to the highest pitch (like a piano keyboard). The vertical dimension represents the combined distribution of head-dominant quality and chest-dominant quality in a singer's mix for a given sung pitch. Depending on the genre, vowel, word, style, tessitura, and other subjective factors, this mix distribution can change. A diagonal line drawn on the chart from a point slightly above the lowest singable pitch and extending upward to the right, ending just below the highest singable pitch, represents the mix interface. The area on the chart above the diagonal line represents the percentage of chest-dominant quality in the mix. The area below the diagonal line represents the percentage of head-dominant quality in the mix. As singers learn to mix during the ascent from low to high pitches through their range, they start with little head-dominant quality in the mix and add more and more as the ascent continues to achieve a smooth, consistent, seamless glissando throughout the compass of the voice (as appropriate for a classical or legit music theatre timbre). As the baseline voice is "tweaked" when singing in various styles, the teacher may recommend a slight adjustment in the percentage of head and chest mix as needed at various points throughout the range, also adding or subtracting nasality as appropriate to assist with blending the mix. Because of the continuum's variability, it may not yield a linear relationship for every singer, every song, or every style. The Mix Continuum reminds the singer that, as one ascends, more head-dominant quality tends to be required for vocal health and comfort. By contrast, more chest-dominant quality may participate in the mix as one descends, especially in commercial, jazz, and music theatre styles. When belting, the amount of chest dominant production and nasality may be increased in the middle voice to achieve the desired timbre. At *no* point does the singer ever need to sing in pure head voice (without the foundation and strength provided by a bit of chest mix) because even the highest possible pitch should still have a touch of chest mix in it. Chest mix may be described to students using the term "tracheal resonance" (really sympathetic vibrations of the sternum and ribs near the trachea), which helps to ground a voice that has a flyaway, fluttery quality in the upper register. Such voices are prime examples showing why mixing head- and chest-dominant qualities throughout the totality of the vocal range is necessary. Likewise, a singer never needs to sing in pure, raw, chest-dominant production (without the elevation of the soft palate that enables a touch of head-dominant quality to participate in the mix) because there should always be a bit of head mix in the lowest possible pitch within a singer's range for healthy singing. The highest and the lowest pitches contain some percentage of both qualities for the maintenance of a healthy voice. Essentially, this continuum ensures that both the thyroarytenoid muscles responsible for producing the chest-dominant quality in singing and the cricothyroid muscles responsible for producing the head-dominant quality remain balanced in their workload and cooperative synergy. As these muscle groups work together, the mixing action at various possible crossover points on the continuum strengthens a singer's flexibility and vocal color options. The continuum also strengthens singers' ability to sing in multiple styles with improved understanding about their own voice's resonance capabilities. The continuum offers a wide array of solutions to both the singer and the teacher regarding how to assist when a pitch, word, phrase, song, or entire role needs resonance adjustment to find the proper mix. The Mix Continuum helps students sing seamlessly across registers when desired, create yodel-like flips in popular styles, add or subtract chest-dominant quality for a superior Broadway belt, add intensity in a music theatre or rock song without causing harm or feeling pain, and navigate a wider path of vocal possibilities, adding to their confidence and artistic control.

Using the Mix Continuum, I have helped thousands of students ease pressure off their voices, belt with less vocal tension, lighten upper tones while adding ring, and manage other tricky aspects of technique throughout a wide range of repertoire and genres. I have also taught music theatre and rock students to "scream" by creating a healthy singing mix that sounds like a scream but minimizes unhealthy stress on the vocal folds, causing no pain. This visual tool helps singers and their teachers make conscious decisions about how to mix to find optimum resonance balancing for a specific phrase or song. The continuum enables students to experiment with sensations of mixing head-dominant and chest-dominant qualities ("light" and "heavy" mechanisms) in various combinations over different parts of their range. Because it has no fixed frequencies, the continuum is adaptable to every singer, whether male, female, transgender, treble, or bass, regardless of age. Because the microphone affects a singer's resonance, more about the Mix Continuum (how to incorporate it into singing with a mic) is included in chapter 9.

Teaching with the Mix Continuum

To illustrate how the Mix Continuum may be useful in the teaching studio, I offer an example. A male student is studying the jazz standard "Everything Happens to Me." He belts the upper tones in a manner that brings his chest voice up to a straining degree, disrupting the smoothness of the line and the mood. In an effort to encourage him to approach the high notes gently, more like Chet Baker would have in 1955, his teacher instructs him to lighten the upper tones and incorporate more head mix into the high pitches of this song. Showing him the Mix Continuum helps him realize how high he was taking the chest-dominant quality. His teacher suggests starting to mix more head-dominant quality into the tone toward the middle of his range, well before he arrives at the highest, formerly belted tones. Working downward from the top to bring the head-dominant voice down into the middle of his voice successfully shows this singer how to lighten the top and strengthen his mix with ample head-dominant production and chest-dominant production blended together. Considering head- and chest-dominant qualities a matter of percentages rather than a "pure chest versus pure head" relationship separated by a break empowers the singer with technical and artistic choice and begins his understanding of the sensations involved in singing with a resonant mix.

Phonation, articulation, and resonance represent important aspects of technique for the aspiring jazz singer. Singers from any genre wanting to sing jazz can adapt to the different requirements of this style easily by achieving a natural, baseline voice first, devoid of stylistic influence. Applying stylistic consideration on the sure foundation of a healthy baseline voice creates a vocally healthy singer regardless of genre. At the same time, jazz singers are encouraged to develop the foundation of good singing technique with regard to coordinated phonation, clear articulation, and a mix of resonance options on which classical singers may have a firmer grasp. Through my Mix Continuum, singers from many genres can experiment with and explore various approaches to resonance balancing while growing their understanding of their instrument and their art.

NOTES

1. Tish Oney, "Onward and Upward with Nathan Gunn," *Classical Singer Magazine*, May/June 2021, 30.
2. William Vennard, *Singing: The Mechanism and the Technic* (New York: Carl Fischer, Inc., 1967), 163.

6

JAZZ STYLE AND ORNAMENTATION

A multitude of different styles exist within what has come to be known as jazz. Some of the substyles of jazz include swing, bossa nova, samba, tango, "west coast" cool jazz, free jazz, and bebop. With all of these, among many other subgroups of jazz, there are myriad ways to approach this genre stylistically. There are also many different categories of ornaments that can be used to decorate tones in jazz music. Several primary styles of jazz and the concept of jazz language will be discussed.

JAZZ LANGUAGE

The language of jazz means many things to many people. Ornamentation, terminology, stylistic considerations, a sense of swing or Latin feel, and other rhythmic emphases within the repertoire of this genre all constitute aspects of jazz language. The use of a breathy tone quality, swinging eighth notes, placing accents in places that propel the swing sense, and using a touch of vocal fry for a specific effect can all transform and enliven an otherwise ho-hum performance into one saturated with jazz language that keeps an audience riveted.

Subgroups and styles of jazz are vital for the jazz singer and jazz voice pedagogue to understand. Distinctions among styles transmit a great deal of information to the audience about the authenticity, experience, or training of a performer. For instance, when singers attempt to swing eighth notes in a bossa nova, they fail to communicate in true jazz language. Latin styles do not treat eighth notes in the same manner that swing or blues styles do. The "long-short" rhythmic pattern of eighth notes in swing and blues (even when notated as straight eighths) strongly suggests jazz style to most listeners, whereas the absolute equivalence of the eighth notes in a bossa nova or samba represent just as much authenticity within the Latin jazz style. It is imperative for the jazz singer and jazz voice teacher to immerse themselves in the various styles inhabiting the scope of jazz. Much like classical singers are expected to have some working knowledge of German Lieder, French chansons, Italian art songs, British/American art songs, and several streams of opera that lay within their Fach, the professional jazz singer must have some experience performing in swing, blues, bossa nova, samba, jazz waltz, ballads, vocalese, and bebop styles. Many more styles exist today, and with the meeting and melding of various world and folk styles, more are derived every year. Knowing the basics of the styles mentioned will help singers build their repertoire, books of charts, and song lists in ways that keep audiences interested and engaged throughout a performance.

Common Styles within the Jazz Genre

Swing

The swing style involves a long-short-long-short eighth-note pattern exemplified in the ride cymbal played by the drummer in a jazz combo or big band during a swing tune. Laying back the second and fourth eighth notes of a two-beat pattern, as if they are arriving late to their place in the measure, is the first step in singing swing. Swinging eighth notes can be described as a tied triplet pattern with the first two notes tied together. Then the downbeats must be deemphasized and the offbeats given light accents. I have several ways of presenting swing to students in an applied lesson situation as well as in group classes or ensembles. One is to build a drum set.

EXERCISE

Ask the student to imitate the playing of a ride cymbal using vocal percussion, "tchhh-tch-tch-tchhh" in a "spang-a-lang" pattern as shown in Figure 6.1. Then ask the student to move to a bass drum (and acoustic bass) pattern on beats one and three, as shown). Third, ask the student to play the hi-hat or sock cymbal pattern on beats two and four. Finally, ask the student to play a syncopated pattern on the toms or snare.

Figure 6.1. Build a Drum Set. Courtesy of Author

In a choral setting, I start with only one layer at a time (the bottom), giving basses the acoustic bass/bass drum pattern. After four measures of establishing this bass figure, tenors enter with the hi-hat pattern. After four measures of bass and tenor playing, sopranos join in with the ride cymbal pattern. Finally, after four measures of the first three parts playing, altos add the snare pattern. Only the basses sing pitches; the rest simply speak syllables with rhythmic precision. When the students get comfortable with their parts, I rotate the parts and have each part "play" each of the other parts until they can change instruments on cue. This builds concentration, swing feel, rhythmic unison, and a heightened awareness of the multi-instrumental role of the drummer in a jazz or swing band!

There are many wonderful historic bands that can teach a student to swing. Some of the swingiest bands in history are the Count Basie Band, Duke Ellington's Orchestra, and Benny Goodman's Band, among many others in and beyond the Swing Era. Great swing singers include Louis Armstrong, Ella Fitzgerald, Peggy Lee, Anita O'Day, Nat "King" Cole, and contemporary singers Diane Schuur and the Manhattan Transfer. Creating a solid listening diet of the finest swing singers in jazz history will better enable modern singers to perform authentically in this primary style of jazz.

Singers should also make a point to listen to leading instrumentalists for every instrument in the rhythm section as well as a wide palette of horn soloists from big bands or swing bands, tracing each instrument's development through major performers of that instrument throughout the history of jazz. Although this sounds like a monumental task (indeed, it is a lifelong assignment), guiding one's listening choices toward music that will educate and refine you will keep your jazz skills and ears at their peak. Great performers must listen to great performers. Choosing at least one instrumentalist from a non-U.S. country per instrument timeline will help open the ears to absorb innovative sounds from cultures where jazz evolved somewhat differently.

Bossa Nova

Bossa nova describes a genre brought to the United States by Brazilian guitarist-singer-composer Antonio Carlos Jobim as a novel subgenre of jazz. This genre, strongly influenced by Brazilian music, is characterized by a "straight" eighth note feel, meaning that eighth notes are equal in length and emphasis, unlike the "long-short" pattern of swing style. Jobim's many compositions, including "The Girl from Ipanema," "Desafinado," and "Corcovado," started a beautifully smooth style of jazz that simmers with percussive energy. Singer Astrud Gilberto's recordings of the bossa nova (e.g., "Corcovado") are worthy of study and will help jazz singers better appreciate the light, precise approach required to perform this style of music. To truly appreciate the bossa nova style, singers are encouraged to listen to native Brazilian singers as well as Jobim's and Gilberto's recordings.

EXERCISE

Help students experience the difference between swing feel and bossa nova feel by having them sing a swing song and switch (on your cue) to bossa nova feel and back to swing. They will sense the tied triplet yielding a long-short, long-short pattern in the swing feel, contrasting with the metrically equivalent "straight" eighth notes in the bossa nova feel. Extend this exercise into a Dalcroze exercise (see chapter 11) by inviting singers to step or clap eighth notes as they go back and forth between swing and bossa nova feel.

Samba

The samba is another Latin subgenre. It possesses an energetic, two-beat feel instead of the four-beat, more gentle sounding bossa nova. A samba can be fast or medium in tempo and is most often scored "in two," (2/2 time) giving the impression that the music is moving at a much faster pace than its easygoing Latin counterpart, the bossa nova. Peggy Lee recorded a humorous song called "Caramba! It's the Samba" and several albums of Latin songs. Her "I Am in Love" from the award-winning *Latin ala Lee!* (Capitol Records, 1960) is an example of a samba that includes several layers of percussion, a common trait in Latin jazz.

Often in jazz, a song that was composed in a particular style or feel is rearranged in another. The bebop giants became famous for reinterpreting old pop ballads at breakneck fast tempos. My favorite way to interpret Jobim's bossa nova "Chega de Saudade" (known in its English version as "No More Blues") is in a samba feel (see chapter 14 for tips on arranging this way). The samba is a rewarding style to include in the jazz singer's set list because it raises the musical energy with its fast-moving harmonic rhythm, active bass figures, often rapid-fire lyrics, and percussive nature. Even when played skillfully in a solo piano style, the samba is an exciting change of pace among swing and other styles. Sambas require an excellent sense of timing and focus on form, so be sure not to program any sambas until you are confident about keeping your place in a fast-moving form. Growing the ability to "feel" music in groups of eight measures is a skill worth developing; it has saved many a lost jazz singer from onstage disasters! It also relieves the need for obvious counting, which is a no-no for any professional musician. Pianists and drummers, take heed. We see your lips moving and are not impressed.

Tango

Really a type of partner dance, the tango (originating in the 1880s at the border of Argentina and Uruguay) possesses a unique, characteristic percussion pattern with a quasi-military "strut" on the snare drum. The tango is played at a moderate tempo appropriate for couples' dancing and is often highlighted with stickwork on the cymbals and snare drum. The tango possesses an emphatic, straight quarter note feel. Less common today, the tango deserves a revival in the jazz singer's set list and is a rewarding style to program for the sake of variety. "Hernando's Hideaway" recorded by Ella Fitzgerald represents a famous example of a tango and clearly displays the mystery and intrigue that characterizes the genre.

Jazz Waltz

The waltz presents a lighthearted contrast among four-beat jazz standards, especially with a swinging eighth-note feel. Abbey Lincoln's lyrics to Freddie Hubbard's "Up Jumped Spring" created a beautiful finish to an already gorgeous instrumental melody and chord progression. Lincoln's recording of this standard is readily available and is highly recommended for singers interested in adding a waltz to their repertoire. The author's "Waltz for Ellie" is a modal waltz written with scat syllables instead of lyrics. This piece should be approached as an instrumental piece with the voice as an instrument. It provides several choruses in which to explore soloing over dorian chord changes. The jazz waltz always rewards the band and audience by adding rhythmic variety and a refreshingly different beat pattern to a lineup of swing and Latin-feel songs.

Ballad

No singer's repertoire is complete without a few ballads. These standby pieces are often played in a slow, usually four-beat tempo and feel. All singers must select ballads that showcase their strengths. When tempo is slow, the key, tessitura, and overall vocal comfort are vitally important considerations because these types of pieces tend to last longer than other songs in the set list. Voices must remain comfortable so that singers may focus on communicating with the audience. When creating song lists, singers are wise to choose a few ballads that are well known but are perhaps arranged in unique ways, as well as lesser-known ballads that deserve to be heard.

Crooners were male singers whose strong suit was ballads. A few standouts included Bing Crosby, Johnny Hartman, and Mel Tormé. Outstanding ballad singers tend to have exemplary beauty in their voices because the ballad offers nowhere to hide. Here is precisely why technical mastery is necessary for the successful jazz singer; ballads expose every flaw in breath management, intonation, diction, phrasing, dynamics, and expression. For these reasons, ballads are among the most difficult jazz pieces to sing well. They also can make or break a set list because the audience will either be riveted or bored, depending on the success or failure of the singer to hold their attention. The energy drops when the tempo slows unless a singer (or the band) can keep the energy simmering without the flashy bells and whistles that up-tempo pieces and multilayered, forward-moving music provide. Studying the artistry of great ballad singers like Rosemary Clooney, Peggy Lee, Sarah Vaughan, Johnny Hartman, and Nat "King" Cole, will go a long way in developing the taste and sophistication that outstanding balladeers must display.

Bebop

An advanced style that eludes many singers because of the sheer difficulty of pitch precision is bebop, originated by saxophonist Charlie Parker and propagated by not only Parker but also trumpeter Dizzy Gillespie and pianist Bud Powell. Sarah Vaughan's career closely aligned with the bebop era. Her ballad singing in particular showcased bebop's trend toward extreme tempos (in bebop, tempi were either very fast or very slow. Vaughan's ballads tended to be extraordinarily slow). Several other singers whose abilities in the bebop genre afforded them inclusion among the greats included Annie Ross, Anita O'Day, and Betty Carter. Carter's live and studio recordings of "Tight" showed a bebop approach to both scat at a fast tempo as well as rapidly delivered song lyrics. Her pitch precision and innovative use of scat consonants allowed the natural flow of sounds out of her instrument as easily as the music was released by her saxophone- or piano-wielding contemporaries.

Transcribing solos by great bebop instrumentalists helps the budding jazz singer attune the ears and tonal memory as needed to assimilate and perform challenging melodies at breakneck speeds, a characteristic of the bebop style. Starting slowly, writing every note, and singing the bebop line one motive or group of notes at a time can help the singer learn bebop at a manageable pace. When the notes can be performed at a medium swing tempo, singers can gradually begin speeding up the tempo, always making sure not to sacrifice precision of pitch or rhythm. If a bebop song is not cleanly performed at its intended tempo, it is not ready for performance. As difficult as this style is to master, it is well worth the effort, and singers will grow their confidence as they listen to, transcribe, and perform solos by outstanding bebop singers and instrumentalists.

Cool Jazz

Cool instrumentalists Lester Young and Chet Baker remain among the most lyrically accessible artists of the cool genre. Young (1909–1959) is generally viewed as one of the first cool artists in jazz history (performing and recording long before West Coast "cool" existed). Young played a style of jazz that diametrically opposed the hot style of his contemporary, Coleman Hawkins. Whereas Hawkins played with a steady vibrato, Young played with almost none, sometimes adding a touch at the ends of phrases for warmth. Hawkins's solos were filled with high energy, but Young's were very mellow and laid-back, almost sounding lazy. Young's long tenor saxophone solos sounded legato and smooth in contrast with Hawkins' bouncier solos. Hawkins and Young represented the "hot/cool" dichotomy in jazz just as Louis Armstrong (1901–1971) and Bix Beiderbecke (1903–1931) represented the same contrast in style so many years before with their common instrument, the cornet. Unlike Armstrong's hot, vibrato-filled playing with an emphasis on virtuosity, Beiderbecke filled his music with lyricism, purity, and mellowness. Beiderbecke was considered by jazz historians to have been the first "cool" player in jazz.

Chet Baker (1929–1988), playing in the 1950s and decades beyond, was himself both a trumpeter and vocalist par excellence. The cool style was exemplified by his very laid-back, gentle, melodic approach, yielding songs that sounded warm, rich, simple, and lush. The cool style leaned away from bebop, giving listeners who loved melody an alternative genre to enjoy during the bebop era.

Free Jazz

Free jazz does not refer to jazz without a cover charge but, rather, to a genre that allows greater freedom from the strictures of form, traditional harmonic conventions, and accessible melodies. It has been said that once you know the rules you are free to break them. This applies to free jazz; I recommend venturing in this direction only after you have already been steeped in the theoretical and structural training of swing, Latin, bebop, the cool school, and other jazz styles. Creating free jazz of quality is far more likely when coming from the standpoint of experience and knowledge of jazz language rather than from ignorance, although sometimes people with superior ears can create jazz (playing by ear) without knowing the theory that others require to excel. Being a lifelong performing artist and an academic, however, I always urge students and colleagues to learn as much as they can and to become musically literate before venturing into such a wide unknown as free jazz. Stretching into this style requires listening to those who did it well. John Coltrane, Ornette Coleman, and Sun Ra were major players in the development of this style.

To improvise free jazz, singers must possess strong confidence in their ability to use scat improvisation (or other means, like connected vowel sounds) with a keen ear for what the band is playing in the moment. Free jazz takes many forms and can be fun for in-class experimentation. Singing "outside" the chord changes is a place to begin, but strict adherence to certain rules learned in an advanced jazz theory course will help the free jazz improviser to make choices that are not merely stabs in the dark but worthwhile solos for singing and studying. To perform free jazz well, advanced theoretical and scalar knowledge (including bebop scales, whole tone scales, half-step-up-melodic-minor-scales that are sung over dominant harmony, etc.) is helpful to know.

JAZZ ACROSS THE WORLD

Jazz continues to evolve throughout the world. Each country where jazz is played has put its own unique national stamp on the music. As the genre moves forward, it is important to remember that although it was first recorded in the United States in 1917 (with elements of it appearing before that in ragtime, blues, and spirituals), it spread rapidly throughout the world and has never stopped growing. Jazz has existed for one hundred years in several countries beyond its country of origin, but tracking the stylistic components of jazz from an international perspective is beyond the scope of this book. The expansive and highly recommended book *The History of European Jazz: The Music, Musicians, and Audience in Context* by Francesco Martinelli (2019) illustrates the vast characteristics of jazz so many countries can now boast in their own jazz histories. Jazz singers are wise to broaden their ears to include jazz musicians, repertoire, and songs outside their own experience. Learning to sing jazz in a language other than English is a great way to start widening the net of understanding for every young jazz singer.

TEACHER TIP

Ask your students what languages besides English they have studied (or possibly have spoken at home). Encourage them to find jazz songs written in those languages for possible study. An additional assignment along these lines is to have students discuss their nationalities or their blending of cultures based on their family trees. For example, if they happen to be Welsh, Irish, and Scottish, assign a project for them to find jazz musicians from those countries—both historical and contemporary artists. Encourage these students to trace the history of jazz in those countries and to become well versed in the diversity of jazz repertoire, stylistic elements, and musicians that reinforce their sense of national heritage. Hold a studio class (or a series of them) in which students perform jazz from countries outside the United States and have each singer share background information about song style, historical context, and artists. Celebrate the diversity of your studio!

Even though jazz originated in the United States, having strong African roots and influences, musicians must remember that the entire Western Hemisphere encompasses America. Canadians, Mexicans, South Americans, and Central Americans have celebrated American jazz in their own unique ways. Learning about the vast amounts of jazz and other improvisational music that hails from these and other nations is a lifelong process. Encouraging singers to start early in exploring jazz from other lands will go a long way toward creating appreciation for the music of other cultures as well as a hugely diverse songbook of one's own.

Starting with music from Brazil will provide singers with a firmer understanding of where a lot of the sounds that have become common to modern jazz originated. The outstanding music of Antonio Carlos Jobim came to the United States in the 1960s. His influence led him to be called "the father of the bossa nova." The more deeply one dives into Jobim's music, the more one discovers a great repository of repertoire well worth exploring as well as a composer whose pioneering spirit started a new style when it became assimilated into American jazz in the United States. It is important to note, however, that the bossa nova is not the same as native Brazilian music. It was created by Jobim when it was melded with jazz in the United States. It is an accessible place to start when introducing jazz from other cultures and includes Portuguese lyrics. Singers are, of course, encouraged to become familiar with the diction and lilt of the languages they perform, and with Brazil having its own unique voice in jazz, learning to sing in Portuguese is a venture worth pursuing.

STYLE IN THE VOICES OF JAZZ MASTERS

The jazz styles of Billie Holiday, Sarah Vaughan, Mel Tormé, Ella Fitzgerald, June Christy, Nat "King" Cole, and countless others became interwoven with the unique qualities of each individual artist. Timbral colors, phrasing, ornamentation, individualized approaches to improvisation, and even the timing of breaths have helped to define an artist's style. To attempt to document authentic style is in itself unattainable using only the written word, so with that caveat, I make no attempt whatsoever to write a definitive missive about learning and teaching jazz "style." So much of musical style for any genre is assimilated through the necessary discipline of critical listening and modeling of great artists—both singers and instrumentalists. Once these disciplines have been consistently pursued, one's own authentic voice may be discovered by the coordination of technique, theoretical knowledge, and creative assimilation of aspects of other artists' performances. The practice of allowing the greatness of geniuses past to trickle into one's own performances helps to keep this fantastic art form alive and well. Developing one's ear and imitative technique, right down to the tiniest shade of nuance in dimensions of rhythm, pitch, articulation, dynamics, timbre, and so on are necessary for developing greatness across all disciplines of music performance, but these elements must also lead toward the development of one's authenticity as a jazz musician.

Building jazz style begins with listening to a large number and a wide variety of artists and genres within jazz. Building style also involves building a jazz repertoire and a jazz vocabulary. Style remains an extremely broad term that defies definition simply because it is much too general to nail down in any singular, succinct form. That said, we may proceed with the understanding that moving from generalities to specifics may be useful to give examples of how many great artists from yesteryear cultivated and mastered their own unique styles. As with many other aspects of this improvisational music, there are no correct, universal answers to the question of style. Duke Ellington's famous quotation comes to mind when discussing this concept: "There are simply two kinds of music—good music and the other kind." For jazz music to be considered "good" it requires that an artist approach it from both a respectful standpoint of knowing and acknowledging the accomplishments and approaches of those who came before, as well as forging one's own path toward an authentic expression of one's uniqueness within the genre. This balance of respecting historicity while creating something "new" (we must remember "there is nothing new under the sun," even in jazz!) must be sought and maintained when artists seek to make their mark on this music. To venture out without knowing something about the history of the art form and how the music has been constructed detrimentally affects one's performance practice just as much as failing to practice improvisation and vocal technique. Like classical music, jazz is high art in the sense that to do it well requires immense preparation, skill, and knowledge. Even with a naturally gifted ear and a pretty voice, to master the art form requires a lifetime of exploration. Even (and especially) consummate performers continue to grow and discover new levels of the craft as they apply themselves toward greater freedom, technique, knowledge, and expression. Celebrating one's milestones and accomplishments while working to improve weaker areas produces an effective mindset for a lifetime of jazz learning and discovery.

THE LISTENING DIET

To develop authentic jazz style, musicians must saturate their ears with excellent music. Selectively choosing the music one listens to remains a common factor among all great musicians. Filtering out music or other noise that does not enhance one's appreciation for beauty, expression, or art is an important step for young musicians wanting to quickly improve their technical and expressive skills. Often the problem lies not with lack of practice but lack of disciplined listening. Active listening to outstanding music remains a necessary part of every aspiring musician's development. Jazz singers are encouraged to listen regularly to singers and instrumentalists who have achieved high levels of artistry. This includes many jazz artists, both living and deceased. Some do-it-yourself jazz singing manuals have included suggested listening lists, but these are limiting and simply a product of my own preferences and listening experiences. All great jazz singers compile their own unique listening experiences and influences. To create a bedrock of jazz repertoire, listening to as many historic and modern jazz artists as possible is recommended. As one grows a listening list, preferences immediately take shape, and a jazz artist begins to understand how every great artist can teach them something. For instance, from tenor saxophonist Lester Young I learned how tone color can be warmed and mellowed, how to back-phrase, and how legato phrasing can be applied to create a "cool" aural painting rich with lush beauty. By listening to recordings of Young's contemporary, Coleman Hawkins (who played the same instrument), I learned how to solo more "vertically" (as a chord-playing instrument would, although playing one note at a time) over chord changes instead of singing in a horizontal, linear, melodic manner. I also learned from Hawkins how a "hot" musician approached soloing. Different musicians can approach the same instrument in entirely different ways and from different angles, with intentions for different creative outcomes. This truth can influence young musicians in developing their own unique approaches to their instruments.

The advantage possessed by every singer is that no other human on the planet has, or ever has had, an instrument exactly like theirs. This adds to the complexity of timbral variety and the myriad of options singers possess for finding their own sounds. It also is helpful for the singing teacher to be reminded that conveyor-belt pedagogy (by which every student gets the same lessons, exercises, and repertoire in the same order) is never appropriate when teaching voice in any genre. The sheer individuality of every human's body, mind, voice, heart, personality, and interests requires individualized, personalized instruction so that the teacher always teaches the person in the room something relevant to that person today. Teachers of voice accumulate thousands of vocal exercises over their lifetimes. I encourage teachers to modify the exercises they love and apply jazz concepts to create their own tried-and-true jazz vocalises (vocal exercises). They also can invent their own to suit each individual student.

TOOLS FOR TEACHING JAZZ STYLE

Back to the Baseline

First and foremost, a teacher must help students find their authentic, healthy, baseline voice. This involves being able to sing freely, with pure vowels, excellent body alignment, and a breathing technique that can help singers traverse long, uninterrupted phrases replete with crescendos and decrescendos. The healthy baseline permits singing with clear articulation and minimal added tension in the articulators (i.e., tongue, lips, and jaw) as well as minimal tension at the level of the vocal folds. A pressed tone is not a healthy baseline—neither is a breathy, edgy, or nasal tone. Finding the balance at "point neutral" where the authentic voice emerges without any "tweaking" or added color must be the top priority of any voice pedagogue, regardless of style being taught (commercial styles especially included!). Singers whose neutral baselines are characterized by healthy, authentic voices can learn to sing a wide variety of styles healthfully, without pressing or stressing the voice. This is not the same as saying all singers must have a thoroughly "classical" technique first. A healthy authentic voice merely means the voice is free, clear, properly aligned, well energized by the breath, able to perform pure vowels, and devoid of any pulling or tugging that certain stylistic efforts may place on it. Seeking a healthy starting point should be the goal of every professional singer every day.

Modification of Classical Exercises

Taking that thought further, I have found that, especially when training a classical singer to sing jazz, starting with classical exercises (to help them find their authentic baseline voice in a familiar musical setting) and then modifying them to swing and scat those same patterns works wonders. Similarly, classical voice teachers can start teaching jazz voice by applying jazz feel and style to their favorite exercises. Both teacher and student experience great satisfaction knowing they do not have to start at ground zero but simply put some jazz swing or bossa nova feel under a scale or pattern. Have the singer perform the exercise with a jazz sensibility instead of an even scale, arpeggio, or pattern. Suddenly an experienced classical teacher is armed with unlimited ideas for exercises. The method books by Marchesi and Concone can be easily modified to a swing or bossa style for the student studying both bel canto and jazz literature. Teaching students to go back and forth between styles will build versatility and instrument mastery, much like placing jazz alongside classical repertoire in a trumpet lesson.

Journaling toward Style Mastery

Not only listening but also verbalizing one's discoveries in a journal or in writing assignments help to cement that which is heard into repeatable practice. Because journaling has been integral to my own personal musical growth as well as that of my students, the reader will see references to journaling throughout this book. Comparative listening journal assignments should be offered to both applied students studying privately as well as to students studying pedagogy in a classroom setting. In these various settings, voice students build a log of their own observations and preferences for particular artists, repertoire, and styles. The act of verbalizing or documenting one's thoughts about listening to music goes a long way in firmly establishing a young musician's development and mastery. If one cannot describe in detail what one has heard, one often forgets it.

The Video Log

Video-recording one's lessons and practice sessions remains an important activity to gain a true sense of everything one projects to an audience during performances. Without consulting video and audio feedback, one can only guess what is being telegraphed to an audience. Fully aware singers practice humility by regularly watching themselves perform (and gently critiquing their own performances) to improve the artistic offering they project. When critiquing oneself, it is of paramount "importance to be kind." As natural as it might be to remember and home in on the aspects you regretted about a concert, work to find positive reinforcement first, as you would when giving a student feedback about a recital. Start with what worked well and gently move toward acknowledging areas that came off less skillfully than you wished. Focusing on jazz style and ornamentation during one watch session is a great way to analyze these aspects of your own performance and to determine whether changes should be made to enhance your shows.

The video log can also be used to increase various necessary skills on a broader scale. How one enters and exits the stage, talks with the audience, displays confidence and correct posture, manages the breath, maintains eye contact with the audience, and sings with good technique can all be studied. The camera is one of the jazz singer's most honest tools for growth. Although it is often unpleasant to watch oneself perform, it is a necessary chore for maximum mastery. Jazz style will develop naturally and completely after singers become comfortable diagnosing and correcting their own mannerisms, visible tensions, and technical flaws with help from a camera. You may believe you are saturating a phrase with a particular stylistic trait, but you may be surprised to discover that it does not translate well to the audience. The video log is like a mirror that shows us as we truly are and not how we believe ourselves to be. This humbling reality also helps us take charge of our progress and forge ahead both in the practice room and onstage toward actually conveying the ideal performance we visualize in all its polished glory.

THE BAG OF TRICKS

All jazz musicians have their own "bag of tricks" to which they add as experience and technique are developed over time, and all come from a unique set of experiences and surroundings that inform their approach to the art form. This repository of colors and devices helps singers develop their signature sound. The sheer diversity of possible approaches to style and ornamentation must be respected whenever teaching jazz voice. As a singer develops and grows in technique, listening diet, ornamentation, stylistic application, and improvisation, the "bag" becomes duly stocked with tools and skills that provide interesting listening experiences for audiences and a wide array of performance options for artists.

Ornaments

Techniques used by jazz vocalists to decorate or embellish the melody of a song are known as "ornaments." These include a wide palette of technical terms that make distinctions among the techniques belonging in this arsenal of sounds. Ornamentation can occur before, during, or after singing a target pitch, depending on the ornament used. Several ornaments used in jazz language will be described here, although many more exist. Listening critically to great masters of the art form will reveal even more ornamental sounds than have been coined and documented by jazz schol-

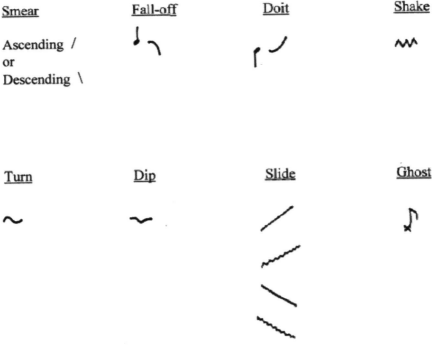

Figure 6.2.   Jazz Vocal Ornaments. Courtesy of Author

ars. I encourage singers to listen deeply to great jazz singing until they can hear and assimilate subtle as well as overt ornaments.

The Smear

A **smear** is an upward or downward slide that connects seamlessly to the next note. It is often termed a "scoop" when critiqued in classical music. A smear is indicated in a musical score with a slanted line or a short, curved line indicating the direction to which the pitch should bend. The ascending smear (notated with an ascending slash [/] above a note) slides up to the target pitch, often starting on the scale tone below. The descending smear (notated with a descending slash [\ ]) does exactly the opposite; it slides down to the target pitch, usually starting on the scale tone above. Both types of smears slide between pitches in an identifiably pop/jazz style.

Ella Fitzgerald and Sarah Vaughan commonly used smears in their singing, especially Vaughan. Several recordings by Vaughan possess her signature smears, which connect the notes together in long, legato phrases. Her commitment to singing smears among several notes in a line helped to create the smooth, connected environment in which her voice operated. The smear, both ascending and descending, was Vaughan's go-to technique that characterized how she moved between notes. Her recording of "You're Mine, You" illustrates this adept, serpentine sliding action that rendered each note a cascade of richly colored sound that poured smoothly into the next.

The Fall-Off

A **fall-off** (sometimes called a "fall") occurs when, at the end of a note, word, or phrase, the singer slides the pitch downward toward an indeterminate low pitch. The name of the technique describes the action as though one's voice is falling off a stable platform to nothingness below. Phonation usually fades after the fall-off reaches a certain low point, although it is possible (although unusual) to end the fall-off by singing a new determinate pitch. A fall-off sometimes serves as an effective end to a section of a piece.

The Doit

A **doit** (pronounced as rhyming with the second syllable of "adroit") represents the opposite of a fall-off in that a singer performs a note followed by an upward slide toward an indeterminate final note. Trumpet players perform doits and fall-offs more frequently than many other instrumentalists, so vocalists performing doits are borrowing the ornament, imitating the jazz trumpet. Doits and fall-offs are frequently used in the vocal jazz ensemble context but not as often in solo settings because this vocal ornament originated within horn sections of classic big bands. When vocalists join together in a vocal ensemble to perform these dramatic ornaments, the effects are magnified much like the effects of the same embellishments performed by an entire horn section.

The Shake

A **shake** is similar to a trill in classical music. A shake, however, occurs when the performer plays or sings two pitches in rapid alternation, sometimes starting slow and speeding up. The shake may occur between two notes a semitone apart, a whole step apart, or even a minor third apart, for dramatic effect. A classical trill has no such parallel but simply consists of extremely rapid alternation between two pitches either a semitone or whole step apart (widening a trill to encompass a minor third is not generally done in classical vocal music). A shake also possesses a slower alternation between pitches than a trill. The listener is meant to clearly hear both pitches during a shake, whereas in the case of a trill, both pitches are sung or played in such fast alternation that it blurs the resultant pitch a bit. When teaching the shake, teachers must take care that a singer does not trill but, rather, sings both pitches clearly with absolute precise delineation between the two. The shake is almost always started slowly and then accelerated, starting on the lower pitch and ultimately landing stably on the lower pitch. No blurring of the pitch should happen. Also, tongue, jaw, and neck tension should be monitored to make sure the head and jaw do not wobble in an effort to change pitches quickly. Sometimes a shake is indicated on a note of short duration in the middle of a phrase. When this occurs, the shake is performed a bit more like a trill for the sake of time.

The globally loved vocal jazz ensemble the Manhattan Transfer has famously performed shakes in this manner for decades. Consider their recordings of "Birdland" when they sing a shake on "everyBOdy heard that word." For the shake to be clearly heard, they waste no time starting it slowly and then accelerating. They simply start to shake at maximum alternation speed at the beginning of that syllable to great effect. As when teaching the classical trill, teachers must develop their own technique in demonstrating and performing this key jazz ornament because, like the trill, the shake requires diligent practice, flexible technique, and strong vocal coordination to pull off authentically and cleanly.

The Turn

The **turn** is similar to a classical mordent. The written pitch is sung followed by the upper neighbor tone, the written pitch again, the lower neighbor tone, and finally the written pitch. This pop and jazz ornament must be practiced so that it can be performed quickly with absolute pitch precision of all five tones and rhythmic equality on each (likened to four thirty-second notes or sixteenth notes, depending on the rhythmic context). Ella Fitzgerald used turns occasionally during her interpretations of jazz standards and sometimes during her scat improvisations. The turn saves the copyist from having to write out four additional notes that anyone with jazz notational sensibility instantly recognizes. A quarter note with a turn inscribed above it should be rendered as described above, delivered as five notes performed in quick, agile succession instead of a single quarter note. The turn is an excellent ornament to employ when seeking ways to present the melody in a novel manner, perhaps on the final chorus before the coda ("tail" ending) of a piece. As with the use of any type of ornament, singers are wise to avoid excess. Thus, development of musical taste plays an important role. Deciding how much ornamentation to use and which ornaments are most appropriate to each situation becomes part of every accomplished jazz singer's modus operandi.

The Dip

The **dip** occurs in jazz when the singer sings the written pitch, drops the pitch slightly, and then returns to the written pitch again, all using a seamlessly connected slide to move from note to note within a short span of time that does not obscure the written rhythm. This ornament is commonly heard in both jazz and pop music. When teaching the dip, emphasis on maintaining jazz style is paramount so that this ornament does not sound like a mistake or a sudden drop in breath support or energy. This ornament is intentional and results in a sense of emphasis or accent being placed on a particular word or syllable.

The Slide

The **slide** can be considered equivalent to a glissando in classical music. Singers sing the first written pitch and then, without ceasing phonation, continue to slide upward or downward until they reach the next target pitch. The notation of a slide is either a long, straight diagonal or wavy line oriented diagonally in the direction the slide is headed (either upward or downward). This wavy notation is ironic considering that the voice remains seamlessly connected by a vibratoless tone throughout the dramatic ornament. The voice must not disconnect from the breath nor from the process of phonation for the slide to be successful. Slides may be fast or slow depending on the rhythmic context. Teachers are encouraged to help singers stay within the jazz style by eliminating vibrato on all slides; they are not portamenti, which, in classical singing, involve sliding while the voice continues creating vibrato. All jazz slides must be absolutely without vibrato.

The Ghost

In the swing style, many times jazz singers vocally imply the second (swung) eighth note in each pair even when it is not notated as a separate note, especially during quarter notes. At other times, just before the onset of a note on a downbeat in the swing style, a sotto voce (under the breath) sound, almost like a gentle, unaccented grunt, may be uttered to emphasize swing feel. Both of these scenarios describe an ornament that jazz musicians call the **ghost**. Ghosts are notated as smaller notes with an *x* in place of the note head on the staff to indicate that the sound is without determinate pitch. If the ghost is taking the place of an eighth note value, it is written with an eighth note flag in a smaller font than the standard notes in the score (like a grace note in classical music, except that it is only implied and not actually phonated). Ghosts require some practice before they sound natural. They are common ornaments in the vocal jazz ensemble and often appear in the performances and recordings of experienced jazz singers.

Teaching, learning, and singing jazz with an authentic approach to style and ornamentation can be approached in a variety of ways. Establishing a basis for jazz language through guided listening and a steady diet of outstanding recordings and performances, studying various common styles within the jazz genre, and building a bag of tricks that includes ornaments and other skills all constitute highly rewarding endeavors for jazz voice pedagogues and their students for a lifetime of jazz artistry.

7

VOCAL IMPROVISATION

Working jazz singers will naturally gravitate toward particular types of improvisation that suit their tastes and abilities but should also be aware of a much wider variety of improvisational tools. The jazz voice pedagogue in particular is encouraged to build skills in demonstrating and teaching more than one type of vocal improvisation. Singers will find, as they explore all of these, that one or more types present great challenges, whereas another type or two may seem quite accessible and even well-developed already. As singers grow more and more adept at improvisation, they learn to expand their pool of ideas and areas of strength.

MELODIC EMBELLISHMENT

The most basic form of vocal improvisation is melodic embellishment. Exactly as it sounds, this is the act of singing the melody in a manner that ornaments or slightly varies the original line in pitch, rhythm, articulation, or some combination of these. Scatting the melody with strict adherence to the written pitches and rhythms represents the first step. When singers can accurately scat all the pitches and rhythms of the original melody, they can begin to vary the rhythm more and more. When comfortable, the singer may begin adding ornaments learned in the previous chapter to the melody with authentic expression true to the style of the great jazz singers in history.

Peggy Lee stands as an expert in melodic embellishment as a form of jazz improvisation. A trouper in delivering the melody as the composer originally intended, Lee also could completely alter the pitches and rhythms of a melody as often as she liked. Listen to her rendition of "My Heart Belongs to Daddy" from the *Black Coffee* album to hear Lee adhere closely to the original melody at first but then embellish it with rhythmic variation. Similarly, Ella Fitzgerald sang her many "Songbook" albums true to the original melodies out of respect for the composers. She resisted her public's pressure to improvise (and especially scat-sing) during these recordings because she wanted to create albums celebrating the composers and not her catapulting vocal acrobatics—a skill in which she had no peer. These "Songbook" albums of Harold Arlen, George Gershwin, Irving Berlin, Antonio Carlos Jobim, Duke Ellington, Richard Rodgers, and Jerome Kern represented Ella's outstanding vocalism with only slight melodic embellishment. These are a wonderful and impressive body of work that singers should use to master the art of singing a song that respects the composer on the first chorus (not changing the music or the rhythms much) and then embellishes the melody on the last chorus. Fitzgerald gave many of these songs once-through treatment without instrumental solos to show how well the raw material stood on its own. This is still quite a legitimate way to present a jazz standard, particularly ballads. Not every song needs an instrumental break or repeated choruses, and smart jazz singers vary the formal design of their set so that the audience cannot predict the road map of every song. Letting a few ballads speak for themselves with just a touch of melodic embellishment can be an elegant rendering of a diverse set of songs.

SCAT IMPROVISATION

Fitzgerald and Louis Armstrong represented two of the strongest scat improvisers in jazz history. Their exciting, "hot" style caused their recordings and live performances to simmer with excitement and energy, and their seemingly endless pools of ideas drew many impressed listeners to jazz. One crucial requirement to become adept at scat singing is listening often to those who did it well. Fitzgerald's outstanding recordings that included scat singing are numerous. Her many live recordings of "How High the Moon" remain particularly famous examples of her scat prowess. Although she quoted several famous songs throughout her improvised solo (duly planning some of the solo rather than strictly improvising it as she went along), various recordings of her performances exhibit that she did improvise a significant amount as she strung together those melodic quotations.

Quotation

A **quotation** in jazz is a fragment of a recognizable melody from a different piece used in an improvised solo. Using quotations in improvised solos is a wonderful way to include the audience in the improvisation because they love to respond to familiar melodies. Although a large percentage of Fitzgerald's scat solos are truly improvised rather than preplanned, it is important to note that Fitzgerald did preplan the architecture of some of her solos, giving attention to the arc of a couple of choruses and using some recurring motives (including quotations) she liked.

Preparation for Improvisation

All great improvisers do some preparatory work on every song over which they intend to improvise. Fitzgerald knew the harmony as well as the melody on which her improvised solos were based, and she gave thought to characterizing each song in the proper light and style. She appropriately used harmonic minor scales over songs in minor keys, and sevenths, thirds, and ninths to define the chords over which she sang. Her sense of swing was so outstanding that even when she stayed close to the written melody, her interpretations of swing tunes have remained the finest recordings of those songs. Improvising never replaces preparation in jazz. On the contrary, one is never ready to improvise a solo until the harmony, melody, rhythm, form, and lyrics of a piece are extremely well learned.

Scat Syllables

When teaching scat technique, the most common question I receive from both students and teachers is "What syllables do I use?" My answer centers on one premise: the original objective of scat singing was to imitate the sound of an instrument playing a jazz solo. When Louis Armstrong first began to sing with scat improvisation in the late 1920s, he was playing a recording date and his lips were tired from having played his horn already for several hours. When the time came for his improvised cornet solo, he elected to sing what he might have played instead, using neutral syllables "ba," "du," "da," and "bu," among others, to give his trumpet chops a rest. Alternate accounts of the origin of scat singing include Cab Calloway's "hi-de-ho" type of nonsense syllables, which he was using in the early 1920s and beyond. Other artists have also made a claim, but more importantly, Armstrong was the first to make scat singing a virtuosic form of jazz improvisation. For a century afterward, singers have worked on their own scat abilities to offer their improvisational ideas to a song's solo break.

Consonant Choices in Scat Improvisation

Until an improviser becomes so adept at creating scat syllables that this new language is second nature, staying close to just a few consonant sounds that approximate the tone of an instrument playing an improvised solo is recommended. These include voiced consonants *b* and *d* and occasionally *v*—all which contain pitch to help keep the musical flow continuous while creating strong delineations among the beats with the percussive consonant sound. As the improviser grows, limits to what consonants sound natural may or may not begin to fall away. The author uses a variety of consonants depending on the context of the solo. Beginning improvisers are wise not to venture far from *b* and *d*, which, even for most experienced improvisers, constitute the bulk of consonants used in scat singing.

Vowel Choices in Scat Improvisation

Certain vowel sounds lend themselves to a greater acoustic amplitude. For this reason I teach my students to use open vowels on the offbeats (in 4/4 swing feel, these would be the second eighth note of every quarter note beat). Acoustically, an open vowel tends to be louder on its own than a closed vowel. Therefore, strategically using closed vowels when singing on the beat is a great way to de-emphasize downbeats so that the accent can be correctly placed on the offbeat. Fitzgerald set up her vowel choices this way, using a lot of "du va," "du ba," and "boo dop" when singing a pair of swung eighth notes starting on the beat. Although it was not always the case, she frequently used open and closed vowel sounds that were acoustically ideal to aid the swing feel in both accented and unaccented notes. When singing this way, singers do not have to try as hard to accent offbeats or deemphasize the "strong" beats because the acoustical properties of the open and closed vowels take care of that difference in volume and carrying power, especially when amplified through a microphone.

Transcribing Scat Solos

Transcribing wonderful scat solos by well-known jazz artists remains a vital tool for developing improvisational ideas. Singers can learn about syllable combinations that work by transcribing the syllables that great scat improvisers have used. Singers need not limit themselves to only singers' solos, though. Transcribing linear piano, guitar, saxophone, trumpet, bass, and other instrumental solos will enable the budding vocal improviser to execute difficult passages with greater ease. Transcribing solos will also enlarge a jazz student's "inner ear" (one's purely mental hearing inside one's head) and harmonic language in ways that will enable greater mastery of scat improvisation. When listening to and transcribing great instrumental improvised solos, the singer should endeavor to use syllables that sound close to how they think the instrument sounds. Simply using "du," "da," "ba," and "va" will help singers begin to build a larger vocabulary of scat syllables. The syllables themselves are not as important as the swing feel (or Latin feel) and rhythmic sense that are prevalent in the song.

Transcribing Hot Style—Armstrong and Fitzgerald

Transcribing the improvised solos of "hot style" vocal improvisers Louis Armstrong and Ella Fitzgerald helps the jazz singer grasp the innovative approaches of two of the finest jazz artists in music history. These jazz pioneers lifted the art of vocal improvisation to a virtuosic level. Each artist offered scores of outstanding recordings of both live and studio-recorded scat improvisations. Their duet albums (*Ella and Louis*, 1956, and *Ella and Louis Again*, 1957) remain two of the greatest collaborative albums in jazz. Studying each artist's recordings in-depth represents indispensable listening and transcription work recommended for every modern jazz singer. Notating not only the pitches and rhythms but also the ornaments and stylistic indications performed by these musically sophisticated artists will instruct the beginning transcriber in critically listening to, identifying, and notating much more than notes.

Transcribing the Coolness of Chet

A terrific example of a cool jazz voice improviser (as opposed to the hot improvisers already mentioned) was Chet Baker. A highly accomplished trumpeter with a mellow tone, laid-back feel, and pleasing sound in both his trumpet and his voice, Baker allowed his playing style to inform his singing style. When he improvised he used scat syllables that beautifully brought out the versatility of the vocal instrument while tastefully choosing pitches and rhythms that created masterful tension and release and outstanding arcs of improvisational expression. Baker seemed to take listeners to a transcendent and meditative world all his own while staying extremely accessible to the average listener. Although he has been criticized by some for low-energy singing, this approach truly worked within his cool style and never resulted in pitch flatting. He showed how a flat, vibratoless *tone* was not the same as a flat *pitch*; Baker was able to keep his intonation in check without adding a great deal of energy or vibrato to his voice. His early recording of "I Fall in Love Too Easily" (1955) demonstrated this understated style. He used a slow, gentle vibrato at the ends of his vocal phrases in the same way he used it in his trumpet playing. Baker was an outstanding example of a musician with dual performance strengths in both instrumental and vocal music, like Armstrong, Sarah Vaughan, and Nat "King" Cole, to name a few, and is one of the most notable vocalists to scat in a decidedly cool style.

Start with the Melody

Scat-singing the melody of a song represents the first step in practicing scat improvisation. Find syllables that sound natural and neutral. Feel free to play with different consonants as long as they allow you to freely express the melody as naturally as possible. Then gradually depart further and further from the melody, substituting a different pitch here or a varied rhythm there. Eventually, with practice, scatting the melody becomes relatively easy and a safe place to start playing with varying pitches and rhythms. As singers become more skilled, they create new melodies further and further from the original. Singers also learn that in certain places in the form (often the bridge), they may need to return to the security provided by the melody, so learning to accurately and authentically scat the melody is a valuable and artistic tool for jazz singers at all levels.

Root Motion

After the melody is learned and interpreted in precise scat syllables, singers are advised to scat the **root motion** of the song, or what the bassist would play (see chapter 12). Find syllables that approximate the sound of a bass: "bu," "du," or "dm" on strong beats, "ba" or "da" on offbeats (swung eighth notes). Scat sounds chosen should mirror the deep, resonant tone of an acoustic bass. Start by singing half notes or whatever note value represents the harmonic rhythm. Harmonic rhythm refers to how frequently the chords change—is it every half note, every quarter note, or every whole note? Move to a walking bass line when comfortable, still scatting on the strong beats and between them moving stepwise by quarter notes from one chord to the next. Listening to accomplished bass players "walk" a bass line is the only way to master this technique. Great jazz singers are also great imitators; be able to sing back what you hear and work on it when you listen to recordings as well as in jazz voice lessons. I like to use a variety of consonant sounds to approximate the sound of pizzicato (plucked) bass. Teachers and students are encouraged to come up with their own sounds from transcribing the solos of great scat singers, listening to exceptional instrumental solos, learning them, and singing along. A string of syllables should flow easily off the tongue, teeth, and lips, and capture the essence of the phrases made by the instrumentalist.

Practice Patterns

All scat singers create patterns consisting of favorite licks and motives they can use over certain familiar chord progressions. Chapter 12 discusses patterns like ii-V7-I and twelve-bar blues that are recommended for beginners to practice when learning to scat-sing. Be able to scat all your scales—major, minor, bebop, blues, pentatonic, whole-tone, and chromatic, as well as all the modes, starting on any given pitch and at a variety of tempos and feels (swing, bossa nova, waltz, etc.). Incorporate sequential patterns based on the scales that are not strictly stepwise (e.g., sing scale degrees 1-3-2-1-2-4-3-2, etc., all the way to the tonic an octave higher). Learning jazz harmonies is central to scat study, so performing scales or arpeggios in the context of a song's chord progression must also be undertaken for each song studied. Advanced singers would benefit from studying Shelton Berg's *Jazz Improvisation: The Goal Note Method* (1998), which is a step-by-step course in advanced improvisation for instrumentalists. Every singer of every style benefits from scale studies. Mastering all relevant scales will equip the budding scat singer with knowledge of what improvised solo strategies work over certain harmonies. It also provides confidence in expressing oneself through the scat language. Don't stop at scales; teachers know a myriad of nonscalar and arpeggiated patterns they use to teach classical voice. Simply set the exercise to a swing beat and scat it instead of singing as a classical singer would. In this way, teachers, students, and professional jazz singers have an unlimited cache of exercises at their disposal. Us-

ing already familiar exercises by adapting them to a jazz sensibility is
the quickest way to adapt one's classical voice studio to accommodate
a jazz voice student.

Guided listening to outstanding jazz recordings can be part of lesson
instruction. Ask students to describe what they hear, being specific about
diction, ornaments, improvisation, rhythm, meter, expression, tone quality, tonal center shifts, and elements of style. There are plenty of books
filled with jazz voice warm-ups, licks, and motives that you can copy and
use, but my advice is simply to listen to great scatters, transcribe their
solos, have students learn transcriptions down to the finest nuance, and
use assigned repertoire to create exercises in arpeggiating harmony in
both swing and Latin styles. Use adapted vocal compass warmups you
already like (exercises that stretch the singer's full range and flexibility)
with scat syllables that easily roll off the tongue and can be modified to
swing or keep a straight-eighth-note feel. Instrumentalists teaching vocalists can hold singers to a high standard for mastering scales just as pianists
do—just keep in mind that scales should be performed within the most
comfortable ranges for your singers as possible at first, gradually letting
them expand outward from the middle comfort zone of their voices. Ear-
training scale tests should also accommodate both high and low voices.
Singing outside one's comfortable range should not be required during an
ear-training test.

Harmonic Mastery

After some work on scatting scales, arpeggios, song melodies, and licks
heard performed by great jazz singers and instrumentalists (remember
those winning motives, write them down, and add them to your performable repertoire whenever possible!), the scat singer is ready to use this
knowledge over a chord progression to create a solo. Starting small with
something familiar is always an important consideration. Begin with
ii-V7-I progressions that repeat many times ("vamp") so that the singer
can arpeggiate each chord, sing the roots, and begin to create melodic
riffs or licks that sound good over those chords. Then change the keys
and have the singer practice this progression in all twelve major keys.
Try switching to a minor tonic and start over for some great mutational
work (**mutation** is the term used to describe going from a major key to its
parallel minor key or vice versa). This device is an important principle to
remember when keys alternate between major and minor tonality. Audi-

ences (and fellow bandmates) love hearing a singer who knows a mutation is coming and sings the major and minor thirds correctly to reiterate it.

Ear Training

Throughout the scat-singing process, ear training remains paramount. Singers should be able to identify what scale degree they are singing (at least as it relates to the tonic key). As one grows in musicianship, one develops the inner ear and can isolate the thirds, sevenths, ninths, and other scale degrees relevant to each chord played in a song. Singers should spend time arpeggiating chords one at a time as they progress through the harmonies of their songs (using scat syllables). This consistent practice helps musicians to fully understand the harmonic structure beneath a melody or solo. The better one becomes at arpeggiating the chords and hearing scale degrees in the inner ear, the more accomplished one becomes at improvisation. Knowing the harmonic progression that is coming before it is played is part of the development of an advanced jazz musician. This knowledge requires many hours of disciplined practice, and this is part of the work that never ceases for working jazz singers. As one adds new repertoire, the process of song learning (pitches, rhythms, harmony, lyrics, phrasing, ornaments, expression, and background of the song) is repeated thousands of times over a lifetime or successful career.

TEXT-BASED IMPROVISATION

Text-based improvisation may be an unfamiliar concept for many readers. It is a term that refers to a style of improvising that maintains the integrity of the original written text, but improvisation of new pitches or rhythms occurs around the intact words. Sarah Vaughan represents a pinnacle of mastery of this form of vocal improvisation, often intent on keeping the lyrics at the forefront of her expression but modifying pitches, rhythms, phrasing, and ornaments to satisfy her creative spirit. Similarly, Peggy Lee was an outstanding text-based-improviser using dynamic contrast, phrasing, back-phrasing, and understatement to create her masterpieces of unique color and style. **Back-phrasing** is an important element of this form of improvisation. First explored by "cool jazz" tenor saxophonist Lester Young (who taught it to Billie Holiday, the first singer credited with using it), this technique is the art of delaying or anticipating a musical phrase from a rhythmic standpoint to vary its delivery, like a conversation ebbing and flowing. Instead of starting on beat one, singers intentionally wait a bit longer before starting their phrase and fit the words in deftly by the end of the musical phrase. An important consideration when teaching back-phrasing it to make sure singers are not always starting late. Sometimes they should begin a phrase early to limit predictability when using this technique. It takes work to become an astute back-phraser, but it is an advanced technique that is worth studying and mastering. Maintaining the integrity of the words (rather than improvising with scat syllables) remains a high priority for many singers, so this form of improvisation is important to acknowledge and authenticate in the realm of jazz voice instruction and performance. It is also usually a more comfortable starting place for beginning improvisers than scat singing because most singers are more comfortable singing song lyrics than inventing their own dialect of scat. Both text-based improvisation and scat improvisation require much study and critical listening to perform well.

Phrasing becomes extremely important to text-based improvisers because they must find new ways to time the delivery of the words and compose new notes to go with them. At every turn, maintaining the integrity of the lyricist's intention remains paramount, unless the singer intends to portray the song in a parody style or with irony instead of in a straight-ahead manner as originally written. Here is where a thorough understanding of harmony and the arpeggios of the chords under the melody can greatly assist the burgeoning improviser. Rather than composing scat syllables along with new pitches and rhythms, the singer can just as creatively set the lyrics to an arpeggiated line, scalar pattern or other motive that fits the harmony. One point to remember about text-based improvisation is that it removes one less variable for the audience. Some audiences do not like scat singing because they don't understand it (or because it is not delivered skillfully in many cases). Text-based improvisation allows the audience to remain connected to the lyrics of the song while the singer improvises, often maintaining a greater connection to the expressive potential of those lyrics.

TEACHER TIP

When teaching improvisation to a beginning jazz singer, start with this form of improvisation. It minimizes the "composing" required in the moment and allows the singer to experiment first with changing pitches or rhythms. Encourage the student to change only one musical element at a time (either pitch or rhythm), while leaving the other intact and then switch! Singers find it easier to start with this approach than with scat singing because syllables often get in the way until they feel like a fluent language.

VOCALESE

Vocalese is a specific type of vocal improvisation that was coined by Jon Hendricks and first performed by the outstanding jazz voice trio Lambert, Hendricks, and Ross. The Manhattan Transfer has also performed this difficult style with great prowess. It is less a style of improvisation than a style of preplanned vocal delivery, but it can be a style of improvising for expert singers. Vocalese is the superimposition of lyrics on top of an instrumentalist's solo and is best illustrated through songs including "Four Brothers," which was originally composed by Jimmy Giuffre in 1947 as an instrumental ensemble piece featuring the four virtuosic saxophonists of Woody Herman's band. Hendricks decided to add lyrics to each instrumentalist's part as well as each player's improvised solo, and the individual parts were sung by one member of a vocal ensemble, yielding a stunningly impressive vocal performance by the Manhattan Transfer on their 1978 *Pastiche* album. Lambert, Hendricks, and Ross delivered a terrific live (video-recorded) performance of a different jazz standard called "Four" at the Festival de Jazz d'Antibes Juan-les-Pins, France, in 1961. Both Hendricks and Dave Lambert vividly delivered clean examples of vocalese at its best during this performance. As shown by these experts, singers must work to cultivate absolute precision in their diction and rhythm to master this style. Because singing text at brisk tempos is necessary for this style of improvisation, scatting the lines first and slowly speaking the text in rhythm (then gradually increasing speed) is a recommended process of learning vocalese. Pitches, rhythms, and lyrics should each be studied and learned separately with great attention given to precision.

TEACHER TIP

As with other aspects of voice instruction, teachers must remove variables for students so they can focus on one aspect at a time. Learning rhythms first, speaking text, adding rhythm to spoken text, and learning pitches at a slow tempo without added text are all steps to guide students through as they work toward learning any song that will include scat or vocalese. Moving into singing a transcribed vocalese solo is recommended after the song has been learned one variable at a time. Only after singers have worked on several examples of previously recorded vocalese solos can they be expected to improvise vocalese on their own. Singer Kurt Elling has composed and performed lyrics to existing instrumental solos to create his own vocalese; his recordings and live performances of this style are recommended study for modern jazz singers. It is a style worth the effort, requiring extremely good pitch precision with wide leaps and medium or fast tempos. Some students find they can improvise lyrics in a rhythmically interesting pattern on the spot. Those students should be encouraged to pursue this style more because it represents a form of virtuosic improvisation all its own.

LYRIC IMPROVISATION

Lyric improvisation involves inventing lyrics in the moment. Often pitches are improvised along with new text. The precedent set for this style of improvisation is most heavily rooted in the blues. For more than a century, musicians have improvised songs, ditties, or tunes accompanying themselves on banjos or guitars as they sang lines of text. Folk traditions of various regions led to the development of the blues, which was a highly improvisatory art form and still is. Blues and jazz have always been related. The twelve-bar-blues is a song form that is often played by jazz musicians and sung by jazz vocalists. Accomplished musicians can build an extended piece of music from this twelve-measure form simply by deciding on a key.

To create text for a twelve-bar form, a singer (in the style of Bessie Smith or Billie Holiday) can think of two short phrases of text that loosely rhyme the last words (even though some do not). The first phrase of text (which fits over four measures) is often repeated before heading to the second phrase of text:

I was with you, baby, when you didn't have a dime.
I was with you, baby, when you didn't have a dime.
Now since you got plenty money you have thrown your good gal down.
(From "Lost Your Head Blues" by Bessie Smith)

The listener will notice that Smith chose to pronounce "dime" and "down" similarly enough that they are accepted as nearly rhyming. This is the essence of lyric improvisation. Sometimes a couplet will not rhyme, and then the singer is forced to find a way to make it work anyway. This type of improvisation is great for poets, actors, and others who are comfortable speaking in public or performing on a stage. Lyric improvisation is a wonderful skill to build for musicians of every genre because one never knows when one will face the unexpected during a public performance. When lyric improvisation is part of singers' skill set, they can work out solutions to tricky performance situations that all professional singers face from time to time. The art of improvisation covers a multitude of mistakes and unexpected moments. Learning to roll with it is the mark of a true professional improviser.

Listen to the Greats

Listening to outstanding blues singers and jazz lyric improvisers is the best way to master this style of improvisation. Bessie Smith, known as "Empress of the Blues," famously improvised several hundred blues songs in the recording studio and in live performances. Billie Holiday also was adept at creating blues lyrics on an impromptu basis (e.g., "Fine and Mellow"). In the glory days of the blues, singers were expected to perform with this creative skill. It is still a worthwhile skill to cultivate in jazz circles; and in classroom situations, it generates a lot of fun.

Singers are encouraged to listen to Ella Fitzgerald's live concert performances; here is where she shined brightest because she responded to her audience and her fellow musicians in the moment, even addressing band mates in the lyrics of her songs. In "Stompin' at the Savoy," Fitzgerald joked with pianist (and fellow master of swing and bebop styles) Oscar Peterson when she substituted "stompin' with you, Oscar, we're through" for the original lyrics of the song. On other occasions, when momentarily forgetting a song's lyrics, she confessed this verbally to the audience in the swinging rhythm of the song instead of singing the song's original words, making her audience love her even more.

TEACHER TIP

Students can select a topic to sing about, think of two relevant rhyming words, and then begin singing along to a twelve-bar-blues progression using those words to end the first and second phrases of text. Encourage students to continue to improvise verse after verse while the music repeats. This builds quick, responsive thinking skills and creative problem solving. When students realize that all they need to create a new verse are two words that rhyme and a storyline idea to connect them, they often become quickly energized toward creating more and more verses. Because the melodies often become repetitive in such lyric improvisations, encourage students to create new melodies over the progressions as they become more adept at improvising in this style.

Lyric Improvisation over Standards and Contrafacts

After successfully navigating improvised lyrics over a blues progression, singers can try it over a familiar jazz standard and see if they can still come up with new lyrics (and a melodically embellished or new melody) that suit the harmonic progression. Singers will create a **contrafact** by doing this. A contrafact is a new song created by using the harmonic progression of an existing song. "I Got Rhythm" by George Gershwin represents the most famous song from which contrafacts have been created. **Rhythm Changes** refers to the thirty-two-measure chord progression from this song. Hundreds (perhaps thousands) of contrafacts have been created over this now common progression. Composers create new contrafacts by writing a new melody, rhythm, and lyrics over an existing song's harmony. "Everybody's Boppin'" is a contrafact of Rhythm Changes written by Jon Hendricks. When lyric improvisation skills are honed, students are free to create any number of newly improvised lyrics over their favorite jazz standard progressions, opening up not only their improvisational abilities but also their compositional ones.

FREE IMPROVISATION

Free improvisation can be interpreted in many ways. For some it refers simply to thinking "outside" the chord changes or venturing into chord extensions (see chapter 12) or alternate scales that are thoroughly explored in other books (I recommend Berg's *Jazz Improvisation: The Goal Note Method* for the advanced improviser). After a student is highly adept at singing within the chord changes of a song, an audience may be receptive to an improviser singing further outside the confines of a standard blues progression or the expected changes. This does not translate into singing "wrong" notes but tastefully selecting places to put a sharp eleventh (when appropriate) or a note outside the appropriate scale that creates tension before resolving to a note within the scale. Free improvisation may be employed most successfully during a third, fourth, or fifth improvised chorus of a song, after the improviser has first proven his or her ability to properly use the notes within the traditional harmonic language. A gradual movement away from "safe" notes to more "outside" playing, followed by a gradual movement back toward that safe space toward the end of a solo is a tasteful way to create an artistic arc throughout one's improvisations.

There are several great free improvising jazz singers worth listening to, including Dee Dee Bridgewater, Betty Carter, and Carmen McRae. Students and teachers are encouraged to listen to these artists to hear what happens after each has sung "inside" the changes for a while and then steps "outside" on a later chorus. This frequently happens in instrumental jazz, and it is wonderful when a singer is accomplished enough to join in and respond in kind. Listening to instrumentalists whose solos consistently pushed the limits of harmony (e.g., John Coltrane, Sun Ra, Ornette Coleman, Chick Corea, and Thelonious Monk) will expand singers' ears and help them tastefully navigate the pathway through a solo when stepping outside the confines of standard chord progressions.

WORLD MUSIC AND IMPROVISATION

As one listens to more and more world music, especially jazz and folk music from various countries, one hears many more ways to explore improvisation. The musics of South and Central America, Africa, the Middle East, Europe, the Far East, and Australia are continuing to create new sounds in jazz with their indigenous instruments, languages, and cultures. Great jazz singers today must become increasingly aware of these alternative approaches to jazz music (as well as folk or indigenous music from other cultures). Although the history of jazz in America is of central, primary importance in how one approaches and teaches modern jazz, one cannot consider only how jazz has been evolving in its country of origin. Our ears, eyes, and sensibilities soon recognize that jazz has influenced other cultures (and indeed, other cultures have and are influencing the development of jazz). We must be attuned toward the fact that jazz is now a global genre.

Each country that sports its own brand of jazz musicians and styles possesses a personal cultural history and relationship with the genre, going back one hundred years in some cases because jazz spread to Europe only a few years after it originated in the United States. Various cultural interpretations of jazz have fueled the globalization of this style over the past century. I strongly encourage students and teachers to broaden their horizons and create ways to incorporate world music (especially music that emphasizes and includes improvisation, like folk music from nearly every country in the world) into their weekly diet of listening. Such brain-expanding activities open one's ears and allow a broader palette of colors to emerge in one's tastes and skill sets. Furthermore, teachers are encouraged to consult their international students for ideas and approaches that would honor their backgrounds and ethnic heritage. This is an excellent way to teach a course in improvisation that allows students to take leadership roles in the instruction process, to instruct their teachers about their native music, and to incorporate music of other cultures into the experience of learning improvisation.

TEACHER TIP

Ask students to consider their ethnic heritage and assign a project of researching, selecting, listening to, and transcribing folk songs or indigenous music from their countries of origin, especially for styles that use some form of improvisation. Have students present selections in a group setting involving instruments that are native to those countries and ask them to explain to the class how improvised instrumental or vocal music from that country could be useful in exploring jazz.

Jazz vocal improvisation may be accomplished in a wide variety of ways. There is no one correct method to learning vocal improvisation, but as in many other areas of music, many teachers (both applied teachers and singers to whom we listen) may provide the most complete education. Broadening one's listening diet, trying different styles of improvising, honing technical and theoretical skills, and practicing diligently using a combination of sources will take the beginning jazz vocalist through an exciting journey of discovery and skill-building that will enhance a lifetime of melodic and harmonic exploration.

8

PHRASING AND EXPRESSION

Vital in the jazz singer's toolkit is honing the art of interpretation through artful phrasing and textual expression. Singers and teachers are encouraged to delve deeply into these to craft unique approaches to the art form. Various examples of these interpretive elements by masterful interpreters of jazz standards enhance an aspiring jazz singer's understanding of the many ways to communicate a text with authenticity and sincerity.

PHRASE TYPES

There exist two primary types of phrases in vocal music: the musical phrase and the lyric phrase. Singers must be aware of both the musical phrases and the lyric phrases within a piece of music to make intelligent decisions about where to breathe, pause, or reach for a deeper meaning within a text. The composer and lyricist work together to establish phrase length and text setting (or sometimes only one of them determines these). Often lyricists add text to an existing theme of music, and sometimes music is added to an existing poem or set of lyrics. Performing vocal music allows jazz singers to combine these to create an interpretive phrase unique to the individual artist. This is often what we mean in jazz singing by phrasing, and it takes many forms depending on the performer.

The Musical Phrase

To become an expert at phrasing a jazz piece, the melodic phrase structure and phrase length (as the composer originally wrote the piece) must first be established. Strong musical skills are built by diligently working through a piece paying careful attention to rhythm, pitch, contour, texture, harmonic progression, articulation, dynamics, and the structure of the musical phrases. Only after a singer truly knows the pitches, rhythms, melodic phrases, and all that the composer wrote should the attempt be made to change any of those elements for interpretive effect. Singers must learn songs strictly as the composer and lyricist wrote them, without any embellishment. As "square" as that may seem to professional jazz singers and students of jazz voice, this is a non-negotiable requirement. It also requires that singers avoid learning songs by listening to recordings. Singers who learn from printed music before allowing recording artists influence their interpretation of a song will become more independent-minded musicians. Often a singer will be shocked at how meaningful the phrases become when simply singing the piece off the page without any added expressive devices, ornaments, or overt stylization.

A mistake many students make involves singing with "jazz style" (or country, pop, music theatre belt, or some other) before the song's pitches, rhythms, words, form, feel, harmony, and melody are well understood. That is akin to trying to break down a complex equation in mathematics without removing any variables. You must first remove variables (learn the building blocks of the song) before adding your own interpretation to it.

The musical phrase can be understood from the standpoint of melody, harmony, and phrase structure. Singers can pinpoint the length of each melodic phrase using clues they learned in music theory courses. Often in jazz, phrases are divided into subphrases. Lulls in the melody's movement, repetitions or permutations of motives, or plateaus where the voice sits for a short pause, sometimes delineate phrases or subphrases in the musical structure. Antecedent and consequent phrases present as pairs within a melody in many standards. Melodic contour (the rising and falling of pitch level in musical phrases) helps determine phrase structure and gives singers clues about where points of intensity lie within a phrase. A melodic phrase sometimes ends at a resting place that suggests finality before a new thought begins. Sometimes the melodic phrase lines up exactly with the lyric phrase in jazz standards, although not always. Understanding the structure of the melody and the location of its phrase delineations is necessary for becoming adept at interpretive phrasing in jazz.

Harmonic progression is important to consider when determining phrase structure, too. Many songs have repetitive harmonies that clearly show phrases or subphrase structures. Here, in learning how to phrase a jazz piece, is where music theory meets real-world application. I overhear too many singers complain that they learn nothing in music theory courses that they will ever use. This misguided belief leads to a weak understanding of theoretical concepts vital to a jazz singer's success.

The Lyric Phrase

Lyricists and poets create textual phrases within a song's lyrics that may or may not always line up exactly with a musical phrase. Such is the challenge for a singer—to make sense of this apparent contradiction. When lyric phrases do not line up, periods or commas may appear halfway through a musical phrase. This simply means a natural pause in speech will not be accommodated in that musical phrase, so the singer must be ready to find other ways to draw attention to the textual demarcations. Church singers may find this to be a frequent occurrence in hymns, which were often poems set to a certain number of measures of music per line. When a comma appears midphrase, the singer may decide to add a slight pause to reflect the mark or add articulation (e.g., staccato) to suggest a lyric phrase has ended.

Rhyme Scheme

Rhyme schemes give important clues to a jazz singer about where phrases begin and end. Do words rhyme at the end of each line? Do lines alternate in rhyme scheme (every other line)? Are there internal rhymes at the level of the subphrase that increase rhyming frequency? Do all the lines rhyme except for the final, titular line? How do these different schemes create opportunities to explore phrasing? The thoughtful teacher can help students discover their own answers as the plethora of implications involved in these questions and their solutions leads to a wide-ranging pattern of possible interpretations and phrase deliveries.

Theme

Many phrases possess themes of their own. How those fit into the overall theme of the song gives the singer virtually endless options for translating the text into musical art. Herein lies the never-ending mining for meaning that the creative jazz singer finds in a single song. Singers who dive deeply into their texts and music never tire of singing songs over a whole career. My interpretation of "Body and Soul" today yields a host of different sentiments now than it ever did when I first sang it at age eighteen. Decades of life experience often mature and hone a song's delivery and meaning, giving the singer a different theme to express than perhaps originally expressed when the song was less familiar. It is important for jazz singers to keep their repertoire fresh as life progresses, adapting song interpretations to remain relevant to self and to the audience as meanings and life circumstances change. Song lyrics remain the same, so songs that were once funny may become ironic; songs that were genuinely sad may become pathetic or cynical. Such is the beauty of the work of the singer, always adapting, always growing.

STEPS TO LEARNING A SONG

How one learns new music can greatly impact one's development of phrasing. Teachers have myriad ways of showing students how to learn songs. I sometimes use different approaches with different students in keeping with their strengths and weaknesses.

Pitches and Rhythms

If students have difficulty mastering rhythms, I ask them to spend more time on rhythmic work first. If pitches are a greater challenge, I ask for more time to be spent learning those. Whenever learning a piece, removing variables one at a time (focusing on only one aspect of the music) is strongly recommended. For instance, when sight-reading a new piece, have the student clap or step the melodic rhythm, ignoring words and pitches. Then reinforce this work by asking him or her to speak (no singing yet) the rhythm on a neutral syllable like "du." This moves the rhythm work from the hands to the voice without the added complexity of adding the full text. I like to have students work out rhythms and pitches separately, before adding any lyrics. Pitches can likewise be learned without rhythm, just singing on a neutral syllable, learning the intervals as the song proceeds. As the learning progresses, I ask students to change the syllables to give them the opportunity to try out different vowel and consonant combinations as they learn a new piece.

Lyrics

When pitches and rhythms are precisely mastered, and the student is singing the piece well from the page, we start looking at the text. I encourage students to write out the text in phrases. Where are the phrase delineations? How many measures are there in one phrase? Where are the rhyming words, if there are any? On first look, what is the overall theme, mood, and meaning of the lyrics? Is the song from a musical, opera, poem, or larger work? I encourage students to research as much as they can about the background of the song, larger work, lyricist, and composer in journaling assignments so that they become as close to an expert about their songs as possible. I explain in my lessons and studio classes that they should not be performing a song unless they are, indeed, the resident expert in the room on that song!

Students also benefit from writing the song as a monologue and practicing it through spoken delivery first, as an actor would intone it without the melodic rhythm added. Later the text can be practiced within the melodic rhythm. When speaking the text feels natural and the meanings have been clarified, work can center back on singing the pitches and rhythms with pure vowels. The song takes on a new layer of understanding as each aspect is isolated and practiced. Students discover the challenges inherent in the song this way and learn to appreciate the independent components of a piece rather than viewing a song as a complex machine with a lot of moving parts.

Articulation and Dynamics

Articulation and dynamics must be addressed before a student leaves the learning stage—all the information provided on the pages of sheet music (or digital images, as it may be today) must be fully absorbed before a singer's "interpretation" of a song can even begin. One cannot interpret what one does not first comprehend. These vitally important early steps must occur so that bad habits do not take root. Some students (and even some working singers) try to "skip to the end" of the learning process, combining words, stylistic elements, pitches, and rhythms before they have mastered any of them, with the end results being sloppy learning, incorrect notes or rhythms (which audiences notice), and lackluster performances. One cannot learn to be even an adequate interpreter of song until the discipline of learning how a song really goes is accepted as part of the process of preparation and practice.

BACK-PHRASING

The art of back-phrasing in jazz hails to the work of tenor saxophonist Lester Young, a master of the cool style. Young taught Billie Holiday the fine touches of back-phrasing, and singers have since taken their lead from Holiday's inventive approach. The text-based improvisational technique known as back-phrasing changes the way a musical phrase is lined up with a lyrical phrase. During back-phrasing, a singer delays or anticipates the start of their sung phrase, entering late or early, making the resulting combination of melody notes, rhythms, and lyrics fit within the nonchanging harmonic structure of the rest of the musical phrase. Sometimes adjustments in melodic pitch are necessary when the original melody creates dissonance over the harmony the band plays because the singer has changed the timing of the melody with its intended harmony. In this way, back-phrasing facilitates and necessitates improvisation. Sometimes the original melody fits fine over the harmony with a delayed start, but other times it does not. The latter case requires a strong ear to correct the pitch by choosing one within the chord, or timing the phrase so that the resulting dissonance can be resolved artistically, with intention.

Back-Phrasing as Conversation

The concept of back-phrasing represents the epitome of extemporaneity in singing any piece of music. The subtle variations in how musical and lyric phrases line up (or fail to line up) with one another mimic the extemporaneous quality of conversation. When listening to a conversation in which two people are invested and fully engaged, one notices the pattern of ebb and flow in their speech patterns. Some phrases draw back, soften, and slow down. Other phrases pour forth with gusto, emphasis, and passion. Each delineates the highs and lows and passions and retreats of human communication. Back-phrasing anticipates and delays the onset of lyric phrases so that they overlap rather than line up directly with the musical phrases they were intended to parallel. The challenge of back-phrasing is to make the phrase flow naturally and with appropriate consonance (or dissonance, if appropriate) despite the new juxtaposition of melody over different harmonic tones than usual. The ear of a singer is greatly tested when practicing this artistic technique.

The Artist's Responsibility

The singing artist willfully accepts the task of not only creating music worthy of the audience's investment of time, energy, or money but also of communicating with an audience on a different level than words or music alone can reach. Truly consummate artists are those who have achieved mastery of synthesizing emotion through the artistic delivery of well-written words set to excellent music. The artist is the living breath, lifeblood, and vehicle through which the composer and lyricist can send their art. Accepting this responsibility on behalf of music creators is no small or trivial task. On the contrary, without outstanding artists to convey the songs, the works of Ellington, Arlen, Berlin, Gershwin, Puccini, Verdi, Bach, and Mozart would not endure—a charge to keep we have as artists! How young artists and tomorrow's young audiences react to great works of art lies in our hands. Without our musical mastery and commitment to beautifying and improving the world with our art, the great music we value and love will be left to theoretical discussions alone rather than soulful performances that inspire listeners and change lives and destinies. Our job as performing and recording artists must not be taken lightly. Phrasing and expression play directly into this great responsibility of introducing beauty and art to a suffering world.

LEARNING PHRASING FROM THE MASTERS

Singers today possess the advantage of having wide access to recordings of an even wider palette of outstanding role models over the past century. How well a singer phrases a text depends in part on how much has been learned and assimilated from great singers in history. Each jazz singer benefits enormously by studying the way expert singers (both historical and contemporary) approached the delivery of a phrase of music and text. Noticing minute details about a singer's timing and treatment of phrases will build the modern singer's arsenal of strategies for creating captivating performances.

Peggy Lee

Peggy Lee became one of the most outstanding practitioners of backphrasing in the history of jazz. She would create new rhythms from those given her by the composer and refashion modes of textual delivery to suit her expressive style. She would not be limited by the notes on the page but would freely interpret a text in a way that suggested the original rhythm, making it sound truly conversational. Lee would take pains to deliver a song in the rhythmic pattern the composer wrote if she were sharing a new composition, but she would treat an old standard more like an old friend, with an original twist on the rhythms and notes that everyone already knew. In this way, she kept the songs fresh, respectfully decorating them with her brilliantly understated vocal style. Her back-phrases consisted of late arrivals to the musical phrase (words were delayed a couple of beats or even a whole measure), or early anticipations thereof.

Ella Fitzgerald

Ella Fitzgerald crafted phrases particularly thoughtfully in her legendary series of albums dedicated to nine Great American Songbook composers: *Ella Fitzgerald Sings the Cole Porter Songbook* (1956), followed by eight more albums dedicated to the works of Rodgers and Hart (1956), Duke Ellington (1957), Irving Berlin (1958), George and Ira Gershwin (1959), Harold Arlen (1961), Jerome Kern (1963), Johnny Mercer (1964), and Antonio Carlos Jobim (1981). She famously refused to scat on these recordings to present the songs as the composers originally intended. Singers are advised to listen to Fitzgerald's respectful treatment of the text and music in these wonderful albums. Instead of leaning on her amazing talent of scat improvisation, Fitzgerald delighted in using other modes of freedom and expression by phrasing her songs with attention to dynamic contrast, delicate ornamentation, logical phrase breaks reflecting punctuation and natural speech pauses, and thoughtful articulation. These albums are a testament to excellent vocalism being paramount first, and improvisational prowess being secondary to presenting a song with integrity and homage to the composer and lyricist.

Mel Tormé

Mel Tormé spun lush, legato lines throughout his career, crooning his way into the hearts of millions of fans. As a Capitol Records artist, he recorded both jazz and pop music early in his career, focusing more on standards in his later years. Tormé could scat precise pitches and rhythms at impressively fast bebop tempi, and he could deliver heart-wrenching ballads with outstanding richness and evocative expression. In both extremes he exhibited an understanding of phrasing that stood out among his peers. Being a frequent duet partner with fellow Capitol Records artist Peggy Lee since his early years at Capitol, Tormé learned from her how to squeeze every drop of meaning out of his phrases, how to hold an audience, how to use microphone technique to his advantage, and how to sing with sincerity and personal investment that audiences loved.

Johnny Hartman

Balladeer Johnny Hartman was an outstanding singer whose recorded works remain highly worthwhile for the aspiring jazz vocalist. Hartman was one of the only singers who could successfully pull off an entire evening of ballads without boring an audience. His phrasing was so beautifully shaped and so thoroughly explored that he became known especially for his incredibly lush performances of ballads. His collaborative album with John Coltrane titled *John Coltrane and Johnny Hartman* (Impulse! Records, 1963) earned a 2013 induction into the Grammy Hall of Fame. This pivotal album showed Hartman's extreme skill as a jazz singer with his own inimitable style. To this day, no other vocal artist has taken his place as a singular ballad singer whose work in only one type of piece solidified his prominent place in jazz voice history. This album is highly recommended for all jazz singers because it pairs two artists whose diverse styles rarely meshed, except on this priceless album. Hartman and Coltrane made history when they brought together Coltrane's progressive jazz with Hartman's Great American Songbook nostalgia and created a new work of art in the process.

Dinah Washington

Dinah Washington's instantly recognizable tone color served her well during her recording and performing years. Her sense of phrasing was steeped in gospel tradition and saturated with expressive devices and alternate note choices all her own. Her recording of "What a Difference a Day Makes" illuminated what a true artist could do with a simple song when she performed it with a tasteful sense of phrasing. Washington's unique vocal beauty and always soulful delivery created lush ballads as well as exuberant swing. Her mastery of putting her signature stamp on a song through magnificent phrasing makes her contribution to the jazz canon memorable.

Nat "King" Cole

Nat "King" Cole, another singer known for his devastatingly beautiful ballads, learned phrasing in part from his experiences and prowess as a first-rate jazz pianist. His piano phrases possessed clarity, simplicity, and melodic freshness, so his vocal phrases mirrored his pianistic phrasing technique with great success. His recording of "Too Young" showed his willingness to back-phrase via the delaying of his phrase beginnings, creating a wonderfully extemporaneous mode of delivering ballads as if he were composing the lyrics in the moment. This added to the sincerity and power of his expression. Cole's lush shaping of phrases using rubato, pure vowel color, and dynamic contrast proved his powerhouse skills as a jazz singer. His dual skills as a pianist and a singer leave no doubt about his central importance to the development of jazz voice technique.

THE ART OF EXPRESSION

Expressive singing requires that the singer be equipped with knowledge about the voice and the music to be sung, strong vocal technique, and a keen desire to communicate through music. The singer's baseline, natural voice must be a healthy vehicle that enables expression by not hindering the singer through bad habits, poor technique, or lack of understanding of the science of singing. Any deficiencies in these areas may cause attempts at expression to fall flat or be ineffectual. Great singers mentioned in this book possessed enough technique to become quite expressive, effective communicators. Not all jazz voice technical approaches are the same, but a singer's technique must work for the singer before an expressive artist can emerge. For instance, the vocal technique of Ella Fitzgerald may not resemble the technique of Joni Mitchell, but in jazz, that is acceptable. Each artist possessed something singularly outstanding that etched their recordings, songs, and performances into jazz history. Starting with an optimized technical base helps enable a budding jazz artist to pursue a long, rewarding career uninhibited by vocal problems or inefficient singing.

First Things First

Anyone who has witnessed the performance of a young jazz, commercial, or music theatre singer who is caught up in expressing text without having a sound command of intonation, breath management, and clear phonation understands the reason for this prioritization of skills. As naturally expressive as a young artist may be, expression without precision, accuracy, and technique is not worth an audience's time or money. Pitch and rhythmic precision, diction clarity, management of the breath, and some degree of resonance balancing are prerequisites for a jazz singer's success. After those specifics are duly crafted through warm-up routines, breathing exercises, voice building work, alignment awareness, theory skills, and lyric analysis, the final touches of expression can be thoroughly explored. Some young singers are extremely expressive naturally long before they learn a healthy, technically sound manner of singing. Their natural inclination toward expressing what they sing can serve them well as they pursue technical skills. In their case, I use methods that encourage them to engage their expressive talent in tandem with a technical skill such as breath management through a long phrase (as emphasized with movement work such as Dalcroze exercises explored in chapter 11). Generally, expression comes more easily to students after they dive deeply into the meaning of texts, so exploring text through journaling can be an important tool for teaching expression.

The Studio Class as a Learning Tool

Another fantastic vehicle for teaching expression is simply facilitating performances for students in a studio class setting. There is nothing better than a room full of one's peers for teaching a singer how to meaningfully express a song's text. Watching other singers whose skill levels vary will teach your students several lessons. Some singers will be strong at expression while others may be too engrossed in their concentration about technique to engage much with the meaning of a song. Still others will demonstrate nervousness that undermines their performance in a way that is often remedied by repeated turns singing a song in studio class, as long as the teacher keeps the environment one of supportive learning.

Having taught university-level Class Voice, Music Theatre Voice Class, Vocal Jazz Master Class, Voice Performance Studio Class, Opera Workshop, Music Theatre Workshop, Commercial Music Combo, Vocal Jazz Ensemble, and Commercial Voice Class, I have laid ground rules for all types of singing classes. First, all students enrolled must sing. This ensures that students giving critiques will also be critiqued by the same singers they have evaluated. Having this rule in place usually creates a more supportive space. My second rule insists that all observers' comments begin with a compliment. Singers have an easier time accepting constructive criticism after they have been affirmed about something they do well. Only after a compliment is offered or improvement commended may an observer offer a comment about something that might be improved. I encourage students to ask each other questions rather than to offer generalizations or sweeping statements. I also caution singers to avoid giving vocal instruction (that's my job!), and I am committed to restating this rule when students break it.

Students love to help one another with ideas to enhance various aspects of performance. Classes often brainstorm ideas to help a singer struggling with a particular line or phrase. After students have spent a couple of semesters watching one another perform, demonstrated improvements can be pleasantly surprising. Even more exciting for me is noticing how a studio class's trust and self-confidence grow in ways that are not as apparent in the private studio. The achievements that only performance situations yield occur at a faster rate when private instruction is coupled with peer performance opportunities at regular intervals (weekly, bimonthly, etc.). Students love to help each other sing well when class is approached as a fun learning forum among friends. This invariably happens when the teacher encourages students to come well-prepared for their performances, to help their peers learn, and to humbly accept peer evaluation that is nonjudgmental. Advanced singers learn to be supportive and accepting of whatever skill level another student currently exhibits. Students not only become better singers at a faster rate when given studio classes than without peer performances, but they also become more observant audience members and more supportive ensemble members. In this forum, singers learn to put down their competitive mindsets and apply teamwork instead, creating a low-pressured learning environment driven by a sincere mutual desire to improve.

Journaling to Deepen Expressive Skills

Journaling represents a vehicle through which a wide variety of singing skills, including expression, can be developed and documented. My students have filled journals with not only their thoughts about text meanings but also with research about background source material, composer summaries, character sketches, lyric studies, historical contexts for songs, and other salient information that enhances a singer's understanding about song texts. Such journaling assignments have always provided positive outcomes for singers in my studio. They gain so much knowledge about their repertoire and the context surrounding it that their appreciation for it grows as their expertise is built. Although most student singers can memorize a song, few remember detailed accounts about composers, lyricists, poems, or shows from which the text was distilled or relevant societal contexts of the composer's time and place in history. Such deep research improves singers' ability to express a text from an informed viewpoint while increasing their interest in the song. Furthermore, this research gives singers information that can be shared with peers in a studio class setting, adding confidence as they realize how much more they know than possibly even the teacher in the room. This "expert" status is vital for student singers to attain as soon as they are able. It can yield an instantly more confident performance of a song as singers relish their advanced knowledge and preparation. Adding music and textual analysis to the journal as a matter of routine can grow a student's understanding about phrasing and theoretical principles that will create more expressive performances. As confidence, knowledge, and song preparation deepen, the student begins to care more about how phrasing and expression should be approached to keep an audience engaged.

Video Recording as an Awareness Tool

Recording videos of student performances remains an irreplaceable tool that grows a singer's awareness more than most other tools. Teachers can encourage students to "just watch" the first time through, maybe with the volume down, so that only visual issues can be addressed. Just as in a studio class setting, students should first notice things that went well. Having students document their improvements and positive outcomes before listing areas in need of work is a vitally important journaling assignment that can accompany the video log. Ask them to consider dress, posture, visible tension, and awkward mannerisms (like arm swinging or chin tilting).

Students should be attuned to things they already do well before they can be expected to take gentle constructive criticism. If all they hear or fixate on is presented as negative, they may develop either an aversion to being corrected or low self-esteem. Teachers must consider the feelings of their students, especially those who are highly sensitive. Earning their trust can only happen when a student feels unthreatened and that trust is usually built by showing affirmations for the student's strengths. The video log can represent proof of the student's hard work. Placing praise as a top priority goes a long way toward building not only trust between student and teacher but also confidence for the developing singer and willingness to receive constructive criticism.

After the visual aspects of the recorded performance have been considered (both positive and those that need improvement), encourage the student to turn up the volume and look away from the video. Placing their attention on the sound without the distraction of watching the video again will help singers focus only on the music. After positive feedback has been given, as well as constructive criticism and solutions for problems that have been discovered (or areas you both agree should receive more attention in the practice room), turn the student's attention back to the video and watch and listen at the same time. This final pass should focus on how well the music and text work together and how successfully the expression of the text came through. These guided watching sessions can take place once or twice a semester in a one-on-one lesson. Teachers can video record one entire studio class and watch each student's performance with him or her at the next lesson. Such valuable feedback is easily accessible via smartphones and tablets that students use daily, so teachers should use this technology in the classroom to facilitate accelerated learning. Students will appreciate your attention to their performances and your thoughtful feedback praising them for what you notice is improving while also encouraging them to grow in areas not yet mastered.

Teaching phrasing and expression requires some experience as a performing artist before one can do it reasonably well. Learning the skill of back-phrasing will provide a host of new ways to deliver a song's lyrics and music by combining them improvisationally. Studying several performances and recordings of outstanding jazz singers will enhance a singer's appreciation of the variety of approaches that yield artistic phrasing and expression. Using a journal and video log will enhance a singer's awareness of performance strengths and areas needing improvement. Exploring phrasing and expression represents a worthwhile, lifelong pursuit that potentially yields a wealth of new approaches and musical outcomes at every performance. Adding layers of knowledge and skill to one's repertoire keeps music fresh and provides rewarding listening experiences for audiences. Those audiences become a group of fans that will return over and over to hear a singer's unpredictable, ever-novel approaches to music they have grown to love.

9

MICROPHONE TECHNIQUE
AND VOWEL SHAPING

The microphone represents half the jazz singer's instrument. This important fact demands that singers who routinely use them possess knowledge and understanding pertaining to microphone manipulation and use. Poor microphone technique can make or break a performance and even a career, so singers must learn how this tool can best enhance their tone and style. Studying the microphone techniques of great jazz singers represents a useful activity for the contemporary singing artist. The mic greatly assists in the artistic formation of vowels and shades of timbral qualities. Great jazz singers capitalize on the microphone's capabilities to create nuance and stylistic authenticity in their performances.

BASICS OF MICROPHONE TECHNIQUE

The singer should hold the microphone one to two inches away from the lips in a position that allows the face to be shown rather than blocked by the mic. The fingertips should gently hold the microphone rather than a full hand or fist clenching it. Singers and technical personnel must work together to find optimum volume levels in the monitors and main speakers so that singers do not need to pull away further than two inches or touch the mic with the mouth to achieve their desired volume. Some mics must be oriented directly in front of the mouth for optimum performance, whereas others can amplify a voice at a variety of angles and from the sides of the mic. A bit of education about various types of microphones will provide singers with important information necessary for developing effective microphone technique.

TYPES OF MICROPHONES

It is helpful for a singer to know in advance which type of microphone will be used at a given performance. **Condenser mics** provide a clear, sweet-sounding, powerful amplitude boost at an ideal frequency range for treble voices and brighter timbres. These mics are quite sensitive and tend to be expensive. They require Phantom Power (48 volts), which is a special type of power available through a switch or button on a quality mixing board, so a singer must be certain that this feature will be available, or the mic will not work. Because portable instrument amplifiers rarely use Phantom Power, singers will not be able to use a keyboard amp or guitar amp to plug in their condenser mic. Some have switches that change their polar pattern from unidirectional to bidirectional (picking up sounds from the front and back, with canceling on the sides) or omnidirectional, which amplifies sounds 360 degrees around the mic, with no cancellation.

Dynamic microphones are durable and able to withstand the wear and tear of rigorous rehearsal and performance schedules, but they lack the boost of a large diaphragm cardioid condenser mic. They do not require Phantom Power, so they can be plugged into any portable amplifier with good results. Dynamic mics are also not sensitive, so they are often used for loud sound amplification (like drums or other rock band instruments) but may not be ideal for crafting nuance in softer jazz singing. They possess a unidirectional, cardioid (heart-shaped) pattern that amplifies whatever sound is in front of it but dampens sounds behind the mic. They are frequently used to amplify sounds in low to midrange, so they are not the best choices for soprano voices because the volume boost occurs rather aggressively where the soprano does not need it (in the upper range, making a voice sound shrill) while not boosting the voice enough in the low range where more volume and clarity are needed. By contrast, this mic does well amplifying male voices whose ranges (except for countertenors) stay in the relatively low to midrange of the mic's sound spectrum.

Ribbon mics represent a much older model of microphone. These give a "vintage" sound and possess bidirectional polarity. They are expensive, sensitive, and delicate instruments that are often preferred for studio performances of strings and voices.

CROSSOVER WORK WITH A MICROPHONE

For Classical Singers

As frightening as close proximity to the microphone often can be for a trained classical singer singing jazz, it is absolutely necessary for many reasons. When the mic is two inches away from the lips, the classical singer learns that the natural amplification present in classical singing must be altered to accommodate the new amplifying instrument. Classical singers routinely maximize their resonance by seeking the singer's formants (acoustic amplitude maximums—see chapter 6) to sing over an orchestra or unamplified in a large concert hall. Softer singing is the first alteration that must be made when singing jazz with a handheld microphone. When classical singers soften their normal tone, it is often surprising how little effort needs to be given to phonate authentically in a jazz style.

For Music Theatre Singers

A music theatre (also called musical theater) belt is inappropriate when singing jazz. There are many instances in modern music theatre when a true jazz style is the sought-after vocal quality for the show. *On a Clear Day You Can See Forever* and *Nice Work If You Can Get It* represent two jazz musicals that require an authentic jazz sound. However, neither the classic, Ethel Merman–style Broadway belt nor a contemporary, pinched, nasal tone will sound natural when singing jazz. Singers can experiment with a breathy delivery and a softer tone that is more spoken on pitch than sung, intimately whispered, or warmly caressed instead of projected forcefully to the back of a large hall. Part of the fun of singing jazz is discovering how much of the tone quality can be successfully sculpted by an outstanding microphone when used correctly.

NAVIGATING THE MIX CONTINUUM WITH A MICROPHONE

The author's Mix Continuum presented in chapter 5 helps jazz singers and pedagogues adjust the resonance balancing necessary to achieve stylistic authenticity and maximum vocal comfort. This tool enables multi-genre (crossover) singing relatively quickly and easily, allowing singers to choose points within the song's tessitura where mixing heavy and light production can be explored and perfected for optimal performance. When using a microphone, singers often must make decisions regarding volume, timbre, resonance, vowel shape, and phrasing for maximum communication and desired effect. Knowing how to lighten the voice by using more head mix will provide the singer with skills to manage stage volume problems or unexpected technical difficulties. Similarly, with practice using the Mix Continuum, singers can simply apply a greater mix of chest-dominant production when desiring greater intensity for a given phrase in the middle part of the range. Experimenting with this tool will allow rock, pop, Broadway, or jazz singers to "scream" by singing with a particular combination of resonance balancing and overtone selection that produces the desired effect with no harmful treatment of the vocal folds. Pedagogues experienced with using the Mix Continuum remember that at no time should unhealthy tensions come into play in the singer's technique. Resonance balancing, vowel shaping, and allowance of certain selected "noise" partials in the tonal mix are all that are needed to achieve thousands of stylistically authentic timbres in a wide variety of genres.

SELECTING MICROPHONES

The first lesson about microphone technique is that not all microphones are alike. There are thousands of types designed for specific purposes and vocal ranges. These yield resultant tone qualities. Female jazz singers are recommended to invest in a condenser mic for intimate rooms. This type of microphone enhances the treble sound in ways that the industry minimum that is widely available (Shure SM-58) cannot. The SM-58 sounds great as a basic, dynamic microphone for instruments or for most male voices (tenors, baritones, and basses), but it creates problems for most female singers (treble voices) because of the bloom of the voice occurring in less-than-optimal areas of the microphone's amplifying range. A soprano jazz singer will acoustically need a greater boost in the lowest part of her range, where the SM-58 is weakest. It will automatically increase her volume as she ascends, making her high upper range distort and sound shrill. It also does a poor job filtering out noise partials. In the male voice, by contrast, the SM-58 does a good job of boosting the voice where the need is greatest in the low and midrange sections of the male voice. This mic allows the voice's natural fullness and ring to soar without distortion in the male upper voice where his volume is naturally louder and fuller, without making him sound shrill. A condenser mic shears off stray upper partials in the female voice while adding warmth and roundness to a naturally bright tone. It also boosts her voice nicely in the weakest area, the bottom of her range. However, a condenser microphone may not be a good fit in noisy areas like outdoor jazz festivals, so having a few favorite mics for each type of performance setting is smart.

Singers are strongly urged to shop around for a microphone that suits their needs and tastes. Try out a few at a music store before buying and sing a variety of songs to gain a sense of what the mic will do for you. There is no perfect microphone for everyone. Trying many types will yield an education in microphone timbre and bloom and help the singer identify the pros and cons of each model. Ideally, the mic that boosts a voice where a singer needs a volume boost without spiking the amplitude in the acoustically strong register areas will nicely complement the jazz voice. The mic should also offer some dampening of unwanted noise and partials that do not enhance the tone. Many modern condenser, dynamic, and ribbon mics are available today for a wide variety of uses. Singers must realize that a high-quality microphone represents a significant investment. Just as jazz instrumentalists must invest in outstanding instruments to create their best performance tone, singers are wise to invest wisely in the instruments they will need.

Another consideration must be the type of performance for which the mic will be needed. Podcasting mics are generally not good for handheld performing, and sometimes a cordless microphone (like a Shure or Sennheiser) is required for outdoor performances or concerts on a large stage where cords are impractical. Given the vast selection of options today, singers may need to invest in more than one microphone to meet all their professional needs. Be sure to research the mics available and purchase a mic specially designed for the job at hand.

SOUND CHECKS

When a singer hands a microphone to a technical director at a sound check (or plugs in the mic), the channel into which the mic is being inserted must be muted to avoid feedback accidents. Monitors should also be muted or turned to low volume when a mic is first plugged in. Ideally a mixing board should be off with channel volumes turned all the way down until after all mics are plugged in. This safe practice saves hearing! Musicians can sustain hearing damage even when the main speakers are turned to low volume if the monitors are turned up when the mic is plugged in. Also, the Phantom Power should not be switched on until after the mic has been plugged into the mixing board. Before handing anyone a microphone singers are well within their rights to politely request that the mic channel be muted and all monitors, mains, house, and PA speakers be turned all the way down. When this directive is followed, then the mic can safely be connected. The correct way to raise any channel or monitor volume level is slowly and gradually. Singers pull away from microphones to correct overly loud volume of their voices onstage. To capture the singer's subtleties, rhythmic intricacies, and pitch variations, the mic must be used at close range. When singers pull away from the microphone, the technical director has no control over the total musical mix or the master volume of the voice, but if it is set too loudly for singers' comfort, they will pull away. A level of trust must be developed between singer and technical director during a sound check (and preferably well in advance via conference or meeting) so that singers and their microphones can be accommodated in a way that captures the artists' brilliance and nuances.

To control the quality of the tone the audience hears, singers are advised to bring their chosen microphone with them to each performance rather than to rely on whatever mics will be provided at the venue. Singers can gently help the technical directors (if help seems to be needed) by communicating their preferred EQ settings and volume preferences for both monitors and main speakers before getting too far into the sound check. Singers should always communicate with the technical director in advance of the performance (preferably in writing) about what microphone will be used, equipment the singer will bring, equipment the venue will provide, and so on. The more information that is discussed in advance about the stage plot, size of the room, and technical equipment and personnel that will be available, the smoother the sound check and performance will be.

MICROPHONE TECHNIQUE AND COMMUNICATION

Mic Distancing

Generally, singing with the mic an inch or two from the lips yields the most consistently optimal distance for good tone production and diction clarity. Holding it against the lips or partially inside an open mouth amplifies unwanted mouth noises that audiences find irritating. Positioning it so that it never blocks the audience's view of the face, just below the bottom lip, tends to be good performance practice. However, sometimes a singer needs to pull the mic away to prevent a sudden surge in volume when singing loudly or at a high range. Audiences appreciate a singer's dexterity with a mic as well as effort toward creating a smooth, consistent vocal line. When, for instance, a soprano or tenor soloist sings a very high note (which has natural carrying properties all its own and does not require a mic to project it throughout a hall), the mindful singer retracts the mic several inches from the mouth. A loud or high-pitched note requires a further distance than a moderately loud or high note. Trial and error with a mic one uses frequently will be necessary to cultivate good distancing technique for the repertoire performed. Each singer's voice and power level are different, and so is each microphone. Experienced singers instinctively pull the mic away when necessary and allow it to stay close when singing softly. Mic distancing will become second nature as one's mic technique and familiarity with a performance mic improve.

Consonant Popping

Another aspect of good mic technique is learning how not to pop consonants. These explosions of air directly into a microphone cause unattractive amplitude spikes. Such unexpected surprises annoy audiences and betray a singer's inexperience. When singers become accustomed to using their own microphone, these accidental, embarrassing moments should be minimal. One may have to work with a teacher and a mic to pronounce *b* and *p* consistently without creating loud explosions that disturb listeners. Sometimes popped consonants actually hurt listeners' ears by creating volume blasts that exceed safe decibel levels, so such habits should be taken seriously by every performer. A mindful technique of speaking and singing gentle consonants (sometimes imploded rather than exploded) into the mic should be fully mastered before appearing in front of an audience. Unfortunately, the problem sometimes lies with the technical staff running the sound board. Those experienced with your specific type of microphone should be able to run an entire sound check, rehearsal, and performance without ever pushing the gain or amplitude to the point of hearing high-pitched feedback or popped consonants. Sometimes feedback can be caused by interference among various microphones and equipment onstage.

Some microphones also are "hot mics" prone to such feedback when the mic is close to the mouth or to speakers or monitors. One should never point the head of a microphone toward a live speaker or monitor because this nearly always causes high-pitched squeals and loud, offensive audio feedback. Singers must learn to be aware of the direction their mic is pointing at all times. Keeping the mic oriented vertically (with the head upright) at one's side when bowing, for example, is preferable to dropping it forward toward the audience right in front of a monitor. Purchasing your own small mixing board or PA system is a good way to practice setting your own mic levels and becoming familiarized with basic protocols at sound checks so that you can help your technical director and band achieve your ideal sound.

Enunciation and Vibrato

Singers will find that when using a quality microphone, much as in normal speech, overenunciating consonants is not usually necessary. Diction clarity is always important but not to extremes when microphones are involved. This will require an adjustment for the singer whose education has included classical voice training. Classical singers are trained to amplify their own voices from a stage, often over a piano, a chamber ensemble, or even an entire orchestra. Such a powerful stream of air tends to be too much for the intimacy of jazz and needs to be reined in somewhat.

Consistent vibrato assists the classical singer in projecting the voice across a wide distance and over other instruments. Because this need is precluded by electronic amplification in jazz singing, vibrato is not necessary for projection in a jazz style. Rather, it often gets in the way of intonation in jazz (especially when harmonies are close and dissonant) as well as delivering recognizable text. For these reasons, vibrato tends to be used minimally for warmth and color in modern jazz singing. However, as long as style and intonation are kept intact, vibrato may be allowable for some singers. Consider Sarah Vaughan and Dinah Washington, two outstanding jazz singers whose vibrato remained relatively consistent in most of their performances. Never sounding old-fashioned, these artists found other ways to sing authentically in a jazz style besides straightening their lush and lovely vibrato.

One of the beautiful aspects of jazz is that no two artists sound the same or achieve artistry in exactly the same way. These points are wise for the jazz voice pedagogue to remember to ensure against teaching only one style or approach to all students. When students possess truly extraordinary qualities (like a gorgeous vibrato), a better approach than ironing out the loveliest aspect of the voice may be to frame that quality with other elements of jazz style that bring out the voice's inherent, natural beauty. Helping students find their unique strengths and maximizing those strengths are two of the most important jobs of every voice teacher.

Diction and Dynamics

Singers who have studied diction ought to have some basic awareness of vowel shaping inside the oropharynx and consonant enunciation at the front of the tongue, teeth, and lips. This awareness assists in creating the proper balance between air outflow (that may create an unwanted sound when amplified in a mic) and gentle enunciation. This balance and tweaking of the airflow and barely audible consonants can do wonders when transitioning from a classical background to singing jazz. Very little sound is needed to sing softly in a jazz style. The "mumble" style popularized by Billie Eilish and others represents an extreme in this direction but illustrates the same concept of singing much more softly than one would when performing on a stage without a mic. Understated singing, perfected by Peggy Lee and later explored by cool jazz singers June Christy, Blossom Dearie, and Chet Baker, is a terrific approach for the full-voiced classical singer aspiring to sing jazz to emulate.

MIC TECHNIQUE OF THE MASTERS

Bing Crosby was the first singer in music history to abandon the shouting posture held by many blues singers that preceded him. Instead of projecting his voice toward a pre-microphone recording device situated several feet away (which the blues singers had to do, by technological design), he sang directly into the (smaller, hand-held) "micro"-phone in a far more intimate style than any singers had done before him. In essence, he was the first to turn the new voice-amplifying device called a "microphone" into a tool for communicating intimacy, as though he and the listener were engaged in a private interlude only they could hear. This explains the gentle, breathy, "crooning" style his singing became, imitated by thousands of other singers, including Frank Sinatra. This historical perspective is important for modern jazz singers to understand so that when they hear Crosby's style of singing they respect the huge ramifications his unique approach meant for the trajectory of both pop and jazz solo singing. With help from advancements in sound technology via the invention of the first microphone, Crosby forged the original pathway to modern microphone technique.

Billie Holiday took advantage of the plethora of colors a microphone could capture. Being a blues singer first and foremost, Holiday was familiar with the shouting approach other blues singers employed and occasionally was known to shout certain words in her songs for greater emphasis and effect. Conversely, she could sing quietly into the mic to create an almost secretive approach to her communication of text. Holiday used a variety of tone qualities (breathiness, clarity, and a gravelly tone) as well as ornaments (like flyaway notes) that the microphone captured brilliantly as a wide array of performance techniques this artist coined as one of the first great jazz singers in history. She also sometimes sang with a tremulous vibrato and other times with a straight tone as though simply speaking on pitch. She placed utmost emphasis on the text, and no emphasis whatsoever on whether or not a tone sounded "pretty." Holiday acted as a poet delivering messages to her audiences, much like Bob Dylan later did in the 1960s. Her sense of phrasing always placed the text's meaning at the forefront and represented a text-based improviser's guru in the art of back-phrasing.

Peggy Lee became famous for singing in a lower range than her soprano voice initially occupied in her late teens and early twenties. This natural lowering of the pitch down into the spoken range changed her ability to resonate over a large ensemble without amplification and enabled her to focus more on communicating the text with style, feel, and musical nuances rather than with volume. Lee famously learned at the Doll House in Palm Springs that singing more softly when her audience became loud made them quiet down and listen. The alternative leads to increased stage volume, which creates a much louder room; shouting, less attentive patrons; and a less musical performance. To emulate Lee's strategy for making an audience listen, singers must encourage their bands to play softer and more musically in direct proportion to escalating noise offstage, which eventually makes the audience more still. Turning up the volume is the knee-jerk response to a loud room, and patrons may even complain that they cannot hear the band. That is the point! Teach your audience to lean in, and they will enjoy the music more because they become attuned to listen.

Sarah Vaughan's microphone technique reflected an artist whose powerful instrument could phonate from a low baritone range through a high soprano. Her impressive consistency of timbre with virtually no audible break at the passaggio (the fixed locus of transition between registers in the voice) remains unsurpassed by other jazz singers. This quality was particularly showcased by her excellent mic technique, which enhanced the smoothness of her voice. Vaughan's mesmerizing vocal beauty and lush richness were amplified mightily by her mastery of the microphone as the other half of her instrument. Knowing how to adjust her own overtones, she could make low notes darker or brighter with a minuscule adjustment of her vowels. She could also season a high note with an operatic timbre by purifying a vowel, using vowel formants to add natural amplification, increasing vibrato, and evening out the volume by gently drawing the mic slightly away from her mouth. Watching Vaughan's many recorded concerts aids a singer's understanding of mic technique, vowel formants, breath management, sheer tonal brilliance and beauty, and consistency of tone throughout the entire vocal compass. Vaughan could also change her tone into a more spoken, emphatic quality at will and often did to express some particular word or phrase.

Mel Tormé (affectionately nicknamed "The Velvet Fog" for his smooth, slightly breathy timbre) mastered microphone technique early in his career and successfully created many recordings worthy of study, transcription, and emulation by budding jazz singers. Tormé became an accomplished interpreter of Great American Songbook and jazz songs using an unabashedly intimate tone quality and hushed singing approach that sounded evocative and sensuous. His pleasing vibrato was always supported by strong breath management, and he could start it and straighten it at will depending on how he chose to deliver a particular phrase. Tormé was a consummate interpreter, using the microphone to crescendo from pianissimo to fortissimo or to deliver sharply articulated scat syllables almost as precisely as Ella Fitzgerald could. His experience as a drummer informed his rhythmic choices, and his high-powered entertainer mindset created outstanding concert performances. Most importantly, his comfort and finesse with a handheld microphone turned his already beautiful voice into a powerhouse of expressive potential and rhythmic interest. Singers are encouraged to listen to the subtle prowess of Tormé delivering one of his many ballads like "That's All" from his 1965 album by the same title. His absolute commitment to vowel purity throughout this ballad offers a persuasive argument toward the value of singing an entire song with only the purest vowels, even in jazz. The resulting beauty of the well-formed vowel was captured in this recording.

Nancy Wilson fortunately recorded several live concerts, and her work as a live performer remains extremely rewarding for the jazz singer to study. Wilson represents another example of an artist who understood how a microphone can enhance a singer's sound via tone quality changes, ornaments, overtones, vowel choices, and dynamic contrast. Wilson depended heavily on the microphone's ability to bring out her nuances, whispers, breathy tone, wide dynamic changes (ranging from pianissimo to fortissimo) and many subtleties that made her renditions of Great American Songbook standards works of art. No two phrases were sung alike by Wilson—the attentive listener remains rapt in her highly original approach of using artistic touches to decorate her lovely natural voice. Wilson's meticulous attention to every vocal sound she made created a catalog of work characterized by beautiful detail. Saturated with her own brand of jazz style, Wilson's beautifully phrased recordings remain unparalleled in mastering the jazz singer's collaboration with the modern microphone to an uneclipsed advantage.

VOWEL PURITY

Singers who understand where in the mouth pure vowels tend to be shaped, along with the role of the tongue in vowel shaping, have an edge on mic technique and vowel resonance. Those singers are also armed with more power over their own instrument, its colors and choices. Knowing the difference between open vowels and closed vowels, understanding the progression of vowel brightness or darkness, comprehending how tongue and jaw position affect vowel purity and resonance, and studying the overtone series all provide the singer with important knowledge and awareness about how the singing instrument works. Jazz singers should know some basic qualities of vowel colors and how to attain them.

Figure 9.1 shows front, middle, and back vowels and where they are formed in the mouth relative to the tongue, hard palate, and soft palate. Singers can become familiar with the chart by speaking down the diagonal from "ee" to "ah" one vowel at a time, feeling the tongue lowering for each successive vowel. Likewise, singers discover that the back of the tongue rises gradually when ascending from "ah" to "oo" upward through the chart toward the uvula in the back of the throat. The tongue's motion becomes clearer when looking into a mirror during these vowel changes. The vowel symbol on the chart below and slightly to the left of "oo" represents the vowel in the word "book." In diction circles we call this the "flying u" because it looks like a *u* with wings! The [ae] symbol represents the sound in "cat." Because singers' diction and working with the International Phonetic Alphabet are beyond the scope of this book, jazz singers are strongly encouraged to study English diction as a separate course.

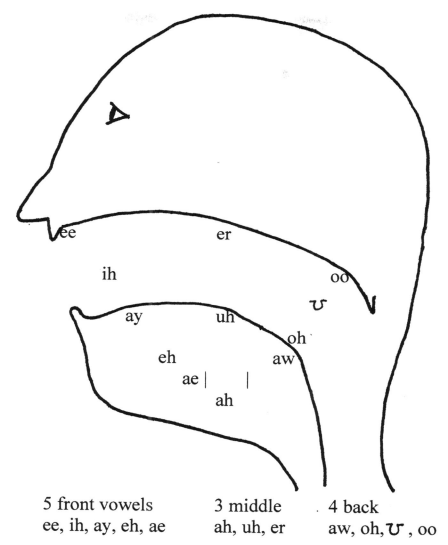

Figure 9.1. Vowel Chart. Courtesy of Author

Impure or sloppy vowels sound even more sloppy through amplification, so the singer must work on purifying vowels, which is in line with first establishing a healthy baseline, natural voice. So often an otherwise tasteful performance is tainted when a jazz singer fails to sing a pure, sustained vowel into a microphone. The longer a vowel sound is sustained, the more attention a singer needs to grant to its purity, form, and shape. Singers are wise to remember that the mic cannot filter out all the noise partials if the singing itself is full of noise. Impure vowel sounds contain noise partials that, when removed by singing with rounder lips or a less tense tongue, or improved head and neck alignment, greatly beautify the tone, the word, the phrase, and the song by naturally boosting beautiful partials and dampening noisy ones.

One important, yet often overlooked, aspect of jazz singing technique is knowing how to sing pure vowels. This is especially important in group singing. Those who sing in choirs and vocal jazz ensembles must learn the vital importance of this concept. In a group, it only takes one singer shaping an impure or mixed vowel among several pure vowels to make the entire group sound out of tune or sloppy. In the same way, a soloist singing with an impure vowel can detrimentally affect his or her own intonation or lose the audience's admiration and attention because of a single objectionable tone. This is why study of vowel purification can be one of the jazz singer's best time investments.

Listening to great singers using beautiful, consistent vowels (and slightly modified, stylized vowels when appropriate) like Frank Sinatra, Doris Day, Rosemary Clooney, and Bing Crosby will illustrate the lush consistency that is possible when a jazz singer pays attention to vowel purity. Obviously, sometimes the singer chooses not to sing a vowel with purity but wants a little noise, warmth, or brightness added to the vowel. This is only possible when singers know how to find the pure vowel first as a baseline and then add the desired color in small amounts until they are satisfied with the resulting timbre. Vocal artists with more color possibilities can paint their songs with more confidence, flexibility, and versatility. It is important to learn how to purify or color a vowel at will. Sometimes simply adding a few shades of brightness to a pure vowel creates exactly the right color that translates into "jazz style." Teachers must help students discover this skill one vowel shade at a time, using both pure vowels and "tweaks" of those vowels with added brightness, darkness, or nasality for different effects. Because every student's instrument is shaped differently, every student's experiments with vowel colors will yield different outcomes.

TEACHER TIP

Help your students find pure vowels by sharing vowel charts, demonstrating pure vowels, and listening to singers whose vowels are consistent and pure. One exercise to illustrate vowel purity and modification is to ask the singer to sing a pure vowel and then gradually brighten or darken the vowel slightly, a little at a time, (using a relaxed jaw, tongue, and lips, without spreading the lips horizontally) until he or she arrives at the next vowel in the chart. Have him or her slowly speak the pure vowels "ah," "eh," "ee," "oh," "oo" in one, uninterrupted line (with no glottal pops between vowels). Start at "ah" again, slowly adding brightness, allowing the back of the tongue to rise up through "eh" to "ee." Then begin at "ah" again and go down through the cool vowels "oh" and "oo" by very slowly adding darkness to the vowel sound while rounding the lips. At all times, be sure the tip of the tongue stays in its "parking place" (resting on the bottom teeth, touching the back of the front bottom lip), where it should always be whenever singing a vowel sound. This exercise illustrates how tongue position or lip rounding turn one pure vowel into another. It also illustrates some of the overtones and partials that are available to the jazz singer as potential "colors" that exist between pure vowels. Singers may find that a particular color of "oo" that suits one song may be different from the overtone spectrum that sounds best for that vowel in another song. Empower your students with more understanding of over-tones and how upper and lower partials (frequencies dampened or amplified by vowel shaping) can be incorporated into jazz singing. With the help of a microphone, these colorizing techniques add variety and authenticity to every jazz singer's repertoire and toolkit.

Implications of Language on Overtone Color Choices

Brazilian songs may reflect more brightness in vowel shapes, while songs in German tend to require much darker vowels. Singing the music of Kurt Weill is a great lesson for the classical singer who wishes to cross over into music theatre or explore jazz sounds in the German language. That Weill song can be taken to a new level by arranging it in an authentic jazz swing style. Consider how that style change affects the color of the vowels that sound appropriate for the song. Teachers are encouraged to challenge their students to explore the plethora of colors, partials, and resonance balancing that various languages can bring to their appreciation of the multicultural music of jazz.

Diction for the Jazz Singer

Correct pronunciation of vowels and tasteful enunciation of consonants will cause audiences to compliment your singing. Good diction requires effort, technique, and experience communicating successfully with an audience. Quality singing delivers a musical message from the vocalist to the audience at a high artistic and emotional level. If the audience cannot hear or understand words because of poor vowel diction or imprecise enunciation of consonants, singers are limiting their ability to reach audience members who want to connect on a musical level. Mindful singers pay close attention to each vowel sound and the essence of their consonants. Such performance practice is not wasted; on the contrary, it is absolutely necessary for consistent, artistic performances, regardless of style. In classical singing, vowels are optimized and carry farther when they are pure. In jazz, part of the uniqueness of different singers' styles lies in their treatment of vowels. First building an understanding about how to attain vowel purity leads to a nuanced and musical acquisition of more and more vowel colors at the jazz singer's ready.

MICROPHONES AND ARTICULATION

Some believe that a microphone reduces the need for a singer to enunciate text clearly. On the contrary, a microphone simply amplifies the sound a person is making, so if the sound itself is not worth hearing, all the audience hears is more of that ugly sound. Singers first must master their articulation if they are to be heard as artistic when using a mic. Poor articulation can lead to muffled sounds, muddy diction, and excess noise amplified through the microphone. Singers whose articulation sounds messy project a lack of professionalism and confidence to their audiences. Those who do not care about communicating clearly lose their audience's attention and respect quickly.

The conscientious jazz singer uses a mic as a tool in conjunction with excellent articulation to enhance communication. The greatest singers of the golden age of jazz possessed such crystal-clear articulation that not a word was missed. Consider Sarah Vaughan and Nancy Wilson, each whose attention to every tiny sound was so nuanced and sensitively shaped that nothing seemed to be overlooked. Every aspect of musical expression worked together to ensure a clear, intentional delivery of the text. Both singers used the microphone as an extension of their vocal instrument. In this way, the mic never obfuscated the singer's intentions or clarity of diction but only enhanced the manner with which the text was enunciated. With practice and good mic technique, contemporary jazz singers can also accomplish this feat.

SUBTLETY IS KEY

Once singers understand how to isolate a pure vowel (or as close as possible) on every pitch throughout their range and how to play with partials that add color to those pure vowels, the possibilities are nearly endless. Each song has its own unique series of vowel and consonant sounds, rhyme schemes, form, phrase structure, key changes, chord progressions, tonal centers, lyrics, moods, themes, and harmonic and melodic structures. With so many variables unique to each song, the palette of tonal colors that can be created to reflect these distinctions through vowel shaping with help from a mic is vast. Singers who keep in mind that subtlety with a mic is paramount will succeed the most in this endeavor. It may be tempting to go for extreme changes as one might do onstage in an opera because larger movements and vocal adjustments are necessary to communicate clearly. By contrast, minute changes will do in an intimate jazz concert or club environment. To remain true to the art form, singers must learn to adjust to a subtler mode of expression including subtler dynamics, vibrato, ornamentation, ways of moving between notes, and consonant enunciation. Remembering the nuances employed by microphone masters Wilson, Vaughan, and Tormé will assist growing jazz singers in developing their own favorite ways to explore mic technique.

Developing jazz singers must select a high-quality microphone that specializes in amplifying their type of voice as a vital step in becoming ready for live performances. Merely using the mics provided by a venue or a band may not yield optimal sound. Singers are encouraged to take time to research and select a mic that suits both the voice and the performance situations for which it is needed. Mastering mic technique involves understanding open and closed vowels, adjusting volume and airflow to avoid popping consonants, modifying vowels, distancing when appropriate, and becoming familiar with one's own preferred sound settings in a variety of concert venues. Becoming an expert in mic technique involves communicating clearly, knowledgeably, and professionally with technical directors. Performing experience, listening to great singers, and practice are the best strategies when seeking to improve microphone technique. Remembering that a microphone represents half the jazz singer's instrument helps to place these considerations into an appropriate context as one works to become an outstanding jazz voice artist.

10

VOCAL JAZZ ENSEMBLES

Choral ensembles of every genre are faced with the challenges of blend, balance, and stylistic authenticity. Vocal jazz ensembles (sometimes called "jazz vocal ensembles") and jazz choirs face these same challenges. Because each member of a vocal jazz ensemble is essentially a soloist with a microphone, achieving a blended, balanced sound is more difficult than in traditional choirs. Coaxing a choir toward authentic jazz nuance is a challenge well worth pursuing.

WHAT IS BLEND?

The concept of blend in any choral ensemble involves a myriad of considerations. When one or more voices or sections "sticks out" of the texture (whether by unmatched vowel color or tone quality), the ensemble lacks blend. When colors in a painting blend together one might see a continuum on which green blends gradually into yellow by the steady, measured elimination of blue from the mixture of colors. Similarly, when a choral ensemble blends well, the timbres and textures of all individual voices are refined by the director toward a communal sound that yields one cohesive, rich tone wherein the individual voices successfully blend into one. Such results typically require many weeks of instruction before choristers become proficient at blending with one another. To attain good blend, singers must be attuned to all the voices around them, as well as to their role in the mix. Singers must be encouraged to listen more and sing out less to find the optimum volume for blending within an ensemble. Listening to the other voices and emulating the director's demonstrations are important components of an ideal ensemble blend.

Vowel Purity and Blend

Ensembles cannot blend until each member sings matched vowels with the other singers. This involves time and energy spent in each choir rehearsal practicing stylistically appropriate vowel shapes as the director instructs, both visually and aurally. Vowels that align regarding overall mouth shape, jaw opening, lip rounding, tongue position, and soft palate height have a better chance of matching between two or more singers than vowels that have no similar characteristics. Directors may wish to add shades of brightness to certain pure vowels ("ah," "oh," and "oo") to achieve a jazz sound.

Vowels Have Pitch

Ensemble blend can be positively impacted when singers realize that vowels themselves have pitch. To prove this point, singers can activate the vowel resonance in their mouths without phonating at the level of the vocal folds.

EXERCISE

Ask singers to release the jaw open with an awareness of the space between upper and lower molars. Have them shape an u vowel (pronounced "ooh") with a released jaw. Then ask each one to lightly tap a cheek until there is tone audible to the singer. Be sure he or she does not tap too hard! It only takes a light touch in the right place in the center of the outside of the cheek to hear a faint tone. Then ask the singer to slowly change the shape of their mouth and lips from u to the more open o (pronounced "oh"). The pitch made by the tapping of the cheek rises slightly. Continue moving through the vowel spectrum to a (pronounced "ah") to hear a marked increase in pitch made by the tapped cheek. Continue lightly tapping, going back down through the vowel spectrum slowly from a to o to u, back up, and down to reinforce that the brighter the vowel, the higher its inherent pitch goes, and the darker the vowel (the closer to *o* and *u*), the lower the vowel's pitch becomes.

This exercise is paramount in teaching both the solo jazz singer and the jazz chorister why vowel-matching and vowel purity are so vitally important to achieve. Because vowels themselves have pitch, any inconsistency in the purity of a sung vowel is augmented by a choir's inconsistent, random vowel shapes in the mouth. Further, the laws of physics require vowel purity for formants to be located, and those are important to know how to access so that jazz singers can capitalize on the additional amplitude (volume) available to them in various performance situations.

BALANCE

Choral balance involves matching volume between and among different voice parts to ensure that no single part is heard above all the rest unless the music warrants that effect. For instance, when the melody is in the soprano part, the supporting parts must be heard but not to an overpowering degree. The melody must be identifiable within the texture so that proper balance between melody and harmony will prevail. This phenomenon also requires sophisticated listening skills by each chorister so that the melody is always audible, even to the harmony singers. All singers should be able to hear every other voice part from their location in the ensemble. Singers can attune their ears to other parts by rehearsing their line along with each of the other sung lines, one at a time, until they are familiar enough with all the other parts to recognize when a part is missing. This rehearsal strategy builds ear training skills as well as awareness of all the musical layers in a balanced mix of voices.

To attain blend and balance, a variety of rehearsal strategies may be employed. Movement study during rehearsal (see chapter 11) helps to teach rhythms, textures, counterpoint, expression, and a host of other performance considerations including awareness of other sections' parts. This awareness is paramount in teaching a choir to pay attention to how their own voices contribute or detract from balance and blend within the ensemble.

Dr. William Dehning wrote a book called *Chorus Confidential* (2003), equally funny and instructive to the budding choir director. He brilliantly explained the difference between blend and balance and how to achieve both in choral situations. Jazz choir directors will find that choral formation plays an important role in how well the group will both hear and sound as a collective unit. Working on ear training helps the ensemble bond as a balanced harmonic instrument. Orienting singers in a manner that addresses their musical strengths and weaknesses, although a challenge, can greatly impact the resultant sound of the ensemble, regardless of skill level or age. Dehning recommended strategically placing large and small voices, and strong and weak musicians, within the ensemble so that lighter voices are not drowned by heavier ones, and so that the finest musicians (often having the lightest voices) can thrive as leaders within their sections. Mixed formation (splitting up the sections into a few quartets) often yields a terrific blend as harmonies are tuned more precisely with dissonant voices standing next to each other. Teaching singers to match the volume of the lightest voice remains a great challenge for most ensembles, and yet, those directors who endeavor to accept this challenge reap a healthier-voiced choir whose musicianship shines above the rest.

AUTHENTIC STYLE

Whenever a singer performs, one primary goal for creating informed performances is to deliver stylistic authenticity. Knowledgeable singers complete necessary research to learn how a style was initially performed. Authenticity involves listening to masters of the style until the approaches they used to interpret art become familiar. These include studying both recordings and live performances within a given style, including outstanding contemporary artists when possible. Imitation (as in transcription study and performance) must only be a starting point when absorbing stylistic qualities. Imitation must give way to incorporation and synthesis of a unique approach for the artist to emerge.

There is a multitude of ways to correctly deliver a sung jazz phrase in a style authentic to the genre. A great approach to fleshing out this goal is to become familiar with as many great jazz artists as possible (both singers and instrumentalists) and note specific qualities that you desire to emulate. Also note specific qualities you wish not to emulate, thus distinguishing yourself from any one singer. Combining traits of many different performing artists helps burgeoning singers begin to coalesce their own distinctive sound and approach to the vast art form we know as jazz.

INSTRUMENTALISTS AS CHOIR DIRECTORS

Only after singers have cultivated an authentic knowledge of jazz style for their own vocal instrument may they be able to transfer knowledge and expertise to an ensemble of singers. It is important to note, therefore, that instrumentalists who conduct singers are sometimes completely unprepared to address the vocal health of singers in a choral ensemble. The vocal jazz ensemble represents a type of choral ensemble. Because the voice is a fragile instrument, only a few seconds of unhealthy singing are needed to cause pain in the body of the amateur or even professional singer. When well-meaning instrumentalists direct a vocal jazz ensemble or jazz choir, they must first be willing to healthfully sing the music themselves. Only then can they truly ascertain what vocal challenges lie before the singers in any given piece. This implies that the director seeks assistance from a professional voice teacher able to teach jazz. Instrumentalists directing singers are encouraged to procure professional voice training, build their own technique and understanding about healthy voice pedagogy, and sing everything demanded of their choristers. If it hurts the director to sing the material in the manner in which it is presented, it hurts the choristers, too, and *correct singing never hurts*. Jazz voice ensemble directors, like any other choir directors, must first do no harm.

SOLO VOICES IN A CHORAL SETTING

Choral singers must be aware that singing in the vicinity of particularly loud voices may either damage one's eardrums or cause oversinging, which quickly leads to vocal strain. Choir directors are advised to keep careful control of volume during rehearsals and performances to protect both the voices and the ears in the choir. Solo quality voices are particularly vulnerable in the choral setting. Because the jazz vocal ensemble ideally includes only solo voices, each of those voices must be considered when planning rehearsals, concerts, long performances, or rigorous repertoire. Directors must be mindful of the expectations and strain they demand from singers so that voices are gently guided toward making the necessary sounds. Great vocal jazz ensemble leaders grow awareness and affection toward softer sounds in jazz music because dynamic contrast in the softer direction (not louder) makes the group sound more authentic and musically polished. Jazz is a nuanced, subtle art form. Jazz vocal ensembles that belt their songs at mostly loud volumes generally do not sound stylistically authentic. Even when emulating big band shout cho-ruses, the outstanding vocal jazz ensemble displays contrasts and taste. Ensembles must learn to sing softly, with stylistic nuance, or they will never sound like they are creating jazz. Because the voices are amplified with mics, there is never a need to require singers to add more volume than they are comfortable adding. In a jazz choir situation, singers do not hold microphones. Area mics can be placed at a few places in front of the ensemble or from above so that no single voice stands out, but, rather, the entire group is boosted and blended. This enables the jazz choir to get qui-eter on some passages and create the soft dynamic nuances that exemplify jazz choral style at its best.

VOCAL JAZZ REPERTOIRE

Jazz choral literature is plentiful and comes in a variety of levels. I recom-mend starting with some basics, including jazz standards by arrangers that understand the beginning jazz choir's needs. As your choir grows in tech-nique and jazz singing ability, your repertoire options will expand. Many online retail sites show grades of repertoire and include recording clips of their charts. As a professional studio session singer for choral music pub-lishers, I can attest that the wide variety of repertoire choices and levels is important for each ensemble director to consider. Some arrangements on the market may be outside your ensemble's vocal range. Others will be tailored toward young singers, so I suggest you do the research and select only pieces that are absolutely right for your ensemble. It is best to explore both music that feels easy and some that is quite challenging to help create an interesting mix for your season. This allows your singers to sink deeply into the easier repertoire (they will love singing it if it feels good and is quick to learn) while also feeling challenged by the pieces that stretch their capabilities. As performing musicians, we need both.

TIPS FOR AN EFFECTIVE REHEARSAL

An effective rehearsal can be constructed in a number of different, ef-fective ways. All teachers develop their own style over time and learn to emphasize various aspects that comprise an effective rehearsal. Always create a rehearsal plan and stay as closely to it as possible to maximize efficiency and cover all that is required to stay on track. A time guide (in minutes) next to each rehearsal segment shows the number of minutes dedicated to that particular warm-up or song. This helps keep the rehearsal moving at a good pace while making sure every piece receives adequate attention. I also include time for a warm-up, which is different every day, to keep singers engaged and listening. The warm-up may include choral blending work (also varied at each rehearsal) and sight-reading. As the rehearsal continues, improvisation exercises, which may be derived from song repertoire, are practiced and songs are rehearsed by testing memory assignments given at the previous rehearsal. This mix of activities provides a structured regimen that singers thrive within while keeping things interesting and somewhat unpredictable.

Emphasize Precision and Authentic Style

While learning music, it is important to remember to practice slowly if necessary, seeking precision. This means if a song's tempo is fast, it should be slowed down considerably for a beginning choir during the learning phase and sped up gradually as the group learns to sing with precision and appropriate nuance. Each pitch and rhythm should be attended to before trying to sing up to performance tempo. Have them sing on neutral syllables while they learn the pitches and rhythms at increasingly faster tempos. Taking out the lyrics and substituting a neutral syllable (like "du") helps the group listen to the chords they are singing, internalize their relationship to the other singers' notes in the chords, and deliver the notes and rhythms without having to think about the text. The text should be added after notes and rhythms have been learned and the group has balanced their parts on neutral syllables selected to help them match some key vowels in that passage. In this way, each song in a group's repertoire can be turned into a balance or blending exercise that can be used during the choral warm-up. Stylization should be approached as soon as possible during the early stages of music learning so that singers understand how to authentically interpret jazz charts.

EXERCISE

Choose a sixteen to twenty-four bar passage from one of your assigned pieces. Have students work on it in sectionals to woodshed correct pitches and rhythms before bringing them back together to sing it again. Keep them singing "oo" or "du," fairly easy sounds through which to start teaching vowel matching. Have the group sing the passage concentrating on hearing all parts equally (this is balance). Then have the group sing the passage focusing on matching the vowel (this is part of achieving good ensemble blend). Then have the group sing it while varying dynamics on cue. This forces them to think about managing their breath as supportively and evenly as possible over a crescendo or a decrescendo, while aiming to maintain the balance and blend they have already achieved together. Then change the articulation back and forth from legato to staccato so they can hear the distinctions and sing with greater awareness of what the notated articulation requires. Finally, have the group sing the passage with the text added, along with the other parameters previously addressed. The text will require a good deal of vowel matching work on the director's part (lasting sometimes several weeks), but this work will be easier now that pitches, rhythms, balance, dynamics, and articulation issues on the page have been practiced.

It is advisable to challenge singers and never bore them during rehearsals. Mindless drills that force singers to sing passages over and over again without changing anything generally create exhaustion and disinterest. Whenever a passage is repeated, the conscientious choral director asks for the ensemble to improve some aspect or to focus on a different facet of the music. This accomplishes the repetition required for learning without boring or insulting the intelligence of the singers.

Memorize All Performed Music

Because singing jazz demands the communication of lyrics, and because singers hold microphones in their hands (so there is no room for choral folders), all performance repertoire should be memorized for each public concert. Also, the improvisational nature of jazz is better served when pieces are completely committed to memory. Each singer should look like a professional jazz singer. Holding a folder of music interferes with that image. Similarly, a music stand, although useful during rehearsals, should be avoided during performances because of the need for communication from singer to audience. A stand blocks communication by creating a physical barrier. Singers must learn to look at members of the audience to effectively communicate jazz lyrics.

An excellent strategy for helping an ensemble memorize a piece is to begin at the end of the piece and work backward, adding a few more measures to the memory assignment each day. Using this principle, singers grow more familiar with the piece as it proceeds so that the ending is strong and well-learned. Beginnings tend to be simple and straightforward in many choral arrangements. Greater complexity often develops later, so singers benefit greatly from memorizing the difficult end and middle of a piece first. By the time the piece is learned, the ending will be the most rehearsed part of the song. Only after music is fully memorized can vocal jazz be expressed and nuanced appropriately. Depending on the level of the ensemble, testing singers in quartets to ascertain their mastery of memorized material can be an outstanding motivator to encourage singers to come to rehearsals prepared.

Exploring Kinesthesia through Dalcroze Eurhythmics

I often use principles of Dalcroze eurhythmics (see chapter 11 for specific ideas) to reinforce memorized music. Singers of all ages remember better when incorporating kinesthetic work into the music study, and they grow in expressiveness and rhythmic mastery by employing their entire bodies as music-learning tools. They also tend to love the physical movement and freedom of body, voice, and corporate creativity that are unleashed during Dalcroze movement work in choral rehearsals. As the group grows in its memorization of material, it becomes excited about the opportunity to finally incorporate movement into rehearsals. I have seen that the more an ensemble explores Dalcroze together, the greater the bond of beautiful artistic discovery that forms among the members.

STRUCTURING THE REHEARSAL

Rehearsals should include a group choral warm-up, some ear training, improvisation work, style and ornamentation skill exercises, repertoire practice, sectional work on repertoire, memory checks, and sight-reading. At the beginning of the semester, more time will naturally be spent sight-reading because all the music (or at least most of it) will be new to all choristers. Later in the semester, after the music is well learned, more time can be spent improvising over chord changes within the assigned repertoire. Jazz ornaments can be built into short choral exercises that the group sings together, both in unison and in harmony with one another.

Concepts can be combined for an efficient practice session working on many aspects of jazz singing at once.

Warm-Ups and Exercises

I recommend starting each rehearsal with warm-ups and skill-building exercises. These can focus on singing the blues scale (or other pertinent jazz scales—see chapter 12), arpeggiating chords and short progressions, performing unison scat lines (Bob Stoloff's *Blues Scatitudes* [2003] is a great resource for these), group vowel matching, ear-training exercises that challenge singers to hold their part in mixed choral harmony, dynamic range-building for the ensemble, and patterns that change from swing feel to Latin feel and back again. An eight- to twelve- measure progression splitting voices into four-part harmony will suffice to provide opportunities to hone intonation, vowel matching, swing feel, straight eighth-note feel, rhythmic precision, and dynamic contrast.

Looping

Using a short, eight to twelve bar passage taken from the group's repertoire, loop (repeat) the sung passage several times without a pause, asking each time for something musically different. Have singers emphasize swing feel and then switch to bossa nova feel. Ask for crescendos and decrescendos or changes in articulation. Have one part sit out (tacet) while the other three parts sing together. This is especially effective for the three non-melodic voice parts so that all singers can hear the interesting harmonies sung by supporting voices. On cue, have sections "mute" themselves, singing inside their heads only as other sections continue to sing. Point to different sections while the music continues to flow, having some parts sing while others rest. Give unpredictable cues to keep singers on their toes, having them jump into the texture midmeasure after a tacet. This is an excellent exercise for developing the inner ear. Singers can learn to sing along in their heads without using their voices, especially when they hear other music playing simultaneously. Work on two harmony parts at a time but not always the same two. Try sopranos and basses together and then sopranos and tenors. Continue to challenge your singers so they do not know your next move. This keeps them having fun and staying engaged and challenged.

Lay It Back

Many books include suggested warmups for choirs and vocal jazz ensembles. I recommend a one-page exercise called "Lay It Back" by Ric Domenico. This four-part choral warm-up (splitting into six parts on the final note) can be used as a short demonstration piece for workshops or public concerts to demonstrate the differences between jazz swing style and bossa nova style (see figure 10.1). When demonstrating this wonder-

This piece may be sung at any tempo in either a swing or even eighth note feel. The purpose of this exercise is to achieve a "laid-back" feel in syncopated music. -RD

Figure 10.1.   "Lay It Back." Courtesy of Ric Domenico. Used by permission.

ful exercise, be sure to ask the group to repeat (vamp) the progression until your cue is given to sustain the final note. Ask them to frequently switch, on your command, from medium swing feel to Latin feel and back to swing, keeping the tempo exactly the same. Designate gestures for each style (hold up one finger for swing and two for bossa) so that singers can lose no time between the transitions. After the group knows it well, ask for scat soloists to improvise while the rest of the group sings softly in the background. Take turns soloing. Have two or more singers perform a scat "conversation" as they react and respond to each other in real time. Point to sections to have them "lay out" and mentally sing until you cue them back in (a great strategy for rehearsing any learned arrangement to improve singers' inner hearing and the group's ability to count and remember pitch). "Lay It Back" can be performed unaccompanied or with rhythm section and is an excellent choice for teaching jazz stylization. Audiences and singers alike enjoy this exercise because it clearly shows jazz ornamentation via ascending and descending smears applied as desired between notes, ghosts before every "doo," and fall-offs on the first three notes of measure four. It also can be used to practice dynamic contrast (as directed by the conductor), elements of blend and balance, harmonized scat-singing, and the difference in rhythmic timing and feel between swing and Latin styles.

Sectionals

Sectional rehearsals can be used to help entire sections learn their music in isolation away from other sections. If there are enough rooms and section leaders who can sufficiently lead a rehearsal for their sections, the choir can split into four groups (SATB) and spend ten minutes on a few selected passages woodshedding their own parts. Usually I lead one section myself and assign a pianist or section leader to lead the others. After each section works alone for about ten minutes, it is important to have them rejoin the whole group to sing those passages with the entire ensemble. If the sectional rehearsal did not seem to elicit improved performance by each section, a few questions may be helpful. Did the section leader run the rehearsal effectively? Were the unfamiliar passages too long to master in such a short time? Was correct piano reinforcement provided or available? Addressing any shortfalls will improve the outcome of sectionals at future rehearsals. Sectionals are helpful for mastering notes in difficult passages and they facilitate bonding within each section as they discover their own unique unified voice. Rehearsing each section simultaneously also maximizes efficiency during choir rehearsals.

Combined sectionals involve more than one section rehearsing together. Frequently, sopranos and altos may be combined while tenors and basses work together. Another helpful sectional can gather groups that share musical commonalities. When sopranos and tenors share melody or texture that contrasts with that of the altos and basses, having the sopranos work with the tenors for a few minutes creates greater awareness across the ensemble about parts that coincide in some way. Sectional rehearsals accomplish much by isolating each group singing the same music. In this independent setting, each can focus on learning pitches, rhythms, vowel shapes and lyrics to unify their section's sound.

BUILDING THE VOCAL JAZZ ENSEMBLE

Lately the terminology referring to a small jazz choral group with handheld microphones for each member has changed from "vocal jazz ensemble" to "jazz vocal ensemble." Regardless of name, this elite singing group usually represents the finest jazz singers among a larger pool of jazz choral singers. I recommend, if there is enough interest to warrant two or more groups, that the ensemble director places less experienced singers interested in learning jazz into a jazz choir where they can learn the fundamentals of jazz singing, style, blend, balance, vowel matching, resonance, and other basics. From that pool, the director can draw out rapidly developing jazz singers to fill vacancies in an elite ensemble, the vocal jazz ensemble. With the larger group constantly supplying somewhat experienced singers, the small group need never suffer with a weak musician on any of the parts. Beginning jazz singers can build musicianship in the large group while more accomplished jazz singers fill the elite group. Both groups can perform at home concerts, building the audience for vocal jazz.

The Vocal Jazz Ensemble Singer

The vocal jazz ensemble requires voices that are strong soloists willing and able to blend with other voices as a choral unit. Singers must possess a discriminating ear that adjusts tuning, timbre, feel, dynamics, vibrato, articulation, and style to appropriately express the text. In well-directed rehearsals each singer is taught to perform consistently and accurately in close harmony with other singers. Building an excellent inner ear (that hears pitch, scale degrees and intonation inside one's head without humming, singing, phonating, or playing an instrument) represents a crucial priority for vocal jazz ensemble singers. Singing in this ensemble requires and builds strong musicianship, vocal flexibility and versatility, pitch accuracy, rhythmic precision, expression, clear diction, the ability to maintain one's part amid dissonance, and an understanding of various feels (swing, Latin, waltz, ballad, etc.). A goal-oriented director can attend to each of these aspects throughout the rehearsal and performance season.

Because every member of the vocal jazz ensemble must have the technique and quality of a soloist (otherwise, giving each member his or her own microphone will be disadvantageous to the overall quality of tone and sound), the vocal jazz ensemble has the potential of being the showcase ensemble for a university, college, or high school music program. This group, when directed properly, can tour and serve as an important recruiting tool for the institution.

A Master Jazz Pedagogue's Approach

Dave Riley, the founder of one of the first collegiate vocal jazz ensembles (originally called the Ithaca College Jazz-Rock Ensemble in 1974) built an extremely successful and noteworthy vocal jazz program in Ithaca, New York. He placed his program's finest jazz singers in a small ensemble reserved for outstanding soloists that blended well together. His vocal jazz ensemble (which the jazz-rock ensemble of the 1970s was later called) became so popular that Riley grew a moderately large jazz choir (around thirty singers) as a secondary group in which he presented the fundamentals of jazz singing and close choral harmonies to more students interested in singing jazz. The vocal jazz ensemble ranged from twelve to sixteen voices, depending on the year and the talent. Over several years of Riley's leadership this evolving group was groomed to perform nationally and internationally at jazz festivals and concert halls. His elite touring ensemble produced several professional jazz singing alumni, including myself. Riley founded the original New York Voices and inspired countless students to teach jazz in their careers as music educators.

As stated already the most accomplished directors of vocal jazz ensembles must be excellent jazz singers themselves. Riley was an exemplary jazz singer and stylist and had previously performed as a professional bassist. This combination of talents enabled him to excel as a professor of jazz and music education. In Riley's vocal jazz ensemble, emphasis was placed daily on ear training, improvisation, sight-reading, ensemble balance and blend, and stylistically authentic ornamentation. Overall, developing great musicianship was Riley's top priority, and he succeeded by blending singers with a variety of backgrounds into his group including those specializing in instrumental music, classical voice, opera, music theatre, jazz, rock, folk, and pop. Having a melting pot of music majors (and the occasional outstanding non-major) in his ensemble enabled the student singers to learn volumes from each other, to lean on one another's strengths, to contribute individually, and to appreciate a wide diversity of skill sets. Such juxtaposition of skills is strongly encouraged for those wishing to develop vocal jazz ensembles at their schools and colleges. Jazz instrumentalists benefit greatly from voice instruction and, when invited to participate in a group context, are often quite willing to do so. They also tend to have soloing capabilities on their primary instruments, which enhance their ability to improvise vocally. Likewise, singers are encouraged to develop their instrumental chops within the ensemble whenever an opportunity arises. One never knows where such multi-disciplined experience may lead.

TEACHER TIP

Encourage your singers to play (however humbly, perhaps) any instruments they know how to play in a rehearsal jam session. Emphasize that this is a safe learning space, and they do not need to be professional instrumentalists to participate. Include instrumental soloing during improvisational training during regular rehearsals and have any singers who can "comp" (accompany) as jazz pianists take turns playing accompaniments for the group during rehearsals when the rhythm section is not present. Build in repertoire that also uses jazz guitar accompaniment and encourage guitarists to participate.

GUIDED LISTENING TO PROFESSIONAL ENSEMBLES

Directors of vocal jazz ensembles and jazz choirs must become aware of exceptional groups from various parts of the world that excel in this repertoire. The Real Group from Sweden is a highly recommended mixed vocal jazz ensemble that has toured and recorded for three decades, as has the

Manhattan Transfer for four. Take 6 and M-Pact are all-male singing groups whose styles are diverse, but always musically rewarding. The relatively new all-female quartet, säje is well worth studying from both a singing and an arranging perspective. Classic ensembles worth emulating include Lambert, Hendricks, and Ross and the Hi-Los. Going further back into history you will discover pop sister groups from the 1930s and 1940s, including the Andrews Sisters and the Boswell Sisters, both which provided impressively high standards of harmony singing that have still not been eclipsed.

Guided listening to strong recordings from these and other outstanding jazz voice ensembles will give your rehearsals an added flair of interest that your members can share together. Engage singers in conversation about what specifically they hear in the recordings you play. Urge them to articulate their thoughts as clearly as possible and to take from those recordings strategies to enhance their own singing, both as a group and as soloists. Encourage your singers to broaden their listening diets and bring in audio samples of both classic and modern vocal jazz ensembles to share with the rest of the group.

EXERCISE

Play an entire song recording by an excellent vocal jazz ensemble of your choice. Have the group quietly listen with critical attention to pitch accuracy, rhythmic unison, dynamic contrast, blend, balance, vowel matching, clarity of diction, articulation, ornaments, and any other aspects you care to discuss. One way to make sure students pay attention is to announce before you play the song that each member will have to come up with an original observation that nobody else in the room has mentioned. After each has relayed what they heard and liked (or noticed, if they did not like the recording), continue to ask questions about the recorded performance. How did the group express the text, or did they? What arranging devices were used, if any, to keep audiences interested (novel beginnings or endings, modulations, reharmonization, interludes, etc.)? Create a series of questions to challenge your singers so that their ears stay open to a wide range of aural observations. Ask "What did you hear?" and "How can we adapt this group's strengths to our own performances?" Try "What can we learn from this ensemble that will inform our interpretations of our own repertoire?" Feel free to allow these questions to create a discussion among many members. Such critical listening practice helps singers explore many ways to talk about music and teaches them to listen more deeply.

Directing the vocal jazz ensemble constitutes a highly rewarding endeavor for the director who has done ample preparation. Attending first to one's own vocal technique is paramount before one can attend to the vocal health and technique of the ensemble members. Routinely addressing concepts of balance and blend yields a group of singers whose listening awareness expands to include everyone in the group. The conscientious director helps singers to unify vowel colors before those colors are amplified electronically. Teaching jazz style and authenticity helps distinguish the jazz vocal ensemble from groups exploring other genres (like show choirs, commercial music combos, or music theatre ensembles). A strong vocal jazz program can be instituted and grown by offering a larger jazz choir for singers less experienced or accomplished (where jazz concepts are introduced) as well as a smaller touring ensemble for elite soloists capable of blending well with other soloists. Constructing rehearsals to attend to rhythmic precision, intonation, improvisation, ear training, sight-reading, expression, diction, repertoire memorization, guided listening, and style (sometimes through the employment of sectionals) will ensure the consistent development of both the jazz choir and the vocal jazz ensemble.

I I

DALCROZE EURHYTHMICS AND VOICE PEDAGOGY

INTRODUCTION TO THE DALCROZE METHOD

Many singers exhibit performance weaknesses in rhythm, pulse, ear training, and expression. Engaging in Dalcroze eurhythmics can remedy these deficiencies while enhancing concentration and emphasizing the fun of making music. Participation in Dalcroze eurhythmics may positively influence the development of musical skills in singers and instrumentalists alike. Jazz voice teachers can employ Dalcroze exercises to challenge their students while strengthening rhythm and pulse, improving ear training skills, and cultivating creativity and musical expression.

Born in 1865 in Vienna to Swiss parents, Émile Jaques-Dalcroze enjoyed a successful career as a music educator at Geneva Conservatory. Dedicated to developing ways of enhancing music education, he founded a method of teaching music using kinesthesia. *Oxford Languages* defines "kinesthesia" as "awareness of the position and movement of the parts of the body by means of sensory organs (proprioceptors) in the muscles and joints." Jaques-Dalcroze noticed that in performance situations his music students had difficulty replicating habits and technical improvements previously acquired in private lessons. Although students learned to perform music accurately, they rarely exhibited musicality in their performances (Westerlund & Juntunen, 2005, p. 112). He claimed, "Many are born with a sense of rhythm, but the power of expression is lacking" (Leck & Frego,

2005, DVD). Jaques-Dalcroze sought to address this shortfall by exploring music through movement, finding that his students often responded with greater engagement, concentration, discovery, enthusiasm, and proficiency when exploring musical concepts from a creative, whole-body approach. His advancements in music education forged the pathway toward greater physical and mental freedom for performing artists.

Although many pedagogues mistakenly assume Dalcroze exercises were intended to teach primarily children (like the Kodaly and Orff methods), Dalcroze exercises are equally effective with adults. The concepts are transferable across generational boundaries and all levels of musical proficiency, from the novice to the seasoned professional. Dalcroze work is relevant in every music studio, whether one is teaching children, Broadway stars, instrumentalists, or singers. Actors and orators also benefit from Dalcroze study. Dalcroze eurythmics work helps singers whose ingrained inhibitions interfere with experiencing vocal, physical, and expressive freedom. Many professionals as well as college-level groups of students and individuals in the context of studio lessons have found that studying Dalcroze exercises positively transforms crucial elements of technique; fills a hole in their musical education; or opens a door to confident, more fully aware stage presence. Nearly every singer who studies Dalcroze in my studio or choral ensemble reports an increased enjoyment of their music because it naturally restores a sense of fun, wonder, and discovery.

Singers who resist or dislike Dalcroze exercises at first seem to need it the most because they incline toward being naturally inhibited about expression or physical freedom during their performances. Some lack self-assurance in some aspects of performance, which Dalcroze makes them face (e.g., their movements onstage or their innate ability to express a text). For this reason, I encourage readers to gently press forward with Dalcroze and trust that good will come from exposure to and exploration of this mind-opening discipline. Much like yoga can improve a practitioner's health and wellness, the practice of Dalcroze exercises can greatly refine and stretch all sorts of musical, physical, and mental skills. It increases body awareness (which every performing artist needs), a sense of physical balance, concentration, command of breathing and singing technique, coordination, and physical freedom during onstage performances. Dalcroze exercises also engage global learning processes in the brain that facilitate creative thinking. Through Dalcroze eurythmics, singers improve their ability to manage the unexpected without interrupting the flow of continuous movement. Singers then can allow for smooth performances amid distractions, without pause or interruption during changing musical situations.

Dalcroze study can help singers begin thinking "way outside the box," which removes musical limitations and constraints common to live performance and even to voice pedagogy. It helps artists and teachers move forward, onward, and upward, with an attitude of discovery and optimism. Dalcroze practitioners learn to eagerly anticipate the next chapter of creativity that awaits. The study of Dalcroze exercises facilitates ongoing musical discovery by teaching artists how to stand on yesterday's discoveries to reach what they seek to attain tomorrow. Dalcroze work gives power to practitioners so that they can own musical attainments and enjoy the process. It provides a conduit for self-awareness and acceptance of one's achievements and development. Dalcroze work reveals measurable daily improvement and presents learning in the guise of a game that entertains when practitioners allow themselves to enjoy it without self-judgment.

The official Dalcroze Method continues to be presented by licensed practitioners as a tripartite, unified program in schools, colleges, and universities worldwide. It represents a multidisciplined approach to music education built on Jaques-Dalcroze's philosophy: the inner ear, an inner muscular sensibility, and creative expression together comprise the core of basic musicianship (Mead, 1996, p. 39). Dalcroze exercises accomplish several objectives in the teaching studio and the classroom. They increase body awareness, establish a sense of inner pulse, provide a release for performance anxiety, engage global and right-brain learning processes, strengthen the inner ear, and build improvisational skills. Dalcroze exercises, often presented as games, combine kinesthetic, aural, and mental processes that create a multifaceted approach to building musicianship, concentration, and coordination. Given the complexity of musical performance, such an approach can be revolutionary in developing myriad musical skills so crucial for the professional singer to master. Because most singers show weakness in some area of technique, theory, ear training, or expression, applying Dalcroze exercises to their regular study regimen can help them solve their own problems and strengthen important skill sets in ways that keep them fully engaged and interested. "Dalcroze exercises . . . prepare the musician to interact smoothly, without interruption, in changing musical situations" (Westerlund & Juntunen, 2005, p. 118). In his book *Songs in Their Heads: Music and Its Meaning in Children's Lives* author P. S. Campbell wrote, "Dalcroze eurhythmics offers a thorough development of musicianship due to its means of inter-mingling the aural, intellectual, and physical selves in its activities. Its results also extend to improved attentiveness, concentration, and motor coordination" (p. 50).

THREE PILLARS OF INSTRUCTION

The Dalcroze method includes three main pillars or tenets of instruc-tional focus: eurhythmics, rhythmic solfège, and improvisation. For the purposes of jazz voice pedagogy, we will focus on primarily the first and third elements and how these principles enhance music learning. In his 1921 book *Rhythm, Music, and Education*, Dalcroze wrote, "Music forgot its origin—which is the dance—and people lost the instinct for expres-sive and harmonious movements in art and everyday life." (Westerlund & Juntunen, 2005, p. 113) Exploring facets of music using kinesthetic movement often results in rapid musical growth for the developing singer. Exercises within these three tenets can be readily adapted to any song or aria, any language (even scat syllables), and many aspects of music: rhythm, melody, harmony, meter, tempo, form, improvised passages, dynamics, articulation, and on and on. One is only limited by the extent of one's imagination, and Dalcroze work helps the singer and pedagogue stretch that, too!

Eurhythmics

Eurhythmics can be described as the study of kinesthetic body motion relating to the expression of music through gesture and movement. "Eu-rhythmics is based on the joint mobilization of mind and body—specifi-cally, on those faculties which enable us to act, react, and adapt to the surrounding world in order to cope with it to best advantage" (Bachmann, 1991, p. 21). One of the principles of Dalcroze exercises is that "sound can be translated into motion and motion can be translated into sound. . . . Eurhythmics teaches the concepts of space, time, direction, level, and shape. Teachers who study eurhythmics also gain skill in the execution of movement, including strength, flexibility, . . . alignment, balance, ar-ticulation, and the dynamics of energy or effort" (Abramson, 1980, p. 62). Eurhythmics work helps singers accomplish multiple tasks, think ahead, and maintain intense concentration. Singers experience a boost of confi-dence accompanying skill mastery, freeing them from self-consciousness, embarrassment, or fear. Instead, the profound joy that Jaques-Dalcroze considered "the most powerful of mental stimuli" fills the singer's consciousness.

Rhythmic Solfège

Rhythmic solfège is the simultaneous application of ear training, sight-singing, and theory skills along with a rhythmic, kinesthetic element. Using the Dalcroze method, musicians experience melodies, harmonies, rhythms, and intervals from a kinesthetic standpoint. (Caldwell, 1995, p. 137). The method allows artists to create their own improvised sounds (rhythmic syllables) according to their instincts. (Johnson, 1993, pp. 42–45). Although this aspect of Dalcroze is an important pillar of the overall method, its use of the "fixed Do" solfège system makes it less attractive than the other two pillars, eurhythmics and improvisation, to many voice pedagogues who are familiar and loyal to the "moveable Do" solfège system. Still, the emphasis on fixed Do encourages the development of relative pitch and ear training for singers. Some exposure to the fixed Do system helps the body and mind work cooperatively to internalize intervals and scales, permanently making neural connections for musical signals. These connections may enhance a singer's capability of matching pitches, identifying and performing intervals, developing pitch and melodic memory, and successfully demonstrating other ear-training skills. Musicians interested in developing relative pitch and improving ear training may be good candidates for exploring this aspect of the method.

Improvisation

Improvisation refers to a specific mental process that creates diverse, unique, expressive, and unrehearsed outcomes in the present moment that are distinctive to every musician. "Improvisation is the study of the direct relations between cerebral commands and muscular interpretations in order to express one's own musical feelings. Performance is propelled by developing the student's powers of sensation, imagination, and memory. It is not based on direct imitation of the teacher's performance" (Dalcroze, 1917, p. 193). In Abramson's words, improvisation is "a way of finding music for yourself and by yourself, a discovery rather than an imitation" (Abramson, 1980, p. 62). Through improvisatory Dalcroze exercises students use all their faculties to participate in creative learning, express feelings through movement and sound, and reduce performance anxiety.

BENEFITS OF STUDYING DALCROZE EXERCISES

In addition to building musical skills, Dalcroze exercises provide a host of other benefits to the singer. Abramson stated that "[e]urhythmics teaches concepts of space, time, direction, level, and shape. Teachers who study eurhythmics also gain skill in the execution of movement, including strength, flexibility, coordination, alignment, balance, articulation, and the dynamics of energy or effort" (Abramson, 1980, p. 62). Regarding the benefits reaped by Dalcroze practitioners, Westerlund and Juntunen, (p. 120) wrote, "A student feels himself or herself delivered from all bodily embarrassment and mental obsession of a lower order." Dalcroze exercises can replace a singer's anxiety and negative mental chatter with the joy of music-making and a revived sense of discovery. Dalcroze work gives the teacher a catalog of creative ideas for strengthening students' musical skills in ways that engage and empower students' problem-solving and self-correcting abilities. These remain crucial qualities for every professional performer.

Practitioners of other body-mind disciplines including Alexander Technique and the Feldenkrais Method attest to the enhancement of somatic consciousness and awareness through kinesthesia. These other approaches to engaging the body and mind with musical work have helped many thousands of performing artists overcome physical or mental obstacles to technical and performance mastery. The Dalcroze method fits nicely with the other two as a discipline worth investigating because each approach possesses its own distinctive strategies and applications that assist performing artists in achieving their performance goals.

APPLICATIONS OF DALCROZE EXERCISES IN THE APPLIED STUDIO

No methodology or prescribed order of exercises is imposed when presenting Dalcroze exercises. Teachers are encouraged to develop their own based on their students' individual needs. Varying activity among different contexts and scenarios represents a major advantage of the approach. This action variance vividly displays the emphasis on improvisation and adaptation to one's rapidly changing surroundings.

Various introductory exercises can be used to incorporate Dalcroze exercises into the applied studio setting.

- Singers can step the melodic rhythm of their vocal lines to better internalize difficult rhythms. This activity grows a singer's rhythmic precision in practical performance.
- A teacher can illustrate changes in meter, dynamics, or articulation by playing an excerpt on the piano and having the student dance the music to depict the changes. The student determines which movements or gestures apply to each type of sound. This challenges students to think deeply and creatively about sounds and how reinterpreting them with physical movement enhances musicianship. This exercise also demands focused concentration over a continuous period of time, a skill that is diminishing more and more as musicians experience increased immersion in modern digital technology. The more singers practice this skill, the less self-conscious and fearful they become about creating movement.
- A teacher can sing a melody and have the student create a dance that reflects the character of the melody. This important exercise draws attention to all sounds that are actually heard.
- Students can sing a melody and the teacher can create a dance to reflect what he or she hears. It is important that the teacher's dance reflects the actual sound performed rather than the student's intended sound. In this way, the teacher communicates physically and visually through gestures how a song's message is (or is not) coming through. Then the teacher can guide the student toward finding ways to communicate more effectively and precisely with the exact nuances intended for each phrase. This exercise shows students the impact of dynamic contrast, thoughtful phrasing, musicianship, expression, and articulation choices upon the audience's sensory experience.

Each of these exercises is not only terrific to use in an applied studio situation but also can be applied successfully in theory, ear training, and sight-singing classes to help students learn intervals or other "left-brain," logical, analytical, or technical concepts. Students who tend toward global, "right-brain," creative processes of learning will more quickly grasp such concepts when they are transferred to their global learning faculties through kinesthesia.

TYPES OF DALCROZE EXERCISES

Basic types of Dalcroze exercises include responsive exercises, quick reaction exercises, embellished walking exercises, and canon exercises.

Each of these can be applied by the voice pedagogue to strengthen particular musical skills in the applied voice lesson. Together, these four categories of exercises provide both the singer and the voice pedagogue with a host of strategies to explore music through movement or quick-thinking skills. Those who apply these exercises into their daily warm-up, skill-building, and teaching routines will eventually yield a significant return for their time and energy investment.

Responsive Exercises

Responsive exercises teach the singer to respond instinctively to music using natural movements like walking, gesturing, and responding in space with sensitivity and precision (Caldwell, 1995, p. 137). Voice teachers can use these exercises to free tension in the singer's body, increase physical awareness, and encourage expressive, meaningful responses to aural stimuli. Responsive exercises simply teach singers to respond to music in the present moment in an intentional, physical way. The exercise described involving the student dancing music sung by the teacher is responsive in quality. The student modifies movements to reflect any changes or distinctive qualities of sounds. An additional exercise in this category involves a student drawing a picture in the air to represent a particular sound, melody, or motif played on the piano. As the teacher plays more contrasting sounds, the student must attach contrasting gestures to each new sound while remembering the gestures previously assigned to other sounds or melodies. Then the teacher plays the sounds or melodies out of sequence while the student performs the attached gestures in the new performance order, as a dance with choreographic motifs connected with a musical passage. The great benefits of growing critical listening and quick-thinking skills naturally lead the learning team to the next category of exercises in the Dalcroze sequence.

Quick Reaction Exercises

Quick reaction exercises teach students to change their response according to a given verbal command or signal. Sometimes more than one signal or command is established, requiring a multiplicity of possible reactions (Mead, 1996, pp. 38–41). Through the incorporation of quick reaction exercises, the teacher enables a student to concentrate intently on the music and react instantaneously to changes in aural stimuli. An ear for critical listening is thus developed as is the student's ability to react instantaneously to changing impulses. Quick reaction exercises provide cues reflecting an instantaneous change in the music (major to minor, slow to fast, triple to duple meter, soft to loud, etc.). An example of a quick reaction exercise that already exists in many voice teachers' strategies is the use of flash cards during rehearsals or lessons. The teacher (or fellow student in a studio class environment) displays an index card with a specific attitude printed on it (joyful, solemn, frightened, bereaved, exhausted, etc.) while the singer performs a song. The singer must adapt facial expressions, gestures, and expressive devices to match the word shown on the card, changing accordingly as new cards are flashed during the performance. This type of quick reaction exercise enhances acting and expression, increases a singer's ability to concentrate in the present moment, and helps the singer think creatively about modifying a performance to solve a problem. This is particularly helpful for students who "get in their own way," whose concentration is focused on negative self-talk or paralysis and fear rather than on enjoying and maximizing the performance in progress.

Embellished Walking Exercises

Embellished walking exercises explore walking and its departure points, length of step, center of gravity, ways of stopping, directional changes, anacrusis and crusis (Bachmann, 1991, p. 21). Crusis represents the "down" beat or strong beat. Anacrusis is the pickup or preparatory upbeat shown by a conductor's upward motion. Teachers show students the concept of anacrusis by lifting the leg and foot off the floor as the upbeat occurs and stepping firmly onto the floor on the downbeat. Repeating these, one foot at a time, while moving the upper body with momentum toward the foot about to take a step will easily show the student how to prepare for the downbeat with the entire body (during the preparatory inhalation). Transferring voice technique concepts to kinesthesia in this way can create bridges in students' learning processes and make previously difficult physical actions related to breath management or muscle tension release in the jaw, neck, tongue, back, or other area of the body much more attainable. These exercises teach body awareness and balance while reinforcing steadiness and duration of rhythm and pulse. Study of crusis and anacrusis through purposeful walking patterns allows students to sense differences in musical accents and energizes their bodies in preparation for singing.

EXERCISE

Have a student step the melodic rhythm of a jazz song he or she is studying by showing crusis and anacrusis with the feet as described. Show long notes and ties by standing still, only stepping changes of articulated pitches and rhythm. As the singing continues, some part of the body should continue to move. For instance, the arms can continue moving forward while the foot steps and then stands for four beats on a whole note. Walking must be smooth and connected, as if the entire body is moving in a legato fashion whenever music is legato. This mirrors the consistent provision of energy afforded by the breathing mechanism during the sung phrase. When music is played or sung staccato, steps may be shorter and punctuated. Keeping knees bent assists the singer in moving evenly and consistently while singing occurs. Singers must be careful not to step beats. Steps only occur when melodic rhythm is articulated and pitches change. Singers do not simply drag the feet along, but instead they become engaged in creating a smooth way of moving from one crusic beat on one foot to the next, using the slightly exaggerated anacrusis shown in the whole body to prepare for the next crusic beat. These exercises help singers engage their voices and bodies more fully without holding tension during sustained, legato singing. Singers have a lot of fun with this exercise, which serves as a pleasant introduction to Dalcroze work through the exploration of crusis, anacrusis, and consistent movement through a phrase. Students may then be asked to step the beat, a subdivision of the beat, or an augmentation of the beat (e.g., half notes instead of quarter notes), on command. These exercises help students correctly distinguish beats from rhythms and simulate complex beat divisions, differences in legato versus staccato singing, tempo changes, and periods of rest, all with kinesthetic tools. This work assists singers in sensing differences in musical accents and energizing their bodies to confidently deliver expressive, precise singing.

Canon Exercises

Canon exercises involve the overlapping of more than one musical idea at the same time. The student responds to the teacher's multimeasure improvisation by imitating at the rhythmic interval of one measure. The student must thereby perform a musical idea while hearing and remembering another (Mead, 1996, pp. 38–41). These exercises develop critical listening and memory skills along with multitasking abilities related to thinking ahead during performance. They help students cultivate the ability to "think on their feet" and build improvisational prowess that helps them cope with changing performance situations. Canon exercises may involve clapping, tapping, humming, singing, or even stepping. Teachers may wish to start with exclusively rhythmic canons at first, gradually building a student's ability to listen to a motive while performing another, before moving on to include pitches. Varying types of exercises in rapid succession keeps students mentally engaged in lessons, mindful of the present moment, and sharp in their listening skills.

EXERCISE

Sing a song in unison with a student singer, asking him or her to delay their beginning by one measure so he or she is singing in canon with you. Then switch and have the student lead, followed by you at the interval of one measure. There is no need for any harmonic alignment as found in performable canons (like Pachelbel's) because the point is to be able to tune out dissonances and distractions while the student performs the given melody. This exercise strengthens a singer's ability to hold one part and stay in a given key. It also strengthens a singer's awareness about other audible music and his or her individual role in a larger composite work.

EXERCISE

Practice scales with students by singing them in canon with one or two measures' delay. Students will be challenged and enjoy scale study more, possibly engaging more fully in scale practice with other students outside of class. This is a wonderful strategy for ear training, sight-singing, and theory classes or preparation for juries in which scales are tested.

APPLICATION OF DALCROZE EXERCISES IN THE VOCAL JAZZ ENSEMBLE

Dalcroze exercises are extremely adaptable to the group setting and can function as an excellent point of focus during a choir retreat when the ensemble works for a day or more on learning music together. These exercises serve to help the singers bond as a unit, having fun and discovering the joy of musical games together as they use physical movement to enhance their singing. I have often used Dalcroze to move students from the barely memorized phase to the fully memorized phase of learning because it is far more difficult for students to move to music while they have to hold sheet music or folders. In eager anticipation of singing with Dalcroze movement, choir members push each other to memorize music sooner. Dalcroze work in group settings creates singers who listen better from within the ensemble, blend better, and are more keenly aware of balancing with other singers. Dalcroze work increases each singer's knowledge about what everyone else in the ensemble is singing because it can be experienced visually as singers watch each other step parts or show different breath phrases through dance.

Embellished Walking for the Jazz Choir

Embellished walking exercises are engaging ways to introduce the Dalcroze method to a group of singers all at once, so the walking exercises mentioned previously can easily be adapted to the choir or vocal jazz ensemble setting. Embellished walking is an effective group activity because students who may at first be self-conscious soon observe their uninhibited or dancer-type colleagues having fun moving to the music and then lose their inhibitions as they create their own ways of expressing legato, crusis, and anacrusis in their own embellished walking style. As long as the material is presented nonjudgmentally as movement rather than artistic-looking dance, most students are willing to give it a try when the entire group is doing it. One advantage to Dalcroze eurhythmics is that, once the principles are understood, the possibilities for inventing new exercises is literally endless. Moreover, exercises can be invented to directly correspond with any repertoire.

Mirroring

J. Timothy Caldwell suggests a mirroring exercise in his book *Expressive Singing* (1995, pp. 51–52). For this exercise each student needs a partner. Partners stand one foot apart, facing one another. When the music begins, pairs of singers begin to move arms, bodies, heads, and feet in synchrony while maintaining eye contact at all times. At first, assign a leader within each pair and then, after a few minutes, switch to allow the other student a chance to lead the gestures. Eventually the objective becomes to develop students' peripheral awareness and micromovement responses so that no leader is necessary, but both bodies move together, as a mirror, simply responding together to subtle or overt changes in motion, momentum, and direction. This exercise builds awareness, trust, and concentration.

Musical Gibberish

Have students invent nonsense syllables (or even scat syllables) to converse with one another. These games require quick, creative thinking that builds improvisational skills. Fostering these skills will enable students to become more confident risk-takers in performance, essential to every jazz musician. Have one student improvise gibberish to a song's music. Then have another student improvise new music to go with a song's text. Encourage students to improvise lyrics to existing music and music to existing text, in a round-robin format during class. Engage every student in this improvisational activity. When teaching scat-singing in the vocal jazz ensemble I often have students sing using collective improvisation ("Dixieland style") all at the same time. This helps singers hear others' ideas and diffuses self-consciousness for those who prefer not to be heard while they explore this new skill. With everyone improvising all at once, no one is listening to anyone in particular, so it is a relatively safe starting point for beginning improvisers. I also like to add a physical element to the exercises when students are ready (like stepping the melodic rhythm being improvised) to add a further dimension of complexity while occupying students' minds with completing instructions rather than judging themselves. As practicing improvisation becomes associated with group fun (and sometimes group bonding), the classroom or rehearsal room becomes less intimidating and more recreational from a psychological standpoint.

Phrase-Breathing

Dalcroze exercises may be designed to improve breathing technique, counting skills, and inner pulse simultaneously. Abramson (1980, p. 62) suggested that students inhale for seven strictly equal beats, resting on the eighth, while staying perfectly in a steady tempo. Exhale in the same manner without dropping any beats or providing any audible taps or sounds for singers to follow. Repeat until the pulse feels regular and consistent. Try changing the number of beats and establishing different pulse tempi. This exercise helps establish a steady inner pulse for an ensemble in addition to stronger breath management coordination. It also creates awareness about the length of phrases and how much energy will be required to sustain each well-supported phrase.

Drawing Shapes in the Air

In his excellent book, Caldwell (1995, p. 40) suggested that students draw shapes in the air with one hand and then add a vocal sound to accompany the drawing. Singers should take care to match the energy of the gesture with equivalent vocal energy. This exercise enables the student to note differences between high and low energy sounds. It also improves expression and improvisation.

Musical Question and Answer

At a 1998 NATS Conference workshop in Toronto, Caldwell described a game in which one student in a group (or the teacher in an applied lesson) sings a wordless improvised melody in the style of their choice (opera, classical, jazz, music theatre, rock, etc.), phrasing the melody in the form of a musical question. Another student responds with a musical answer consistent with the style first demonstrated. This game determines which students need more exposure to certain musical styles and reveals deficiencies in harmonic or rhythmic understanding. By practicing this game, ear-training skills are developed along with rhythmic skills and improvisational confidence.

Tug-of-War

A Dalcroze-inspired expression of the classic tug-of-war game is an effective group exercise for building awareness of phrasing and breath management for an entire choir or even for one singer in a lesson. It can be approached in a variety of ways depending on an ensemble's needs and the arrangement of the piece to be sung. Set up two rows of singers facing each other. Tenors and basses stand in one row in two separate sections along one line, and sopranos and altos line up opposite them. Have a pianist play the accompaniment of a vocal jazz piece and as singers mentally sing their parts, ask them to visually and physically show the length and location of breath phrases by pulling on an imaginary rope in a tug-of-war with the other singers facing them. The inhalation is represented by a release of the rope and a rapid forward reach to grasp the rope exactly at the moment phonation begins. The rope is then pulled slowly, with evenness and a sense of smoothness and resistance in the body, throughout the entire length of the breath phrase. As long as singing continues in that phrase, the rope continues to be pulled back toward the singer's body. At the moment the phrase ends, inhalation occurs again, and the rope is released while the body reaches forward. The rope is once again grasped at the precise moment phonation begins. This exercise teaches rhythmic precision, length of phrases, steady release of air as a phrase endures, and corporate unity within sections. All altos, for instance, should be showing exactly the same phrase lengths, points of grasping the rope, and timing of lunges forward to regrasp the rope at each inhalation. This is a wonderful way to visually show singers where their phrases begin and end, and how important it is for the entire group to breathe in synchrony. It also teaches how to pace one's breath to last throughout a long phrase. The longer the phrase, the slower the pull must be so that there is still movement happening as long as singing continues. My choirs have loved these exercises because they are mentally and physically challenging and are often difficult for singers who assume their musicianship and breath management are already outstanding. All singers can improve skills every day, and Dalcroze work creates enjoyable ways to help a vocal jazz ensemble, jazz choir, or any choir make musical strides together.

By employing a variety of Dalcroze exercises and games, the voice teacher or jazz choir director encourages the simultaneous refinement of a plethora of musical skills. Particular skill deficiencies may be targeted by using exercises that challenge the student or group in that one area. Dalcroze exercises teach students to discover solutions to their musical difficulties. "What the student discovers, the student remembers" (Caldwell, 1995, p. 137).This power to solve one's own problems remains a key objective, the value of which cannot be underestimated in music education and performance.

The Dalcroze method founded by Émile Jaques-Dalcroze significantly benefits the field of voice pedagogy by offering a fun, challenging medium through which music can be explored and practiced. The integrated study of this discipline through a variety of exercise types builds a singer's sense of rhythm and pulse, ear training, and artistic expression (Oney, 2017, p. 39). Dalcroze kinesthesia work often grants singers heightened awareness, decreased tension, improved concentration, and a reduction in performance anxiety. These added benefits, in addition to building musicianship, further establish the relevance and importance of the Dalcroze method as a valuable tool within the fields of voice pedagogy and music performance. The method's emphasis on rhythm and improvisation greatly enhances the exploration of jazz in particular, thereby enabling the development of more rhythmically competent, confident improvisers. Teachers interested in blending musicianship, expression, and pleasure into their pedagogy are encouraged to plunge into Dalcroze work because it proves itself as equally valuable to both the applied jazz voice lesson and the jazz voice ensemble rehearsal. "Through rhythm it is possible to bring together the mind, body, feeling, music, and all forms of arts in a conscious human experience. . . . The teaching of rhythmic movement, although based on music, is not solely a preparation for musical studies; rather, it is a more profound education of general culture" (Westerlund & Juntunen, 2005, p. 118). Dalcroze eurhythmics exercises assist both singer and voice pedagogue in addressing and resolving a multitude of musical and performance challenges while enhancing the experience of creating musical art.

12

JAZZ THEORY AND INSTRUMENTAL APPROACHES

In the world of jazz performance, singers have frequently been stereotyped as being less proficient in jazz theory, musicianship, and general musical knowledge than their instrumental colleagues, too often for good reason. Many jazz singers do not know how to create an arrangement, transpose a jazz standard into their optimal key, rewrite an introduction or coda for their unique performance, or knowledgeably direct a band, although I have noticed this general state of things finally beginning to change. Such deficiencies in training and education no longer have a place in modern performance. Although a few famous singers of bygone eras may have succeeded in maintaining a lucrative performance career without ever developing the ability to read music, such ignorance will not likely yield success in the field of modern jazz. In a jazz band, the singer's role is not simply to deliver the melody but to perform using one's voice as an instrument capable of improvising an entire chorus (or three) and to provide contrapuntal interest throughout the texture as the other instrumentalists do in the moment. Developing a working knowledge of scales, modes, and an intimate understanding of the chords ("changes") that make up one's repertoire cannot be underestimated. It is to the contemporary jazz singer's advantage to grow in jazz theory knowledge and to acquire a listening diet to match (or even exceed) that of one's instrumental colleagues to attain the highest possible performance excellence.

Collegiate jazz singers are well-advised to enroll in a formal jazz theory course after meeting standard prerequisites in Western music theory, sight singing, and ear training. To cultivate strength in jazz improvisation, a few basic jazz scales are prudent to know. Each scale plays a role in developing jazz performing artists, so teachers can present the scale itself and then engage students in performing exercises that grow their proficiency. The emphasis on the understanding and practice of a variety of scales and modes within a jazz voice lesson is akin to the importance of major and minor scales, arpeggios, coloratura runs, and vocal exercises practiced in a classical voice lesson. Scale study serves specific purposes. The development of the inner ear along with a singer's ability to precisely and instantaneously tune the voice to external pitch references are important outcomes of such study.

SCALES AND MODES

Jazz voice students benefit from regular practice and testing of major scales as well as natural minor, melodic minor, and harmonic minor scales. Teachers are encouraged to help students learn their scales by testing each type of scale in a wide variety of keys as part of their jazz voice lesson warm-up or assigned work during each lesson. Such regular work on scales will help singers become more adept at singing distinctions among scales and modes while also improving ear-training skills necessary for every jazz singer. As a jazz voice pedagogue I have required my students to present three scales per semester at juries, demonstrating proficiency with more advanced scales or modes in each successive semester (e.g., freshmen may sing major and three types of minor scales; sophomores sing modes; juniors add pentatonic, blues, whole tone, and chromatic scales; and seniors sing bebop scales and other advanced patterns). This ensures that singers add scales according to their skill levels and theory training. Because scale knowledge and performance precision of scales and arpeggios are vital to every jazz improviser for creating viable solo ideas over various harmonic structures, scale study remains an indispensable part of every jazz singer's performance preparation.

The Pentatonic Scale

The pentatonic scale consists of five tones (hence, "penta"). The tones correspond with major scale degrees 1, 2, 3, 5, and 6. In the world of solfège, these tones are sung as Do, Re, Mi, Sol, and La. The C pentatonic scale, therefore, contains C, D, E, G, and A. All other pentatonic scales may be found by transposition of this scale. Interestingly, the pentatonic scale can first be presented to students by noting the relationship among all the black (ebony) keys on the piano—the ebony keys comprise the Gb pentatonic scale. See figure 12.1 for notated examples of the pentatonic scale. A staple in blues repertoire, the pentatonic scale is an excellent, accessible scale for many beginner-level singers.

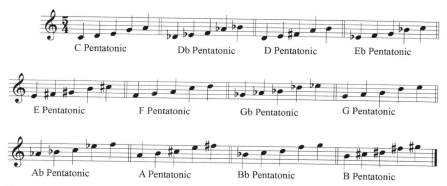

Figure 12.1.   Pentatonic Scales. Courtesy of Author

Modes

The **modes** correspond to the Gregorian modes of early church music and are taught in basic music theory. Familiarity with modes is crucial for all jazz musicians due to the reality that there is an entire genre of jazz music ("modal jazz") based on this ancient organization of tones. Not only that, but entire sections of many jazz standards can be thought of as compatible with a particular mode. For example, dorian or aeolian modes are often played over minor chords or long stretches of minor chords, and the locrian mode is played over half-diminished chords. Singers knowledgeable about modes bear a distinct advantage over those that simply guess while they are improvising. Figure 12.2 displays each of the seven modes used in jazz. These modes are transposable into all twelve major keys. Although the example shows the modes pertaining to the key signature of C major, any other major key signature can be used as long as the mode reflects the sharps or flats of that given key.

The **ionian mode** consists of all the tones of the major scale, starting and ending on the first scale degree ("Do" in solfège) and, therefore, is

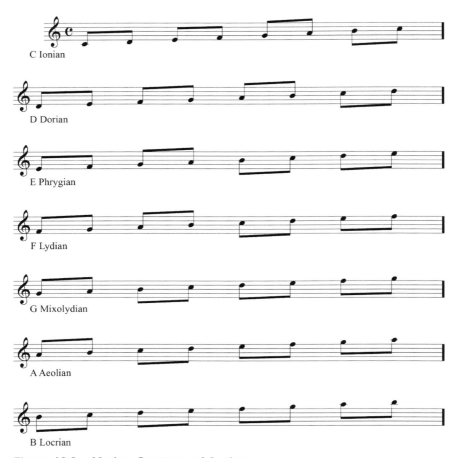

Figure 12.2. Modes. Courtesy of Author

identical to the major scale. The **dorian mode** is found by playing a major scale beginning on the second degree ("Re") and playing stepwise to the octave above that pitch. It consists of the natural minor scale except that it possesses a raised sixth scale degree. That single deviant pitch gives the dorian mode its distinctiveness apart from a natural minor tonality. Because it contains a flat third, it is considered one of the minor modes.

The **phrygian mode** functions within a major scale starting on the third scale degree ("Mi") to that same pitch one octave away. This mode is notable for its first interval being a half step. It is considered one of the minor modes because the interval between the starting pitch and the mode's third is a minor third. The **lydian mode** is considered a major mode and can be played with all the tones of the major scale starting on the fourth scale degree ("Fa"). It is most notable for its raised fourth scale degree (constituting a tritone from the mode's tonic pitch and creating a whole-tone scale with the first four notes). The **mixolydian mode** may be played within the major scale from the fifth scale degree ("Sol") to an octave away from that note. It is one of the major modes and may be played over dominant harmony because it consists of a major scale except that it contains a lowered seventh. The flat seventh gives dominant (major-minor) chords their characteristic sound, and the same is true of the mixolydian mode. The **aeolian mode** is played from the sixth degree of a major scale ("La") to an octave away from that starting pitch. It is considered a minor mode and is *exactly the same* as the natural minor scale. The **locrian mode**, often used in minor keys over a ii chord (because the ii in a minor key is half-diminished), begins with an interval of a half step. It starts and ends on the seventh scale degree of the major scale and includes a diminished fifth between its starting pitch and its fifth modal degree. A minor 7(b5) chord thus often signals the impending arrival of a minor key tonic, which triggers the experienced improviser's awareness that the locrian mode would fit over this passage.

Learning the major and minor modes on all white keys first is strongly recommended to memorize the intervals of each mode using an easy pool of pitches—only white keys—before transposing to other keys. In time, the advanced improviser will learn to navigate the modes in every key both by ear and by pitch recognition on a score. Mastering the recognition and performance of each mode is necessary for the aspiring jazz singer. Assigning exercises using each modal pitch collection helps singers recognize and use them with ease. Eventually, performing permutations of each mode (singing modal patterns over appropriate chord changes, arpeggiating and transposing the mode, creating short motives using modal pitches, etc.) becomes possible for advanced jazz singers.

Bebop Scales

Bebop scales are useful to know within the bebop genre or anytime fast swing is employed. These scales add one chromatic tone to either a major or minor scale to facilitate the performance of chord tones on strong beats. They also add an additional half beat to the playing of the entire scale (when one plays one eighth note per scale tone), delaying the arrival of the octave tonic so that it occurs on the downbeat of a measure instead of halfway through beat four of a 4/4 measure. Traditional major or minor scales possess only seven tones, so the bebop scale's additional eighth places the consonance of each chord tone on the beat where it belongs. This adjustment facilitates a situation advantageous to a jazz performer's timing when performing at brisk tempi. The added tone allows the natural flow of chord tones to continue undisrupted through endless runs of scales, for which the bebop style is particularly known. One can hear the bebop scales played when listening to the primary founders of bebop, Charlie Parker and Dizzy Gillespie. Virtuosic jazz singers Ella Fitzgerald and Sarah Vaughan, well versed in the bebop style, also used bebop scales in their scat solos with relative ease.

The **major bebop** scale adds a "sharp five" (#5) to the seven original tones of the major scale, creating two additional half step intervals (instead of a whole step) between the fifth and sixth degrees of the major scale. This allows the sixth scale degree (commonly used as an added color tone in major chords, particularly in early jazz) to land on a strong beat along with scale degrees 1, 3, 5, and 8 (when played as a string of eighth notes starting on beat one), creating a more colorful set of tones than one could obtain using the traditional major scale. This scale is appropriate to play over major harmony. See figure 12.3 for notated bebop scales.

The **mixolydian bebop** scale adds a flat seventh (b7) to the seven original tones of the major scale, creating two types of sevenths for this scale, thus toying with both the mixolydian mode and the major (ionian) mode. This added tone allows the flat seventh to land on a strong beat along with scale degrees 1, 3, 5, and 8 (when played in the manner described previ-

Major Bebop Scale

Mixolydian Bebop Scale

Dorian Bebop Scale

Figure 12.3. Bebop Scales. Courtesy of Author

ously). This bebop scale supports the sound of a dominant chord and so is appropriate to play over any dominant harmony.

The **dorian bebop** scale adds a major third to the dorian mode, creating two types of thirds for this scale (major and minor), thus exploring the scale's defining third. This bebop scale allows for a colorful alternative to other minor scales when playing over minor harmony or, especially, the blues because this genre toys with the relationship between the major third and the flat third or sharp nine (a "blue" note).

The Blues Scale

The **blues scale** is a particularly useful scale to know when singing jazz. Every tone in the blues scale may be sung over any chord in a standard twelve-bar blues progression. To properly use this scale, it is necessary to know not only the scale tones (see figure 12.4) but also the structure of the twelve-bar blues progression. The blues scale may be found by using minor scale degrees 1, flat 3, 4, sharp 11, 5, flat 7, and 1. On the descending blues scale, I find it helpful to name a "flat 5" in place of the "sharp 11," reminding students that these are enharmonically equivalent tones, which may appear in a jazz piece in either b5 or #11 form. When considering chromatic solfège syllables, the blues scale is sung in the following pattern: Do, Me, Fa, Fi, Sol, Te, Do. In the descending scale, I have my students sing "Se" instead of "Fi" for reasons previously described. It is an important distinction that a complete blues scale only includes seven tones including the top tonic (rather than eight in the major scales, minor scales and modes). It also contains some skips (from 1 to flat 3 and from 5 to flat 7) as well as a couple of chromatic tones (4 to #11 to 5).

Scale degree   1   #9   4   #11   5   b7   1   1   b7   5   b5   4   b3   1

Figure 12.4.   Blues Scale. Courtesy of Author

CHORD PROGRESSIONS AND FORM

Jazz language includes certain common chord progressions and formal designs that jazz musicians must learn as they study the art form. Blues form and ii-V7-I progressions constitute standard harmonic frameworks that support thousands of songs in the jazz genre. Familiarity with both of these must be honed and mastered to become conversant in these ubiquitous types of passages and form.

Blues Form

The blues was so critical in the development of American popular music in the early days of the twentieth century that it maintained its own identity, and it is still developing today. The **twelve-bar blues** (see figure 12.5) is a common form in jazz music, and it inhabits an entire genre within the jazz idiom, so the mastery of this important progression serves as an excellent starting point for many singers desiring to increase their jazz feel, stylistic tools, harmonic understanding, inner ear, and improvisational ability. The basic twelve-bar blues possesses only three types of chords, which makes for an excellent training ground for those inexperienced with jazz. Twelve measures of music are divided into three phrases containing four measures each. The first phrase introduces the tonic and

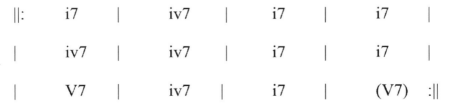

‖:	I7		IV7		I7		I7	
	IV7		IV7		I7		I7	
	V7		IV7		I7		(V7)	:‖

Minor Blues

‖:	i7		iv7		i7		i7	
	iv7		iv7		i7		i7	
	V7		iv7		i7		(V7)	:‖

Figure 12.5.   Twelve-Bar Blues Form. Courtesy of Author

subdominant chords, most often notated in Roman numeral form with one chord per measure: I—IV—I—I. The second phrase places a greater emphasis on the subdominant, creating the following progression: IV—IV—I—I. The final phrase at last introduces the V7 chord quality, touching on the others previously introduced before preparing to repeat the entire progression with the assistance of the V7 chord, which turns the harmony back toward tonic: V7—IV—I—(V7). Because several repeats of the entire twelve-bar progression are implied for blues songs and constitute correct performance practice, the final dominant chord often appears in parentheses, meaning it should be played only if one intends to repeat back to the beginning. On the final chorus, that parenthetical dominant chord is not played. The tonic, I, is played instead, often with an added flat seventh to accentuate the bluesy nature of the piece. Blues is often played with all dominant quality chords, as shown in figure 12.5. Minor blues results when the tonic and subdominant chords are mutated from major or dominant seventh to a minor-minor seventh chord quality.

One is advised to listen to early blues singers like Bessie Smith and Billie Holiday to hear typical blues patterns and stylistic qualities. Generally, a singer would sing a two-bar melody over the first two measures of the blues, wait for two bars, and then repeat that process over the second set of four bars, displaying that the same melody and identical lyrics served the music well in both phrases even though the harmony was changing. In the final four bars of the progression, the singer most often changed the melody and the lyrics, although there are many cases in which the melody was the same for all three sets of four-bar phrases. The absence of a moving vocal line in bars 3-4 and 7-8 of the twelve-bar form gave the instrumentalists accompanying the singer an opportunity to "answer" the singer's statements after each musical idea was expressed. This give-and-take, or call-and-response, texture is a standard blues convention and has remained in contemporary blues performance practice. It is also commonly used in other forms of jazz.

EXERCISE

Sing the ascending and descending blues scale while a twelve-bar blues progression is played. Notice that the unchanging scale matches the harmony well, even though the harmony changes in every phrase. Next, modify the scale using an arpeggio or motive (using the same pitch material in the blues scale), and sing this same, unchanging figure over the entire twelve bars. This will grow awareness of how transferable the blues scale is over I, IV, and V7 chords. As this gets easier, more freely modify the scale and create new motives.

The ii-V7-I Progression

The chord progression that tends to be played more than any other in jazz is the ii-V7-I progression. Having a basic knowledge of this progression and a keen familiarity with it so that one recognizes it instantly whenever it appears in a piece are crucial for every jazz improviser. Part of the charm of this ubiquitous chord progression is that it encompasses three of the primary triads in jazz music (major, minor, and dominant) in just three chords and is endlessly repeatable. For scads of ii-V7-I exercises and accompaniment tracks for practicing, students are encouraged to procure some volumes from Jamey Aebersold's huge library of play-a-long books and CDs. No other publisher offers nearly the depth and variety of song selections, styles, and composer collections designed specifically for practicing jazz as the Aebersold catalog. I recommend these volumes to all of my jazz voice students, starting with easy songs and topics and gradually moving into more and more challenging repertoire. They are excellent self-study tools and students have fun performing along with the first-rate rhythm section that performs accompaniment tracks on the CD that match the keys and lead sheet arrangements of the songs printed in the book. Not only are these volumes valuable for learning to improvise with a band, but they also are invaluable for learning how to read and create a proper jazz lead sheet.

MOTIVIC IMPROVISATION

Arpeggios and Chord Inversions

Instrumentalists skilled in improvising are aware of many permutations available when one has mastered scales in all twelve major keys, minor keys, modes, and other types of scales. Creating broken chords (arpeggios) is an excellent way for an improviser to outline the harmonic foundation on which an improvised solo is built. This is a crucial skill to master in root position chords as well as in all chord inversions. Sometimes the improviser has to establish or reinforce the harmony for the audience (or the band!), so knowledge and skill related to performing a chord one pitch at a time becomes essential. For instance, I have frequently performed live jazz in non-traditional combos and duos and have often had to perform (sing) the bass lines or the chord outlines so that my partner on the stage could perform a solo over a solid harmonic foundation. Or, occasionally the chord progression is unknown to the instrumentalists (or perhaps an error occurs during which band members find themselves at different points in the piece), so the ability for a singer to reinforce the most important chord tones (thirds and sevenths) lends great assistance to the ensemble. Occasionally a fellow performer may get lost. In those instances, it is most helpful to be able to set the group back on track (skilled singers can do this) by arpeggiating the correct chord progression for that part of the song, reiterating root motion or bass lines, and rhythmically timing the chord tones in such a way that will help guide the others through the arrangement. Mastering these skills requires years of practice and continual striving for betterment of one's performance and improvising skills. One of the joys of being a jazz musician is that no two performances are the same! One never knows what challenges may lie ahead on tonight's stage. For the skilled improviser, such unknowns create valuable energy and not performance anxiety. To achieve this, ample preparation is essential.

Concomitant with knowledge of scales and arpeggios is adeptness at creating patterns and permutations of those scales and arpeggios. Only rarely does an advanced improviser actually use a pure scale in an improvised solo; more often it is appropriate to adjust the scale into a pattern of some kind that allows the audience to hear a scalar or arpeggiated passage that has been tweaked by improvisation. Practicing such patterns (much like the practice patterns espoused by Mathilde Marchesi and others of the bel canto tradition) will ensure that performers have those tools at their disposal whenever the need arises. Creating more and more possible combinations of those patterns and practicing those also creates a greater repertoire of improvisational resources for the budding improviser. This truly is an instrumental approach, as accomplished instrumentalists and teachers of instrumental jazz have understood since the art form began that mastering the fingerings, patterns, and theoretical understanding involved in delivering virtuosic patterns can only be achieved through diligent practice of scales, arpeggios, and practice patterns. For this reason, I encourage teachers of jazz singers (and singers themselves, of course) to employ in their daily practice regimen some effort toward mastering patterns of permutated scales and arpeggios.

Sequences and Step Progressions

Sequences and **step progressions** are commonly used in motivic improvisation. A sequence is a musical idea (also known as a "motive," or small collection of notes) that is repeated in a series, often in conjunction with movement of the initial pitch by step. A step progression occurs when the starting pitch of the motive moves up or down a step from the original statement of the motive that appears first in a series. Each time the motive is repeated in a series, the starting pitch continues to move away from its original pitch in a stepwise manner, hence the term "step progression." Practicing the sequence or step progression concept helps to create improvisations that audiences immediately appreciate because they remember a motive that has been repeated, and they love to notice patterns an improviser uses. An avid listening audience marvels that an improviser can transpose a motive so quickly and easily to match the moving progression of the chord structure, which is constantly in motion in a piece of music.

Sequences and step progressions have been widely used in classical music for hundreds of years. They represent an effective tool to assist in teaching improvisation, particularly over musical passages having stepwise ascending or descending bass lines or short chord progressions that are immediately transposed up or down a step (like iii – vi –ii – V7, which is itself a sequence and step progression pattern). Look for opportunities in your music to use sequences and step progressions, as they will abound! Once the ear and brain open their awareness toward these opportunities, the intelligent implementation of patterns, motives, sequences, and permutated scales and arpeggios will help the aspiring jazz improviser to excel in creating a plethora of possible solutions for what to sing over a particular progression.

THIRDS, SEVENTHS, AND EXTENSIONS

Many jazz pedagogues have taught that the most important tones in any jazz chord are thirds and sevenths. This statement comes from the fact that thirds and sevenths define the quality of a chord. Major chords become minor by lowering the third by a semitone. Major chords become dominant chords by lowering the seventh (from major to minor). Masterful use of these chord-defining tones constitutes important early work for every jazz singer and instrumentalist as each develops soloing capabilities (improvisation is often called "soloing" in jazz jargon). Training the ear to isolate the third and the seventh of a chord requires practice and careful attention to harmonic progressions, but the results make such work worthwhile.

EXERCISE

Play a major seventh chord and ask your student to sing the root. Transpose that chord to several other keys and have the student practice hearing and matching the chord root. Once this skill is fairly well performed, have the student sing all the roots in a twelve-bar blues progression, modulating to several keys. This enables the singer to practice performing the root motion inherent in the blues.

EXERCISE

Play a major seventh chord and ask your student to sing the third of the chord. Modulate to several other keys, scrambling the pattern to force the student to isolate the third using their inner ear. Change the chord quality to minor and dominant to give the student further practice distinguishing and tuning thirds of varying qualities. Repeat this exercise, asking the student to sing the seventh of major, minor, and dominant chords. Focus on one chord quality at a time until the student is ready to sing thirds and sevenths that appear in a series of mixed quality chords.

Chord **extensions** refer to those notes above the octave that are included in a chord, namely ninths, elevenths, and thirteenths. Ninths are colorful notes in jazz harmony and are often excellent choices for a singer to perform over a major or minor tonic chord, as when performing the final pitch of a song, for instance. Ninths create a beautifully unfinished effect to a final tonic chord, leaving room for a bit of improvisation (or "noodling") at the end of a jazz piece.

Elevenths are sometimes used within minor chords to add color. They are often the colorful notes in major or dominant chords that set up 4-3 suspensions (or "sus" chords). A suspended chord can be used to create tension leading to resolution over major harmony by suspending the eleventh over the root (creating a perfect fourth instead of a major triad), which resolves downward by half step to the third (because the eleventh scale degree is one octave higher than the fourth scale degree). The natural eleventh is not used in major triadic harmony (except for suspensions) because it is not a chord tone; it clashes in an unattractive way that sounds wrong, and it leads the ear away from the chord root. The eleventh can be used when exploring quartal (nontriadic) harmony or stacks of fourths at advanced levels of improvisation. In major and dominant harmony, the eleventh can be raised by half step to create a sharp eleventh. The sharp eleventh creates a lydian sound due to the whole tone scale that ascends stepwise from the root to the #11.

The thirteenth (one octave above the sixth scale degree) is sometimes used in dominant harmony to add color. In major harmony the sixth is often coupled with the ninth to create "six-nine" chords. Chord extensions add beautiful colors to chord harmony and are important tools for the developing jazz singer to understand, isolate, and use in performance.

Singers must note that C6 is a *major* triad with an added major sixth above the root, whereas C13 is a *dominant seventh* chord having the same added pitch (because the thirteenth is one octave above the sixth scale degree). Similarly, CMa9 is a *major* seventh chord with an added ninth (D), whereas C9 is a *dominant* seventh chord with the same added ninth (D). Studying jazz theory will stretch and hone a singer's knowledge base and help gather ideas for crafting compelling improvised solos. Spelling jazz chords correctly, hearing their distinctions, and arpeggiating them accurately are necessary skills for every jazz vocalist. Singers and teachers are encouraged to create their own exercises performing series of arpeggiated chords and chord inversions. I have often required students to perform various jazz scales (whole-tone, blues, pentatonic, bebop, or modes) and arpeggios of jazz chords at their lessons and juries, making scale-singing and arpeggio precision a regular part of their evaluations. Holding singers to this high standard (alongside their instrumental counterparts) helps them master theory skills so they are as drenched in rudiments of jazz harmony as their bandmates.

HEMISPHERICITY

Another concept attributable to an instrumental approach is hemispheric-ity. This concept has been extensively explored and documented by Joe Riposo, an outstanding jazz educator, saxophonist, composer, arranger, and author. In his book, *Jazz Improvisation: The Whole-Brain Approach* (1989), Riposo describes creating an environment in which jazz students can exercise both hemispheres of the brain simultaneously. Truly, a "left-brain, right-brain" designation represents a simplistic understatement of the complexity that innervates the entire brain organ. Both hemispheres engage and interact during both analytical and creative activities. How-ever, this model is sufficient to give the musician a visual representation of the different types of thinking required for successful improvising work. Riposo describes the role of the "left brain" in using logic, organiz-ing facts, and analyzing chords, scales, modes, and song forms. Riposo then suggests that all the knowledge accumulated by the left brain can-not, by itself, facilitate improvisation. He presents a persuasive case for the necessity of "right brain" activity, replete with spatial learning, aural processing, performing in "the zone," and strengthening the inner ear, to combine with the knowledge, organization, logic, and analysis of the left brain to finish the job.

According to this model, musicians who learn a piece by sight-reading and studying a musical score tend to be left-brain-dominant musicians. As they develop their skills, excellent music readers tend to rely less on their ears to help them play music, whereas musicians who play by ear without reading music tend to be right-brain-dominant musicians and learn to rely on memorization. At early ages musicians tend to favor either music reading or playing by ear and so rarely have opportunities to strengthen both left- and right-brain learning as they develop their skills. Riposo challenges members of each camp to combine their brain hemispheres by engaging the musically weaker side of the brain to achieve a more com-plete ability to translate facts and knowledge about music theory (from the left brain) into improvised music that sounds good and reaches new heights of aptitude and creativity (from the right brain). This combinato-rial approach strengthens the weaknesses of both types of musicians and raises the level of musicianship and improvisational abilities of all who read this wonderful book.

EXERCISE

One area that Riposo emphasizes in presenting this material is the necessity of playing a song by ear after only seeing it (or sight-reading it) once. The brain is then forced to fill in the gaps that it does not recall, thereby creating improvisational bridges throughout the mind's memory of a song. Practicing this skill enables the gradually improving improviser to remember more and more of a sight-read piece after the first reading and to make up the rest with good results. Students are, in essence, forced to improvise to get through the song's form, even if their attempt barely resembles the original piece. The point, obviously, is not to regurgitate what has been written down, or even to approximate most of the original piece, but to rely on one's ears, theoretical knowledge, creativity, past experience with chord progressions, and improvisational experience to create music with little starting information. I recommend introducing this exercise to intermediate or advanced improvisers after they have mastered a few scales, some jazz repertoire, and basic knowledge about keys and standard progressions. I also highly recommend this method to excellent sight-readers who are less comfortable memorizing or improvising music, as well as to musicians that use their ears to memorize quickly and play by ear but do not read music well. This book does a great service to all musicians by teaching how to use the parts of our brains that our natural tendencies and instincts may have neglected, resulting in the enhancement of our total musicianship.

TRANSCRIPTION

When beginning jazz improvisers are ready, they should begin early in their study to work on **transcription**. This is a concept that instrumental jazz teachers present to their students on a regular basis, but many singers have never attempted it, to their own detriment. Transcription (similar to dictation) is the process of writing down music that is heard on a recording or in a live performance. The resulting chart or musical score is called the transcription, as is the process of creating it. Writing a transcription requires a discriminating ear that can detect precise pitches, rhythms, and chords played by an instrumentalist, band, or a vocalist. It also requires strong music theory skills to navigate this advanced type of dictation. The process of transcribing music hails back several centuries when composers' apprentices learned to compose music by transcribing live performances and copying manuscripts written by their masters.

The Value of Transcribing

The skills obtained by mastering the art of transcription cannot be overstated. One gradually learns how to notate rhythmic passages, pitch collections and chords at a high level of aptitude, and how to create one's own original music and arrangements using the ideas gleaned from the scrutiny of high-quality musical performances. One also learns to be much more precise about one's own performances by listening to and internalizing the outstanding solos others have performed. Transcribing is a skill well worth pursuing and is indispensable for jazz musicians of all types.

To teach the art of transcription, one should begin with a song fairly easy in chord progression, melody, and form. Four- or eight-bar phrases having fairly typical, straightforward progressions (like ii-V7-I, a twelve-bar blues progression, or "Rhythm Changes" would be good places to start). Once students know the theoretical form of a chart, their first transcription assignment could be to transcribe a song in that style. For example, after introducing twelve-bar-blues form and having students study a few blues songs, try giving them a transcription assignment within that form. The chord progression and form would not be difficult to notate, but the melody, rhythm, lyrics, and other distinguishing characteristics of that piece would be unique among other blues songs. When completed, students may transpose the transcription into a comfortable performance key. Once teachers begin giving transcription assignments to their students, they notice how quickly ear-training skills, understanding of jazz chords and theory, and improvising abilities improve.

The Process of Transcription

When transcribing, start by notating the bass line to determine the underlying key, root motion, and chord structure. Then write down the melody that corresponds in time with the chord roots you have notated. Listen to the qualities of the chords as the song progresses and see if you can reproduce them on the piano or guitar—does the third over the bass note sound major or minor? Students will use the ear as well as logic to fill in chords within longer progressions and will learn to quickly identify those more familiar progressions such as ii-V7-I, circles of fifths, and passages using blues progressions. Knowledge of and the ability to identify chord qualities, various scales, and the circle of fifths assist the transcriber in completing this initially difficult activity. Roman numeral analysis helps greatly too because it takes on a new layer of relevance when the theoretical meets the practical in the act of transcribing music.

One can quickly fill in the harmony of a progression that sounds diatonic after one determines the bass notes (which are often the roots of chords). Knowing the chord qualities of all the triads built on that key's scale (major, minor, or modal) is also useful information. Transcription helps students appreciate what they already know about music theory, how different aspects of theory work together to form a core of helpful knowledge, and why that knowledge is relevant to the music they wish to play.

Another reason to pursue transcription is that it forces a singer to truly listen critically—at a microscopic level—to music for the purpose of analyzing, notating, and performing it. A frequent context in which beginning improvisers are given transcription assignments involves transcribing an improvised solo recorded by a veteran jazz musician—a thirty-two-bar improvised solo played by Lester Young, for example. After writing down each note and rhythm Young performed for a particular song's improvised solo, the student learns a plethora of skills and can more easily sing or play back the solo. The reproduction of a veteran musician's performance is a major benefit of honing the skill of transcribing. Once a student can sing a thirty-two-bar solo performed by Young, including his requisite smears, glissandi, articulation, back-phrasing, dynamics, and subtle nuances, the student has absorbed much more than just notes, rhythms, and correct notation. The student has, unconsciously perhaps, absorbed some aspects of the unique voice of that performer. A student thus climbs inside the brain of a master musician for a moment, performing the same music the master created when he or she was in "the zone." The more singers transcribe and incorporate outstanding improvised solos into their own performances, the stronger their improvising skills become.

Through transcription we learn the mannerisms of the jazz masters, their go-to passages, their "bag of tricks," and we make them our own. We are not in danger of imitating an artist slavishly if we transcribe passages performed by a wide variety of artists because this is how an artist develops their own improvisational sound or voice. Only by learning from the genius of others can one's authentic voice be discovered and cultivated. We imitate the best sounds from our favorite artists and systematically add to that collection of tools by transcribing music we love from saxophonists, trumpeters, trombonists, pianists, guitarists, singers, and even drummers. This practice will help us carve out a distinctive sound that is never lacking in ideas. We are endlessly improving as we add more and more transcriptions to our repertoire.

Jazz singers frequently perform over progressions that many of their favorite musicians have played. Knowing *what* they played when they faced that progression gives singers material to consider when they wish to say something original. Modern singers may organize a song slightly differently to make it their own, or they may quote a musician directly. Either way, singers put transcription exercises to practical use while growing both their library of possible solutions to the puzzle of improvisation as well as their confidence in doing so under pressure. The discipline of transcription proves that a little planning goes a long way in creating original art.

Students learn melodic and harmonic dictation in theory and ear-training courses, so a jazz voice teacher's supplemental work (teaching and honing transcription skills during lessons) will go far in strengthening skills already developing in those areas, while proving to student singers how music theory remains relevant to their future professional work. Conversely, a singer's work in theory and ear training classes will help refine their work in the voice studio. This teacher loves to see information and skills overlap from course to course because a student's education jumps in relevance whenever that phenomenon occurs. Transcription is a fabulous way to link music theory to music performance, and it is absolutely necessary in the toolkit of every jazz musician, whether instrumentalist or singer.

Singers learn myriad techniques and stylistic nuances by studying the work of great performing instrumentalists whose mastery of these skills is readily apparent. Louis Armstrong first performed vocal improvisation in a manner that approximated the sound, style, and note choices he played on his cornet. Scat-singing originated when singers (especially Armstrong) imitated the sounds of instruments playing jazz, so a melded theoretical and instrumental approach to scat singing is highly apropos in today's jazz landscape. It is literally where we began one hundred years ago and where we ultimately hope to land as vocal artists.

13

MINDFUL SINGING
AND MENTAL TOUGHNESS

The concept of mindful living has been circulating in pop culture for several years. Scores of books have been written on developing mindfulness to alleviate stress, develop mental focus, and accomplish myriad goals without distraction. Multitasking, by contrast, has recently been discouraged by experts who insist that tasks are performed more efficiently and effectively and with heightened job satisfaction when workers focus on performing one task at a time. Experts have suggested that people who concentrate on doing one thing well and then move on to the next task experience less anxiety and overwhelm in their daily lives. Singers coordinate and mentally process many aspects of performance simultaneously (physical sensations of breathing, singing, and physical alignment; visual feedback from the audience, conductor, or fellow performers; memory recall of music, words, song order, and cues; and many others). For this reason, singers must learn to be mindful and aware while they give their full attention to singing during every rehearsal, practice session, and performance. The brain only successfully performs one task at a time, so it behooves us to be disciplined about refraining from engaging in distracting activities during singing practice certainly when performing in public. Herein lies our motivation for developing mindfulness in the studio, in the practice room, and onstage.

PRE-PERFORMANCE MENTAL PREPARATION

Developing mental focus to coax the voice into its proper pre-performance state is a craft worth pursuing. Many fine voices have been damaged simply by singing without first warming up and thus failing to stretch the tiny, delicate, intrinsic muscles of the vocal apparatus as well as the sizable network of extrinsic muscles (the masseter muscles, the tongue, the shoulder muscles, back muscles, and more) that exert force on the vulnerable vocal organ. Singers are wise to create a warm-up routine they enjoy and use it faithfully before every performance, rehearsal, or practice session. When a singer becomes committed to an easily accomplished routine that is integral to vocal health, the voice becomes healthier, stronger, and more reliable.

THE VOCAL WARM-UP ROUTINE

The warm-up routine need not be something a singer performs exactly the same way every day. Because creative minds tend to prefer variety and freedom over regimented methods, the teacher is wise who suggests categories of exercises rather than specific drills to practice by rote. I personally need the flexibility in my warm-up routine that allows me to invent new exercises depending on how my voice is feeling or what it needs to do each day. I have developed a categorical series of exercise types that work wonderfully for all my student singers as well as for myself—from beginners to professionals and youth to adult singers of an advanced age.

Healthy singing generally cannot occur within a body that is tense. The first order of business, then, is to invite a sense of relaxation, elongation of the muscles, and release of tension into the entire body. Starting with physical stretches, we open up the body, the chest, and the back, while elongating the spinal column. I guide my singers through many different types of stretches on different days. Here I will share just a few.

I like to begin with stretching the arms over the head, reaching upward one hand at a time while inhaling slowly, then reaching the other arm into a stretched position over the head while exhaling. These are great for both teacher and student to do in the applied studio or in a choir or opera rehearsal to warm up a group of singers. Repeat these until you have stretched both arms over the head one at a time, several times (never stretch a muscle beyond what feels comfortable). I then have the student roll the shoulders gently in circles, bringing them up toward the ears, then down toward the back, and sliding forward toward starting position, completing a circular motion. Repeat the circles in the opposite direction, sending the shoulders forward and down, then sliding back and upward before falling forward to complete the circle. Try this moving the shoulders together synchronously and then in alternation with one shoulder forward while the other is back, continuing to move in circles.

Another great exercise to open the chest and stretch the shoulders is to squeeze the shoulder blades together and hold them there for a few seconds and then release. Repeat and notice that the sternum lifts when shoulders squeeze together. This lifted sternum represents the absolutely correct, open chest posture for singing, whether seated or standing. Many jazz singers attempt to sing with a collapsed sternum, sabotaging their potential for sustaining long phrases, managing the breath, and maintaining good posture, so this exercise is excellent for creating awareness about the sensation of sitting, standing, or singing with a properly high sternum.

McCLOSKY'S POINTS OF RELAXATION

A series of exercises I love to use are based on McClosky's Six Points of Relaxation. The McClosky Method is an internationally known method of singing that emphasizes physical relaxation for optimal vocal technique. The six points include the facial muscles, the tongue root, swallowing muscles under the chin, jaw (masseter) muscles, muscles above the larynx (from which it dangles), and the neck including sterno-cleidomastoid muscles. Singers are encouraged to attend a seminar on the McClosky method to dive more deeply and familiarize themselves with all of the benefits this method offers.

To warm up the muscles around the vocal mechanism, start by massaging the face with both hands, making small circles with the fingers. Massage the temples, forehead, cheeks, bridge of the nose, and areas under the eyes, above the mouth, the lips, the chin, and face. Pay special attention to any areas you know hold tension. For me, the temples, the area between my eyes, and the temporomandibular joints (TMJ) need particular massaging. After a minute or two, your face should feel more relaxed. Move on to stretching the tongue root by extending the tongue out of the mouth as far as it will go. Hold it far outside the mouth for about ten seconds and then relax. Repeat four or five times, always gently opening the jaw and working to extend it a little further out of the mouth each time, holding it long enough to feel tension release at the root of the tongue. Then the swallowing muscles can be massaged by placing the thumbs under the chin and gently palpating the soft area under the jaw. Lightly press the thumbs straight upward, one at a time, into this soft area. Try swallowing as you do this and then try speaking, continuing to gently massage the area with the thumbs. Notice how much tension collects there when you speak or sing! This warm-up exercise increases a singer's awareness about where tension remains. After a minute or two of releasing the swallowing muscles, grasp the bottom jaw at the chin between one forefinger and thumb and gently move the lower jaw up and down with the hand (not by flexing your jaw muscles!) Try moving the jaw at different speeds, being careful not to click the teeth together. Also be aware that a proper jaw release occurs by the lower jaw swinging gently down and back, pivoting at the hinge, not driving downward in a straight line toward the floor or jutting forward. The forward jut creates serious problems for many singers and is to be avoided at all times. This exercise, when done with the awareness of rocking the jaw down and back, enhances proper jaw alignment and freedom from tension. After a minute or two of creating space between your molars by letting the hand open and close (and quickly flutter) the jaw, move on to the muscles around the larynx. Allow yourself to gently yawn—this opens the back of the throat and allows the larynx a moment to find a low, relaxed position. Begin this stretch with the sensation of the larynx feeling low and wide and not high or tense. Gently place both hands alongside the larynx as if a physician were palpating the glands in the neck. Gently massage these muscles laterally, moving the larynx slightly to the right and left (only moving it a few millimeters) by massaging the muscles from which the larynx dangles. After allowing these muscles to relax for a minute or so, proceed to the neck muscles. Drop the chin to the sternum, feel the weight of the head stretching the muscles in the lower neck and upper back. Then rotate the head to the right as if the head were a doorknob that you are turning. After holding this stretch for a few seconds, bring the chin back to the center of the chest and continue rotating to the other side, turning the doorknob the other way. Repeat this series until the neck muscles have attained an adequate stretch. Return the chin to the center again and slowly lift the head. Assess the quality of the relaxation you achieved by doing a "bobble-head" motion (gently bobbing the head up and down as you glide it to the right, center and left through your head's range of motion). Be careful not to tip the head too far back; it should not exceed a few degrees above parallel with the floor at any point during this exercise. All McClosky exercises emphasize a gentle performance of each relaxation point.

The six points of relaxation may be explored throughout one's practice routine and literature study to ascertain which areas may harbor tension while a singer sings. I suggest randomly doing one of the stretches while you proceed through vocal exercises and later, during song practice. These exercises are wonderful in isolating problematic areas of tension as well as relieving that tension. With months of mindful work, that tension can be released using this method.

BREATHING EXERCISES

After releasing all physical tension that the singer brought into the studio, the teacher can work on engaging the breathing mechanism. Warming up the abdominal muscles and intercostal muscles is recommended before beginning any serious voice training, rehearsal, practice, or performance. The singer's daily warm-up routine should address not only the laryngeal musculature but also the breathing mechanism, while relieving tension in the back and opening up the chest cavity. Creating mental awareness about the body's alignment and breathing is necessary for every performing artist. Use a mirror whenever possible to match the sensation of correct form and technique with the eyes' informed correction.

The Breathing Stretch

A key exercise I developed for waking up the body and reminding the breath how to engage correctly I call the Breathing Stretch. Stand up straight with sternum lifted, aligning the points of balance. Inhale for six slow counts while you gently lift straight arms up (in an outward, upward motion) over the head, keeping shoulders low and relaxed and the breath low. Suspend the breath with the glottis open for four slow counts. This phase should feel like you are a hot air balloon suspended and floating over the earth. Then exhale for six slow counts while you allow the straight arms to descend, retracing the same path in fully extended orientation, stretching the arms and shoulders down and back. During the exhalation keep the sternum lifted. When the arms reach the sides of the body, suspend the breath once again, avoiding the inhalation for four counts before repeating the cycle. Inhale for six, suspend for four, exhale for six, and suspend for four. The final phase of suspending out may feel strange but is a reminder that we will not drown or faint if we wait a few more seconds before inhaling. It allows us to mentally control the breath even when the body wants to take in air. At no point should the glottis close or a singer feel muscles holding or tensing. There are many instances when a singer would like to breathe but cannot until the current phrase has been completed, so this exercise helps both body and mind adjust to the sensation of being at the end of the breath for longer than a moment. This exercise has expanded the breath capacity of hundreds of singers in my experience and is highly recommended for creating a relaxed, trustworthy, reliable breathing technique.

Breath of Fire, Step One

While using the breath of fire exercise explained in chapter 4, a singer can cultivate mindfulness and increased body awareness. Beginning in a seated lotus or cross-legged position on the floor, take a moment to find a relaxed place there from which to begin. Place hands face up on the knees and begin to pant with the mouth slightly open and jaw fully released. This is a good time to scan the body and make sure alignment is in check and that the jaw is dangling open in a downward, backward swing from its closed position. The jaw should never feel forced or pushed backward or forward. The lower jaw naturally pivots down and back from the hinge. The lower abdominal muscles empower the panting motion by flexing inward toward the spine on each exhalation but simply releasing (not pushing forward) on the inhalations. This exercise has been monumental in illustrating the physics of singing for many of my singers. Slowing down the pant, the teacher can demonstrate that the only flexion happening in this cycle is on the exhalation. The inhalation is merely the result of the muscles letting go, releasing all tension, and bouncing back (without any effort on the singer's part) to the original position. We do not have to pull air in; the body's vacuum automatically pulls the air back in as soon as the abdominal muscles relax. Start by slowly and audibly exhaling while flexing the abs toward the spine. Then, let go of the abs and watch them pop back to their original orientation as air silently fills the lungs! When students first experience this phenomenon they often display joy as a light bulb illuminates in their minds, finally "getting" how breathing technique should feel. Indeed, the more a student masters this relaxation phase during every inhalation, the greater and greater stamina they will develop and the less tense they will feel as they try to manage their breathing during song performance.

Breath of Fire, Step Two

Once the pant has been mastered at a slow tempo, increase the speed until it resembles a quick pant like that of a dog on a hot day. This requires great control over the abdominal muscles and a true release of the muscles on every inhalation. At first, students may feel frustrated at the difficulty, but over time, as long as they understand the premise and practice daily, it will get easier. The goal will be to be able to continue panting this way for a couple of minutes without cessation. As singers become more adept at this and more flexible, the body can actually regulate the amount of air on the intake so that they can adjust accordingly when they sense the need for more or less air for maximum comfort. This level of gauging the system may be attained after many months or years of developing this abdominal flexibility. As one gets more advanced, one can employ the intercostal muscles as well as the abdominal muscles in regulating the comfortable amount of air in the lungs at any given time, even at a fast panting speed.

When ready, the singer should close the mouth and pant through the nose, focusing on a noisy exhalation followed by a silent inhalation. When practicing this, attention should be placed on a completely relaxed abdominal release on every inhalation, proper jaw alignment (space between the molars with no jaw jutting or pressing), and an elongated spine. Some advanced singing teachers and yoga teachers can perform this exercise for seven or more minutes without pause. During the breath of fire cultivating awareness about releasing one's bodily tension and focusing entirely on the breath remain most important.

Hissing

Another breathing exercise I use is a series of hisses while a singer is in a standing position. In a medium tempo with a quarter note—quarter note—half note pattern, hiss *s* three times through the teeth (without clenching the jaw or tongue). Repeat this several times using a steady beat, always being sure to move the abdominal muscles gently and subtly toward the spine during every *s* while fully releasing the abs between the hisses. An easier way to think of it is that each *s* occupies an eighth note followed by an eighth rest. On the rests, the abs release and air rushes into the lungs silently without the singer drawing it in. As a second stage of this exercise I perform it double-time: [s]-[s]-[s]-[s]-[ssss] with an extended hiss on the end (in the same tempo as the previous exercise but using four eighth notes followed by a half note). Breathing at the end of the quarter note (cheating it by an eighth rest to give time to inhale without stopping the rhythmic pattern) will reinforce the correct movement of the abs throughout this breath cycle: abs move inward during the full duration of the long hiss and then fully release as soon as inhalation begins. These exercises are great to do as the Breathing Exercise portion of a daily warm-up. Different exercises may be given on different days to give the singer a few different breathing tools to add variety to their regimen.

MINDFUL PRACTICE

Mindful practice can include a variety of musical activities. Mindfulness, of course, refers to one's attention remaining on what one is doing in the present moment. Cultivating a mindful approach to singing, practicing, score study, analysis, language and diction mastery, and bodywork will assist the aspiring vocal artist toward a career in which mental focus is an absolute must. The benefits of singing mindfully are myriad: freedom from being easily distracted, ability to remain disciplined for long periods (which is necessary for learning a lot of music), attentiveness during rehearsals, and mental toughness for performance situations, to name a few.

Mindful practice, in my estimation, also includes elements of music study that are necessary for every performance which are outside the realm of a classic definition of "practice." When students think of practice, they generally think of warm-up drills, scales, repertoire run-throughs, and the like. But there are many other ways to practice that help them learn music even when their voices are tired, ill, or compromised. Much can still be accomplished when the vocal instrument needs to rest. With mindful practice, a singer dedicates time toward what the voice needs on a given day. Sometimes the voice really wants to move; other times it may wish to grow its dynamic control through crescendi and decrescendi. Daily practice can be a delightful exploration of what the voice is willing to attempt or hone each day, and it need not be boring, regimented, or unpleasant. Listening to one's instrument within the housing of the whole body allows the singer to cater to its voice's daily needs.

Several types of practice approaches include vocal workouts, diction study, visually studying the text, looking up meanings of unfamiliar words or phrases, and speaking text meaningfully as if it were a poem or extemporaneous speech. Other elements of effective practice can center around specifically challenging aspects of a piece. If a song is difficult to count, speak it while you conduct it, keeping careful track of where the beats are in each measure. If melodic pitches create problems, work on linking the melody together in a string of short motives. Background study of the origin of a song is always an educational, worthwhile activity—does it come from a musical or film? In what context was the song originally presented? Who is singing and what are the character's objectives during the course of the song's drama or storyline? Who is the target audience? These questions and many more that occur to the mindful singer when he or she begins digging into a song's meaning are worthy expenditures of time and effort because they lead to deeper levels of understanding which audiences greatly appreciate.

Nonsinging Practice

One main discovery of mindful practice is that it involves much more than phonating. Putting set lists together, visually reviewing arrangements, playing through chord progressions, working on piano chops, creating new arrangements, working on breathing exercises, writing song texts several times to memorize lyrics, visualizing a successful performance while mentally reviewing music and text, and experimenting with new ways to start and end a piece of music can all be considered aspects of practice that are necessary and beneficial to the developing (or working) jazz singer. None of these tax the voice at all. Mental practice, in fact, is highly recommended during days when the voice is tired or resting (e.g., immediately before or after a performance). Visualizing success in one's stage performances is a highly encouraged practice that builds confidence.

As long as the singer's craft grows on a daily basis, various activities related to mastering the art form can be considered practice, even when resting the voice. Wise teachers assign nonsinging musical work when a singer must rest the voice or is vocally tired. Singers are advised not to skip scheduled lessons (except when a student has a contagious illness) during periods of voice rest. Instead, valuable lesson time may be spent working on diction, rhythmic mastery, kinesthetic exercises to build musicianship (see chapter 11), text memorization through journaling, or researching song, composer, or lyricist backgrounds. This teaching moment enlightens a lazy singer that enormously important singing work can be accomplished without phonating at all! It is also appropriate to give nonsinging students lessons in breathing and posture when singing is inadvisable. These habits inform singers that they cannot always take a day off from thinking about vocal work just because they should not phonate. Instead of singing, other relevant work can be efficiently accomplished.

A singer's downtimes are crucial for practicing transcription, analyzing the harmony of a piece, reharmonizing a jazz lead sheet, or sequencing a recital song list giving attention to varying key, style, meter, tempo, and feel. Singers are encouraged to brainstorm other ways to accomplish necessary performance work in their practice sessions without overtly taxing the voice. This creativity in the practice room helps musicians stay consistent and healthy while steadily growing throughout their careers.

Creative Practice

Singers may create different ways to practice using play-along activities that provide accompaniment; Jamey Aebersold's wonderful Play-A-Long series of books and recordings are excellent resources. Other approaches to practice include singing in unison with oneself while improvising a solo on a piano or guitar, analyzing a song's music using Roman numeral harmonic analysis, or studying phrase delineations and melodic contour. Singers can dive into how the lyrics meld with the music and how the music reflects the meaning of the text. They can investigate the composer and lyricist, what political or historical relevance the song may have, and any background information available. The depth to which a musician can explore layers of a song is literally endless and only limited by one's imagination. When singers think outside the average parameters of song preparation, they learn much more about a song than they perhaps realized there was to know! The physical act of singing a song only scratches the surface of the many forms of practice that developing into a true jazz artist requires.

Journaling toward Mindfulness

Teachers would be wise to apply these suggestions for expanding students' practice routines in regular journaling assignments. Over many years of teaching university-level voice, music theatre, and jazz voice instruction, the process of journaling has remained an essential tool for enabling students to be responsible for their own daily progress. Those students who embraced journaling made noticeable improvements at every lesson. Those who took the journaling assignments less seriously or did not do them at all failed to practice efficiently and show improvement on a regular basis.

There is no end to the types of questions and assignments a practice journal can successfully explore. It becomes not only a log of assignments students routinely hand in but also a means through which they ask questions about practice habits, songs, and technique. Journaling gives students a medium for recording vocal progress, repertoire discoveries, research, successes, failures, performance reviews, rehearsal plans, listening assignments, fears, and goals. Journaling is an excellent way for a teacher to get to know students, their musical and mental needs, and their practice habits outside of the studio. Journaling can be a lifelong pursuit that helps singers to stay mindful about many facets of their art.

MENTAL TOUGHNESS

The concept of mental toughness is a trait every professional singer needs to cultivate to be capable of delivering a consistently strong performance amid life's surprises. This trait is extensively explored in the wonderful book by Shirlee Emmons and Alma Thomas, *Power Performance for Singers* (1998). Voice teachers can guide their students through exercises to help them become more confident performers who learn from every rehearsal, private lesson, and performance opportunity. Mental toughness involves establishing a routine of performance preparation, mindful performing, visualization of ideal performances prior to a concert, and critically analyzing performances after they are complete. The professional performing artist relies on mental toughness to proceed through a concert with clarity and concentration. This is particularly useful when "the show must go on" shortly after a performer is bereaved or during a bout of depression or illness. Mental toughness helps the singer focus on technique, diction, expression, and stagecraft rather than on their life circumstances or other distractions.

Sometimes singers must adjust their performance plans to practice self-care. This may mean switching performance nights with another artist when possible or swapping out a few sad songs from the song list for some lighter material. With mental toughness and self-care, singers can often get through a performance and even shine when enduring difficulty in their personal lives. As unfair as it may seem, sometimes performers have to keep their grief or physical pain to themselves so that a concert can proceed successfully. This harsh reality of show business may actually help heal the singer from an emotional affliction.

Singing does so often bring healing, so I encourage singers to sing even when they do not feel so inclined. Wise words I once was told by the legendary voice pedagogue Dale Moore went something like this:

"There will be days in your life when you won't feel like singing. Those are the days when it is most important for you to sing!" This is yet another display of mental toughness. Singers who can rise above their feelings of listless disinterest and be disciplined enough to gently practice on a consistent basis will grow more and more resilient with each passing day. Resilience is a necessary component of mental toughness that must be cultivated for a durable career.

Teaching Mental Toughness

How does a voice pedagogue approach the topic of mental toughness with students? I have found that building singers' confidence while building their technique is a wise undertaking that will aid them in growing mentally prepared for the unique challenges inherent in the life of a performing artist. Journaling assignments that demand focus and reflection on one's practice habits as well as evaluating one's own performances can help. I also found that requiring voice majors (whether classical, jazz, commercial, or music theatre) to sing for each other and provide performance feedback builds phenomenal tools for rapid improvement in technique, stagecraft, song preparation, and confidence as long as the teacher provides a strict and consistent set of boundaries.

The Studio Class

The forum in which all of my voice students gathered every couple of weeks to sing for one another became known as "studio class." This was an extra class period I provided so that my students could prepare for juries, recitals, auditions, and opera or music theatre roles in front of a supportive peer audience. Each student was required to sing for the rest of the students one to four times each semester (unless there was a medical reason that prevented their participation). Students signed up to sing three to five times each semester, based on their major, year in school, and number of songs they needed to perform that semester, whether for jury or recital. Students were required to perform each song from memory. This encouraged students to be well prepared for juries long before jury day arrived. If accompanists were provided for their lessons, those accompanists needed to be present to play for the singer's studio class. This afforded additional rehearsal and performance opportunities for the pianists as well as the singers, with free coaching provided by me. My students were always prepared for their jury performances well in advance if they followed these guidelines and made time in their schedules for these extremely beneficial class times.

Students were also given strict rules about feedback they were allowed to provide. No one but I was allowed to offer advice about vocal technique. Comments had to be framed within a positive light starting with a compliment. I always began the feedback stage following each singer's experience with "What would you like to say to _____ about the performance?" After becoming accustomed to the supportive, safe environment, students felt comfortable offering compliments and observations about noticeable improvements, and even asked questions delving deeper into translations, expressive techniques, and history behind the songs. Singers were required to know and share translations of all songs in non-English languages, as well as a bit of history behind each song. I made a point to prepare them in case they were asked by a faculty member in a jury situation to clarify the settings or other information about their pieces. I explained that prepared singers present their repertoire as relative experts, as if they are the most knowledgeable people in the room about the aspects of that song. This presented a challenge most of the time when I probed students with questions about the composer, setting, or story behind the piece to demonstrate how much I expected them to be able to share with the group.

When responding to others' performances, singers were asked to balance observations about what the singer could improve with a compliment about what went well during the performance. This practice not only lowered anxiety for each singer, but it created an environment for accelerated learning because students built trust with one another in the studio class experience. They could experiment and know their peers were cheering them on. They learned to listen and watch performances with a critical but empathetic ear and eye, and they learned how to communicate specifically about music and singing. Many things were taught and learned in the studio class environment that could not be taught in a private lesson or practice room. The addition of the supportive audience created a fantastic learning environment where all singers would arrive in anticipation of the beautiful music they would hear and leave with practical, salient ideas for improving their own performances.

Although many classical teachers may have such studio classes programmed into the voice curriculum, many jazz voice teachers do not. Encouraging jazz voice students to meet together and explore various ways of performing their songs is as valuable to them as studio classes are to classical voice majors. To adapt the studio class to accommodate jazz, a teacher might ask students to prepare a song with a guitar accompaniment for the first class (and invite a graduate jazz guitar major to accompany). For the second class, the teacher may invite a jazz piano accompanist to join the singers, and so on. While it is often good to let students determine which songs they perform at various points during the semester, I always encourage my singers to plan on singing their most difficult songs in front of their peers as early in the semester as possible. This gives them more time to hone and strengthen their performances and make them performance-ready before jury or recital time arrives. I also sit down several months ahead of a recital with each student and create a memorization timeline to make absolutely sure he or she has a plan that enables the student to perform with fully memorized text, pitches, rhythms, dynamics, articulation, and phrasing.

Huge boosts of confidence often occur for jazz voice majors in studio class or voice class environments because it is here, in the laboratory among their peers, that singers try the skills and techniques learned in private lessons. Regular lesson attendance coupled with several studio classes each semester facilitate marked improvement for the students who apply themselves.

Beyond the Classroom and onto the Stage

In addition to all this, jazz singers must be fully aware and rehearsed regarding how the accompaniment will sound, how the form of their piece unfolds, how to lead the band, and the finer points of handling themselves onstage. Improvised segments must be adequately rehearsed and worked out with full knowledge of the chord progressions. Providing jazz voice students with a variety of performance scenarios in a plethora of rooms, outdoor venues, and ensemble combinations will help to bolster singers' performance chops and ready them for whatever performance situations may arise. This is crucial preparation for all great jazz performers.

Mental Toughness of the Masters

Sarah Vaughan, Ella Fitzgerald, and countless other professional musicians have demonstrated mental toughness in their live performances whenever they sang in high-temperature surroundings (like under hot lights). Before the days of modern air-conditioning, musicians often had to hold a handkerchief in one hand to wipe away the sweat from their faces and brows. Delivering great shows amid obvious physical discomfort proves that a singer can focus on the music in the moment with ample mental toughness. Another example occurred whenever Fitzgerald forgot lyrics and improvised them instead of allowing her lapse to negatively affect her performance. She was determined to deliver her songs creatively and beautifully regardless of any temporary memory slip. Many fans considered these "lapses" the best parts of her concerts; they certainly displayed her genius. The finest jazz singers must work toward cultivating an improvisational sense adept enough to improvise whenever the need arises. Although text memorization must not be minimized in importance, when a memory lapse does happen, an instrumentalist misses a cue, or any number of other performance emergencies occur onstage, it is the experienced improviser with mental toughness that saves that musical moment for both the band and the appreciative audience.

Improvisation as a Tool to Develop Mental Toughness

Mental toughness can be increased as improvisation skills develop in a singer. Singers who are confident improvisers do far better in unexpected performance situations than those lacking improvisational skill. I confronted this truth as a twenty-one-year-old having my first international opera experience. When singing the role of Mozart's "Susanna" in Rome, I resorted to improvising text in Italian because my scene partner forgot his lines. For several measures in the fourth act of *Le Nozze di Figaro*, I sang Figaro's part (note to reader: always know the music assigned to the musicians around you!) and I improvised to fit the situation until my embarrassed compatriot jumped back onto the moving music train after several measures of sitting in stunned silence. The Italian audience generously applauded me afterward, remembering the moment and appreciating my impromptu solution to a potentially awkward and disastrous conundrum. The conductor approached me later to thank me for "saving the performance," as he fully expected a train wreck when the actor stopped singing his part. I was an accomplished jazz musician and knew how to improvise in the moment when I deemed it necessary. Looking back, I am thankful for that skill and for the mental toughness to take such a risk and pull it off successfully. Unexpected situations arise frequently during live performances. Programs like Opera Works have taught hundreds of opera and classical singers improvisational skills that have helped them become confident, mentally tough performers. Singers must be ready for a multitude of unexpected performance scenarios. Happy is the singer whose improvisational prowess exceeds the need for such abilities in the present moment.

Flow State

Mental toughness and mindfulness combined create the recipe for success that many artists call "flow state" or being "in the zone." This super-creative state of relaxation and attention facilitates creative spurts of disciplined concentration and unbridled artistic freedom. Flow cannot be attained in a medium of anxiety, distraction, or lack of preparation. Texting, scrolling on a device, checking email, or indulging any other distraction while practicing or performing music results in lack of focus, less effective practice and performance, and appearing scattered and unprepared before one's audience. If a singer must improvise over a passage of unknown chord changes, for example, flow state cannot be achieved. Likewise, if a singer is cramming to remember lyrics five minutes before the show, finer points of the performance like pitch precision, nuance, dynamic contrast, expression, and musicianship may suffer along with the delivery of correct text. Every audience, including a jury of voice faculty, deserves a performance free from wrong notes, rhythms, form mistakes, or other gross imperfections. The composer and lyricist deserve clean, artistic renderings of their songs at each performance of their work. Every band, singers included, ought to thoroughly know their music exceptionally well before presenting it in public. The more a singer prepares for success, the more likely success will meet the singer onstage on a regular basis.

The value of both mindful singing and mental toughness to a professional singer cannot be overstated. Singing mindfully may be accomplished by turning complete attention to one's breath, lyrics, or music. It can also be enhanced by focused study on diction, textual analysis, relevant background information about the song, composer, or lyricist, and any number of other nonsinging activities that render one an expert song stylist. Completing preparatory work well in advance of the performance date allows for the singer to sleep without anxiety and fully focus on making music in the moment. One of the most wonderful aspects of being a successful performer is awaking rested on the morning of a performance knowing that all the work has been done and all that is left is to show up and sing the concert. When mindful singing has been achieved, a singer has mastered the notes, rhythms, dynamics, articulation, chord analysis, and all other musical aspects necessary for a successful performance before arriving at the venue. Mental toughness can yield a strong performance when the singer devotes all energy toward immersion in creative moments that the music brings forth. Together, these two complex skills can add vitality and confidence to a well-prepared performance, making it thoroughly enjoyable and possibly even brilliant for the performer, band, and audience.

14

ARRANGING AND BANDLEADING

The most marketable jazz singers in the modern world possess more than just excellent singing skills. To pursue performance as a viable career, additional skills in arranging are increasingly practical and helpful. Becoming a competent arranger requires music literacy and a solid foundation in music theory. Bandleading constitutes yet another recommended area of expertise for the working jazz singer. Once the singer has prepared the voice, the "book" of arrangements must be prepared, and finally, the singer must learn to lead effectively on the stage.

THE JAZZ SINGER-ARRANGER

The modern jazz singer's arranging skills determine how well prepared he or she can become when readying for a performance. Few singers can afford to rely exclusively on the written song arrangements others write to build their book of charts. Singers whose arranging prowess shines stays far more marketable over time than one less capable of presenting their own music arrangements in live performances. Unfortunately, the dearth in competent jazz singer-arrangers has propagated the bias that when singers bring a "book" of their own to an engagement, the band should expect chords to be inaccurate, forms to be wrong, and any number of aspects of musicianship to be shoddy and poor. Although I cannot remedy this shortcoming in a single chapter of a book, I urge the reader to invest in a jazz arranging course or two at a university and to become aware of my column, "Anatomy of a Standard" at *All About Jazz*, which explores musical and textual analysis of jazz standards.

"Anatomy of a Standard"

The column has been invaluable to jazz teachers, performers, and students alike because it displays the outstanding workmanship behind Great American Songbook standards, suggesting reasons why they have endured as works of art. The marriage of music and text was not a chance happening within the songs that have become standards in the repertoire of every jazz musician. This marriage involved intentional pairing by the composer and lyricist that can be better appreciated with a bit of knowledge and analytical skill. Singers must learn how to analyze a piece of music to notice patterns and noteworthy aspects of its construction. This is the first step in understanding how crafting an arrangement can beautifully frame repertoire in ways that express one's unique voice and creative spirit.

Mastering theory skills is step one toward becoming a competent arranger. Cultivating strong transcription skills is step two (which requires outstanding ear training). With these tools, aspiring professional jazz singers can be on the road toward creating the book of arrangements truly tailored for their own voice, personality, and skill set. No other arranger can perfectly cultivate this for you, so it behooves you to dig deeply and develop the skills as early in your career as possible.

A Case in Point

I have loved my career as a singer-arranger-composer, and I would not have changed a thing as I look back on decades of singing my own music. I began learning the art of arranging while yet a teenager and created my own charts (song arrangements) on pages of manuscript paper by hand. I still do this from time to time, although I more often use notation software now for ease of reading and digital storage of charts. The ability to create my own harmonically correct, unique, and formally interesting charts has played an enormous role in my career as a jazz performer at festivals and on performing arts center stages, in one-woman shows and cabaret, and as a big band and symphony pops soloist. Today I accept commissions to create tailor-made concerts for large venues seeking jazz bands with a singer for concert series, cabaret stages, jazz festivals, and symphony pops concerts. Although the reader may not aspire to do nearly this much in terms of arranging, I encourage every jazz singer to become a good enough arranger to know how to transpose a song into your preferred key, add your own composed beginning and ending, modify the feel and tempo as needed, and create a professional-looking (and sounding) arrangement. Without arranging skills of your own, you will always be dependent on a "musical director" or pianist to do this work for you. I have always encouraged my student singers to rise to their potential as competent bandleaders whose musicianship matches or exceeds that of the instrumentalists they hire to play with them. Without the ability to arrange and authoritatively lead a band, a singer will always be viewed as a "sideman" (or woman) and never a leader.

The Same Brain Principle

Arranging for one's own voice is a particularly rewarding endeavor for a professional musician. It represents a blending of logical and creative activities undertaken by the same brain (writing a chart specifically for one's own voice to sing) rather than having someone else do the practical theory work. Peggy Lee, for example, wrote 270 songs for her own voice to sing, which enabled her to play to her own strengths. She explored source material and styles that particularly interested her. When the same mind that writes or arranges a piece also performs the piece, beautiful things happen and audiences notice. When singing a piece you arrange, you instinctively know that arrangement better than the others on the stage and automatically become the resident expert on that chart. You also have complete control over preferred key, tempo, style, feel, introductory and final chord progressions or motives, and expressive devices that you can apply as you craft the arrangement to reflect your best singing work. As your arranging and theory skills improve, those reading your charts will grow in their respect for you and their trust that your charts will be correct, clear, and musically worthwhile. These are important bridges to build with your band, even if you only perform with them once.

Piano Skills

Singers are strongly encouraged to pursue some measure of jazz piano training so that their arranging skills may grow. Although a singer may never aspire to accompany himself or herself or be hired as a jazz pianist, piano training will greatly inform his or her choices of how to harmonize transcribed melodies, create chord substitutions that make sense, and compose introductions and endings that beautifully frame lead sheet arrangements. These finishing touches are absolutely necessary to be taken seriously as a musical professional in jazz circles.

When I hear jazz players talk about only playing "head" arrangements (memorized lead sheets of standard chord changes) as if there were no other way to play jazz, I instantly realize that I may be dealing with people whose own arranging skills have never been developed. Although it's fun to jam, call a tune, and just play it however it comes out, that is not the norm in the context of most professional, world-class jazz concerts. A well-crafted arrangement leaves some room for improvisational solos but creates a clear road map that proves the arranger-musician has put some time, effort, and energy into framing and interpreting the song uniquely. The arranger's added attention to the chart makes the audience appreciate this new rendering of a favorite tune. Many musicians can play "Rhythm Changes" by heart but presenting it in the context of a terrific arrangement is part of the fun and challenge of performing at a professional level. Playing jam after jam of unrehearsed standards, while important for the development of a student musician's ears, repertoire, improvisational abilities, and stage presence, should not be the final goal of the concert jazz musician or the recording artist. Beyond the jam session, self-written arrangements that are professionally polished grace every serious jazz singer's book. For many jazz artists, a professional concert appearance or recording date is neither the time nor the place to call a series of "head" arrangements, hoping that everyone stays together and comes up with workable endings without a plan.

CONSTRUCTING A PROFESSIONAL ARRANGEMENT

Every good arrangement has an original, notated beginning and ending, is written in the preferred key of the singer, and possesses a clear road map of the form with double bar delineations between major sections of the piece (e.g., every eight bars in a thirty-two-bar AABA-form standard). A good arrangement also indicates "Concert" in the upper left-hand corner, which means the chart is in concert key (for C instruments). Transposing instruments should have their own charts in the correctly transposed key so they don't have to sight-transpose while looking at a concert chart. The designated part is indicated in the upper left corner of the first page (e.g.,

"Trumpet in Bb," "Alto Sax in Eb," or "Concert," etc.) so that charts for each instrument are prepared (transposed if necessary) and placed in each player's book.

Use the Right Changes

My chord changes for standards tend to be consistent with the multiple volumes of *The Real Book* published by Sher (or a transcription from a recording). On some occasions I have specifically reharmonized passages to align with alternate chords I want played. Singers are wise to note that when playing with a new band, using harmonies that are consistent with the accepted changes of standard tunes is smart. I recommend that student singers use tried-and-true chord progressions available in *The Real Book* before venturing into reharmonization. I encourage all jazz singers to study advanced jazz theory so they can become well versed in "reharm," arranging, orchestration, transposition, and basic jazz piano skills—all that will enhance singing and bandleading abilities.

Transposing for Instruments

Arrangers must be familiar with what transpositions their band members need. Trumpets, tenor saxophones, and clarinets play Bb instruments. This means that their charts must be transposed up a major second from the concert key to match the tonality played by C instruments (piano, guitar, and bass). So, if your arrangement of "My Funny Valentine" begins in concert A minor (no sharps or flats in the key signature), a trumpeter or tenor saxophonist would need to read it up a step in B minor (two sharps in the key signature) to correctly play it on their instrument in concert with the rest of the band. Piano, guitar, and bass can read from "concert" charts, although the bass reads an octave higher (when in bass clef) than the pitches being played, so it, too, is a transposing instrument (down an octave from concert key). This means that when bassists read C3 (one C below middle C), they actually play C2, which is an octave lower. Understanding these realities is important so that the singer-arranger can be more cognizant of the tonal parameters of each instrument in the band and keep written arrangements within comfortable, viable ranges for all instrumentalists. Studying a bit of orchestration does wonders for brushing up on transposition skills needed to create workable arrangements for the variety of instrumentalists with which a singer may eventually collaborate.

The Road Map

At the beginning of the arrangement a few basic items must be indicated. Meter is generally only shown in the time signature at the beginning (until a change of meter occurs), but it is helpful to carry key signatures down to the beginning of every stave so that players remember in what key they are playing. This is particularly helpful whenever a song has been transposed out of "standard" key into a tonal center more comfortable for the singer-arranger. Because songs meander through various tonal centers, instrumentalists appreciate having the reminder about what the tonic key is at the beginning of each line. Tempo and feel must always be shown just above the first measure, and the song title should be centered at the top of the first page and shown centered at the top or bottom of each successive page followed by a page number (i.e., "My Funny Valentine, p. 2). I like to write "Intro" flush left and above the first measure of the Introduction (if there is one), and I also write "Coda" at the start of the ending, even if a coda sign is there. I use form delineators A, B, C, D, and so on with boxes around the letters to show rehearsal sections. I end my arrangements with the word "Fine" in the correct place under the final measure so that players know where the end is located. There are so often repeats in jazz music, or a "*dal segno*" (D.S.), which takes the player back to a previous place in the chart, that the ending measure must be clearly marked whether it is situated as the final measure or somewhere else. Sometimes the D.S. leads to a song ending midway through a chart. The standard practice of creating clear form delineations makes rehearsing and discussing the chart easy and straightforward.

Setting up the chart to have four measures per line is a great practice when you intend to include chord symbols above the staff, the melody on the staff, and lyrics below the staff. All this information should be present for each of your vocal charts because they give your band members plenty of information at their fingertips. Charts that omit the lyrics, for example, leave some players wondering where the singer is because they cannot follow any words if someone's counting goes awry. Lyrics help instrumentalists follow the singer and serve as a memory aid for a singer when preparing songs for performance. I also recommend notating the melody, even when it is well known. Instrumentalists can use this notated melody to create a melodic improvisation when they play an improvised solo. Because vocal charts are often transposed to different keys for different singers, notating the melody in the singer's key represents a courtesy to the band. I have heard some instrumentalists complain, especially at jam sessions, about a singer's chosen keys. Singers are encouraged to consider the instrumentation of the band by avoiding keys that will be overly difficult to play. For example, guitarists play in sharp keys more often than flat keys, so one is wise not to hand a guitarist a piece in D-flat unless there is ample time to rehearse it. Whenever possible, a singer is wise to move a song in a complex key to a key that is easier to play (having fewer sharps or flats in a key signature) because, although this week you may be accompanied by a jazz piano veteran who can play standards in every key, next week you may be accompanied by an undergraduate who has never previously heard the song. I encourage students to write arrangements that are easily read and performed by everyone so that a chart only needs to be written once.

Know Your Band

Singer-arrangers should know their transposing band members' limitations; an alto saxophonist must add three sharps to the concert key, for example. Handing that instrumentalist something in the concert key of B major would cause the player to sit out and not even attempt to play that chart. Being a conscientious arranger means that you may have to sacrifice a bit of comfort to accommodate the people reading your arrangements. Although F# Major might seem like a perfect key for your voice, it will not be comfortable for anyone else, so the chart should be moved to either F or G. Further, the tuning of the band suffers when members are forced to play outside of their strongest keys. Learn to adjust, adapt, and choose reasonable keys for your colleagues. Concert keys of C, F, Bb, Eb, G, and occasionally D (unless it will be played by an alto saxophonist) give singers plenty of variation without sending the band into distant keys where members do not wish to play. The farther the key is into remote tonal areas (e.g., C flat or F sharp), the harder it will be for the player to read the part and play it in tune.

Sometimes, no matter how conscientious a singer may be about choosing reasonable keys for their songs, a chart winds up on the song list in a difficult key. There are multiple ways to solve this problem. One is to transpose the song to an easier key a half step away. Another solution may be to consider your instrumentation, and if your pianist loves to play in D-flat (like I do!) let him or her play in that key with you as a duo and give the other members of your band a rest. This adds variety to your song list, too, by changing the texture and giving your audience a break from the same combination of players song after song. As a bandleader I love finding ways to feature one band member at a time, so I routinely plan vocal-drum set duets, vocal-bass duets, and vocal-guitar duets. This practice provides instrumentation changes, periodic rest for the band members one at a time without taking a break, and opportunities for the audience to hear instrumentalists featured on a more intimate, focused level. Know your instrumentalists' favorite keys and play to their strengths, as Duke Ellington did when writing arrangements for his band.

Arranging Tips

Some clever introductions or endings include imitative, canonic passages; some consist of short motives found within the melody of the song; and others incorporate the seldom-performed introductory verse that was originally written to open the song. Introductions need not be four or eight bars in length; trying a five-measure or nine-measure introduction provides added interest for the band and the audience. This practice can be a good way to make charts less predictable and to challenge the band. Melodic motives often provide good source material for introductions and endings. A well-constructed introduction can sometimes double as an interlude. I suggest making the commitment not to use "stock" endings that are ubiquitously played at jam sessions. Instead, listen to contemporary arrangements of standards and work on making endings unique.

EXERCISE

Write a five-measure or nine-measure introduction using a melodic motive and see how it adds distinctiveness and quality to your arrangement. Try including interludes between verses.

Arranging as an Essential Practice

Arranging skills should not be considered optional in contemporary jazz. Arranging for one's own band has become part of the measuring stick of every quality jazz musician. Jazz as an improvisational art form necessitates bringing one's own "voice" and creative ideas to one's repertoire. Thoughtfully arranging one's songs creates the opportunity to introduce yourself both to your audience and your band as a highly skilled, unique jazz artist that defies comparison with other artists. Because advanced arranging concepts lie beyond the scope of this book, I strongly suggest taking courses or lessons with an arranging teacher to build these necessary skills.

PLAYING WITH STYLES

One of my favorite roles as an arranger is to take a song that was written in a particular style or feel and change the feel. For example, sometimes I will modify a ballad to become a tango, which works well when both are in 4/4 meter. The tango feel "dresses up" a minor-key ballad, adding a touch of sophistication and mystery. Another favorite way to rearrange a ballad (or swing tune) is to reconstitute it into a three-beat pattern and turn it into a waltz. This requires a bit of mathematical adaptation, of course, to accommodate all the beats necessary to keep the essential character of the melody intact. Creating waltzes from ballads is an easy way to refresh and revitalize your repertoire. The livelier feel of a jazz waltz allows a singer to enjoy more ballads in a song list without keeping the energy low and tempos slow. It is important to note that a singer can (and should) still swing in the waltz feel. Where harmonic rhythms in four were written at the level of a half note, they become transformed to a dotted quarter note for a waltz, creating a syncopated division of the measure into equal halves. This gives the waltz a lilting, mobile character that is fun to play. Often, a full measure of waltz can stand in the place of a half measure of 4/4 swing; the singer-arranger simply should play with the timing and discover what works best for the flow of the lyric as the music moves from a four-beat pattern to a three-beat pattern.

Another adaptation I often use to modify my swing tunes is to play them with a straight-eighth note (Latin) feel. This yields a new, simmering twist to a well-known song. Ballads can be sped up to a fast bebop feel (like the bebop players often did in that era of jazz history), but if this arranging option is chosen, the arranger must be sure the lyrics do not become impossible to cleanly sing. Many lyrics are set to sustained rhythms spread over several measures, but others are syllabic, meaning that every melody note has its own syllable of text. When this is the case, bebop lyrics become extremely fast and difficult to deliver, so trying an arranging idea before committing to it is strongly advisable. Sometimes at bebop tempos I like to double the harmonic rhythm (a compositional device called "rhythmic augmentation"), making the song feel fast while allowing more measures to deliver the lyrics over slower-changing harmony. In this case a half note harmonic rhythm for a ballad would become a whole note harmonic rhythm when sped up to bebop tempo. Remembering that a singer must deliver lyrics in some semblance of good form will help create a bebop chart that sizzles without causing the lyrics to become lost and unsingable.

Peggy Lee turned Rodgers and Hart's ballad "Lover" from the Broadway musical *Babes in Arms* into a fast samba and created a hit. This was an early example of an artist-arranger modifying the tempo and feel of a jazz standard to reflect the individuality of the singer performing the song. She also succeeded in creating much more aggressive and sultry textual overtones than the original version had with her choice of having several percussionists imitate galloping horses. The resulting arrangement took an innocent song from an old musical and turned it into a highly suggestive recording for the period. Lee's take on "Lover" perfectly illustrated the way artist-arrangers can affect the historical trajectory of a song in the jazz standard canon as well as cement their image as a music innovator.

BANDLEADING

Learning to effectively lead a band should be part of every working jazz singer's skill set. Though years of experience are the best teacher, several areas deserve particular attention for the burgeoning bandleader. Finding the balance between nurturing talent and creativity while keeping musicians on task can be tricky work. Effective bandleaders learn to encourage their musicians toward their greatest potential while also earning their respect. Outstanding bandleaders gently but firmly expect excellence and help band members deliver it. Mutual respect must be part of every ensemble. Stage etiquette often comes into play in conjunction with being a supportive band member and knowing the difference in roles.

Starting as a Sideman

Sidemen (as nonleaders or band members are generally called in professional circles) need to be shown respect as well as to show respect for the leader. This means not contradicting or offering to improve the leader's ideas or suggestions. The leader makes decisions for the band. Questioning, arguing, or contradicting the leader do not add strength to a band; they only weaken it and force the leader to take a more aggressive stance. Learning first how to be a cooperative, supportive sideman is the first step toward developing one's own leadership skills. Singers are wise to avoid a confrontational attitude and always show professionalism.

Sidemen must be prepared with music learned when they show up for rehearsal. If the music was sent in advance, a singer must be sure to solidly know it and be ready to perform it at the start of rehearsal. Sight-reading during a rehearsal is only appropriate if the music has been handed out at the rehearsal. If a leader has asked for something specific from you, show that you can take direction and cooperate. Becoming a trustworthy and excellent bandmate must be a singer's first priority; nobody wants to work with someone who creates trouble or slows down a rehearsal. Stage etiquette is demonstrated in part by how cooperative a bandmate you can be.

Introducing the Band

An important aspect of bandleading includes knowing how and when to introduce band members. Often in jazz it is appropriate immediately after an improvised solo to say the name of the player to draw the audience's attention toward that person. This practice is best saved for a natural pause in the set, like on the final song before a break. Introducing the band can also be done when speaking directly to the audience as the final song is introduced. During bows and applause at the end of the concert one more effort should be made to introduce the band. Some bands like to play a final song that serves as "exit music" like a blues that can be improvised for a number of choruses until all the speaking is finished. In this way the band puts a strong ending on the set. Such considerations are important to work out in advance. Bands should rehearse an encore in addition to their sets, in case an audience requests it. Another alternative is to arrange "exit music" specially designed to overlay the applause as the band gets introduced. Giving each band member a short bit to do in this music can serve as a professional finish at the end of an excellent show.

The Book

A singer's book refers to any number of organizational systems used today to present charts to a band. Some singers use three-ring binders with songs in alphabetical or numeric order. Other singers (like myself) bring only charts that will be performed that evening. I pull from a master book for each instrumentalist, each of which contains hundreds of alphabetized arrangements. I put the selected charts into separately labeled file folders.

One file ("book") corresponds to one member of the band, with charts arranged in performance order for that instrument. I have separate, mostly identical books for guitar, piano, bass, and drums, and a transposed book for Bb instruments (trumpet, tenor saxophone, or clarinet) plus a book for alto saxophone (an Eb instrument). This type of organization ensures that all members of my band have their own copies of the music I expect to play, and each generally sees the same instructions and road map on every chart. I prefer writing tailor-made lead sheet arrangements showing chord progressions, melodies, lyrics, articulation, dynamics, and original beginnings and endings. Every player in the band reads essentially the same chart, tailored to their needs.

The Song List

Before each concert I create a song list and pull the charts from each large book, placing them in performance order so I can begin creating a gestalt of the performance flow in my mind. The song list shows the number of sets and the precise order of songs in each set. This requires that I spend time before each concert placing every instrumentalist's book in order, only bringing charts that will be played at that particular concert.

Singers are wise to spend considerable time planning their song order for each concert in their schedule. Audiences do not want to hear the same songs in the same order every time they come to see you unless you are doing a specific show with an advertised theme or title (like a tribute show paying homage to a particular singer or composer). When selecting repertoire for a performance, consider your audience, the venue, the time, and other important considerations. If playing in a theatre, you are smart to plan patter or comments between songs or groups of songs (sometimes thought of as miniature sets), which will put a professional shine on your musical performance. Also, consider the average age and demographics of your audience before selecting repertoire that might alienate anyone. Planning music that keeps people listening is an art form in itself. Starting with something up-tempo begins the concert at a high energy level, which excites the audience. Following that with a medium-fast swing tune keeps the energy high and helps listeners relax into the groove the band has set. Next, a conscientious singer changes the feel or tempo. A medium Latin song or a jazz waltz in the third song spot keeps the energy strong while providing a change. A ballad comes next, which allows the built-up tension to release before starting the cycle over again. A singer is wise to modify the tempo and feel frequently enough to add interest and unpredictability to the performance.

Keys are important as a song list comes together. Audiences, believe it or not, experience tiredness of the same key if it is repeated even once, except within a medley (more than one song flowing uninterruptedly to the next song). Juxtaposing distantly related keys next to one another in a song order constantly refreshes an audience's ears and prevents listener's fatigue. This requires a singer to be a savvy enough arranger to set songs in a variety of keys. Singers must not get stuck in the rut of putting every song in Bb or audiences will be perpetually bored and not take them seriously. Keys matter.

The Rehearsal

At band rehearsals songs should be rehearsed in performance order, at least talking through the form of each arrangement and pointing out tricky spots within each one. Any challenging beginnings and endings should receive special attention. Rehearsals should start and end on time and be focused on the music. Rehearsals do not require all the sound equipment that will be used at the concert, but they should allow players and singers to hear one another to get a true sense of what the blend should sound like. Rehearsals should provide the band with all the information they need to deliver a polished, informed performance in concert with the rest of the performers.

Band Etiquette

Certain characteristics make for great band relationships. Punctuality, reliability, respect for others, a sense of humor, consistently good preparation, and musical excellence help to create good rapport among band members. Leaders must maintain a patient, supportive attitude that can also keep members on task. Although this may be hard to develop, it is worth the effort. Professionalism and mature leadership are equally important; the unexpected will happen and when it does, rolling with it will help provide a band with the confidence that with you at the helm, they can accomplish anything. Politeness, appropriate dress, and dependability go a long way in the music business, and word gets around about attitudes and experiences. Jazz musicians talk freely with and about one another, so strive to be that singer-leader with which band members throughout your region love to collaborate.

Stage Presence

Behaviors and skills singer-bandleaders should develop as they work on stage presence include mindful walking, standing, sitting, and moving on the stage; engaging the audience with light humor, stories, or background information about songs; and using meaningful, natural gestures. Singers will develop stage presence in different ways. Some never tell stories or even talk to the audience, yet still succeed as masterful communicators. Singers should be sure to let the music do most of the talking. Many singers make the mistake of talking too much and singing too little. Preparing and rehearsing dialogue, video recording one's practice sessions, and watching recordings of rehearsals and performances enhance overall performance skills. Improving one's stage presence represents an important priority in performance preparation for every singer-bandleader.

Singers must consider arranging and bandleading skills to be as important to cultivate as vocal technique and repertoire development. Honing those skills through formal instruction or experience will enhance the total performance in practical ways. Building a repertoire of quality arrangements, creating effective song lists, and becoming an excellent band member are necessary before bandleading can be successful. Finally, developing one's stage presence provides a professional finish to the behind-the-scenes work that every jazz artist must undertake.

15

ARTISTRY AND PEDAGOGY— PUTTING IT ALL TOGETHER

The coordination of body, breath, mind, voice, and heart is where the key to artistry lies. True artists must hone their vocal technique, energize the tone with breath, maintain mental focus, and express the text and music with sincerity, musicality, excellent preparation, and nuance. Likewise, a thorough understanding of how to teach voice from the perspective of healthy habits, energy efficiency, and physical freedom creates a bedrock of understanding for the jazz voice pedagogue. All voice teachers assemble their own collection of general truths, exercises, patterns, and systems that they glean through the years from their teachers, from books and articles about singing, from workshops and master classes attended or watched online, and from valuable experience on the stage, in the practice room, and in the teaching studio. All of these sources form a composite technique and method that can be used for training many voice types having a myriad of distinct qualities. How to instruct singers to attain vocal freedom is a universal concept that teachers of every singing style must undertake. As with athletic training, the process of training to become a true artist requires years of study in a healthy direction to produce lasting results.

THE COMPLETE SINGING ARTIST

Complete singing artists modify their singing approach according to the particulars of the setting. Outdoor gigs with symphony pops orchestras may require a fuller tone quality than a small, intimate room with just a piano accompaniment. In large ensemble situations, the singer must make timbral adjustments to purify vowels to find formants that will help the voice carry above the orchestra, even when using a microphone. When the venue is large, the voice must carry further. Sarah Vaughan, capable of singing operatically in range and volume when the venue called for it, frequently let her audience hear the fullness of her beautiful, unrestrained instrument. Possessing a broad dynamic compass and displaying it regularly, her artistry shined in both large and small venues.

Likewise, the singing artist knows how to play with overtones to accommodate different performance situations. Sometimes when singing with a new technical engineer at the mixing board, a singer is challenged with levels not being exactly right. By manipulating overtones and brightening or darkening vowels, a singer can improve the EQ settings the audience hears without involving the technical director. Employing a touch of nasality can bring the tone forward into the mask. Using an "inside smile" (feeling a lift in the cheeks and smiling with facial muscles just under the eyes) can brighten vowels and clean up enunciation while making the face look more alive and engaged. The experienced singer finds ways to troubleshoot and make the best of the situation at hand because there is no perfect performance or performance situation.

Becoming an artist is not a given for every singer. To become a true artist means to master several aspects of voice technique, musicianship, and communication through years of training and disciplined practice. An artist makes sacrifices to place art and self-care on higher priority levels than most other facets of modern life. Singing artists give up things that are detrimental to their health or wellness. Singing artists make commitments to diligently and consistently care for their instruments by abstaining from habits, foods, and substances that cause vocal harm or compromised singing. These vary from singer to singer but may include alcohol, dairy products, gluten, acidic foods, tobacco, soft drinks, drugs, certain medications, and late-night gatherings in noisy rooms. Artists must protect their ears from unnecessary noise and avoid crowds and loud events that might damage hearing. Artists avoid speaking over room noise, shouting, and exposing the vocal organ to known allergens like pollen during allergy season. Singing artists wear face masks to filter out pollen on high-allergy days, and they wear masks indoors during pandemics involving respiratory pathogens. Professional singers take precautions seriously because they take their voices and physical health seriously.

THE SINGER-ENTREPRENEUR

Entrepreneurial singers succeed by creating work for themselves. To ensure career sustainability, it is smart to pursue a wider palette of training that forces singers to develop other related skills. A degree in arts management following a degree in voice may enable singers to fund their passion more substantially than having two voice degrees. Being able to record and edit video for other artists may create an excellent business venture for the singer who is skilled in recording and editing technology. Singers that compose music may register their titles with a performing rights organization like ASCAP to collect performance royalties when their music is performed or recorded. In these times, developing multiple skills and multiplying streams of income are essential practices for a sustainable career in the arts.

Many of the finest high school choir directors possess solo quality voices. Many of these multitalented artists sing to supplement their full-time income as music teachers. Others assume administrative occupations, putting to good use the discipline and systematic problem solving that playing music well requires. Others may occupy careers in the recording industry, music publishing, music agencies, publicity, music technology, or other related vocations. The pursuit of a musical education yields many more pathways than simply a career as a full-time performing artist, and modern music programs at universities and schools of music are wise to require students to minor in business, arts administration, or other helpful disciplines. Forward-thinking, prudent singers identify and develop additional areas of expertise to ensure employability later. Singers are wise to major or minor in fields that expand employability and to obtain practical work experience through internships, summer jobs, part-time work, or assistantships within those fields.

ALTERNATE PATHS

Many singers make the difficult decision to turn toward another career path because being an artist means total dedication to a craft at the expense of other pursuits, some mentioned previously. Many follow another career path because a performance career does not guarantee sustainable financial compensation. Those singers making tough choices are to be highly commended, for they can still contribute beauty and art to the world without the pressure of maintaining a full-time career as a performing artist. Countless singers with advanced degrees in voice grace community choirs and church choirs, direct high school music programs, and serve as arts administrators. Part-time singers occupy myriad other employment positions in local communities into which they pour their considerable talents. Trained singers are vital to the local community arts scene. Local and regional arts organizations and houses of worship provide avenues for singers to consistently enjoy sharing their gifts.

A COMPLETE PEDAGOGY

For those who become teacher-performers, learning to organize the studio and the instruction that occurs therein remains an essential priority. Teachers gain efficiency and effectiveness in their pedagogy through simple planning. A primary aspect of such studio organization involves keeping careful notes about every lesson and student.

Record Keeping

Various methods of documenting lessons assist the modern voice pedagogue. In whatever manner one chooses to accomplish it, attention should be paid toward noting what material is taught, rehearsed, and presented during each lesson. Goal setting remains a high priority for the voice teacher, and discussing goals with students helps them to develop achievable goals for themselves. Using the lesson log, the video log, and the repertoire list can help a young teacher focus on immediate needs for each lesson while keeping an eye on the big picture of longer-term goals.

The Lesson Log

As students begin learning breath management, posture and alignment, and other aspects of voice instruction in the university setting, I have found it necessary to keep careful records of every lesson taught. In my twenty-six years of university-level applied teaching, I have used a lesson log template (see figure 15.1). At the top of a sheet of blank loose-leaf paper I place the student's name, year, current semester, contact information, major, and degree program (bachelor of arts versus bachelor of music, for instance, is an important designation to indicate at many institutions because these two degrees have different requirements and

Student Name   BA / Jazz Voice Performance
Contact phone/email   Freshman   Fa21

1) 9/8/21. We talked about previous singing experience, his goals for the semester, and worked on alignment. I presented the Points of Balance and basic breathing technique. Assigned "Come Fly with Me." Asked him to scat melody and perform major, natural minor, and blues scales next time. [Grade: 95]

2) 9/15/21. 5 minutes late. I reiterated the lateness policy and suggested he re-read syllabus. Reviewed breath management and tension release (tends to breathe high in chest). Worked on melodic precision in "Come Fly with Me" and checked 3 assigned scales. Having some trouble with blues scale, so I also assigned 12-bar-blues in F for next time. We talked about blues form and how the scale fits in every phrase. [Grade: 88]

3) 9/22/21. "Come Fly with Me" is memorized. Worked on clean onsets, discussed breathy and glottal onset production. We worked on singing root motion of the harmony and embellishing melodic scat. Blues scale sounds much better when singing it over 12-bar-blues. I played a recording of "Shulie a Bop" (Sarah Vaughan) and he discussed what he heard (vertical, harmonic approach to scat-singing, rhythmic and pitch precision). Assigned a 16-bar transcription of this for him to complete by the end of the semester. Collected journal. [Grade: 91]

9/29/21. Canceled due to illness, submitted doctor's note. Give makeup.

4) 10/4/21. STUDIO CLASS #1 (makeup for 9/29). After group warmup, he performed "Come Fly with Me" for class, completely memorized. Improvised a 16-bar solo and used text-based improv for the rest of the tune. Received good feedback from class about adding more expression and releasing shoulder tension. [Grade: 94]

5) 10/6/21. Talked briefly about studio class performance, collected journal, worked on notating transcription more accurately. Needs help hearing and notating rhythms. Worked on singing the transcribed solo and improvising lyrics to the 12-bar-blues using the blues scale. [Grade: 90]

6) 10/13/21. Assigned "Bye Bye Blackbird." Should learn melody on scat syllables and be able to sing root motion next week. "Come Fly with Me" is coming along well—venturing beyond melodic embellishment for solos. Can now arpeggiate chord changes throughout the song and is nailing the root motion. Assigned pentatonic and whole-tone scales. [Grade: 95]

7) 10/20/21. Ten minutes late. Arrived rushed and stressed, so we spent more time on breathing and gently warming up. Ran through "Bye Bye Blackbird" for the remaining 5 minutes. Collected journal. [Grade: 82]

Figure 15.1. The Lesson Log. Courtesy of Author

expectations). I then list each actual lesson taught, entering the date and the number of the lesson for that semester (lesson 2 of 12, for instance). For each lesson I write brief notes about any discoveries made, improvements, particular struggles, technical aspects I covered, and repertoire rehearsed, numbering accordingly down the page as I add lessons. I also indicate what assignments were given that day. Each lesson description takes two to five lines, depending on how in-depth I wish to go and how much was accomplished, or what concerns arose.

If a student misses a lesson for any reason I indicate that next to the date. If the absence is unexcused, the lesson is numbered and factored into the student's grade as the syllabus requires. If the absence is excused (again referring to the syllabus and departmental guidance), I indicate that next to the date but only give a number to the makeup lesson that will be offered at a later date, often via a studio class. I use studio classes as group makeup lessons for those who have excused absences so that my limited time can be spent teaching well and facilitating performance opportunities for students rather than trying to make up ten students' missed lessons on my own time. If a student is late, I indicate that in my report so that I can factor that into the final grade as stated in the syllabus and so that I can account for the time that was missed if we fail to meet our goals. Students are expected to arrive to lessons warmed up, but I still guide them through a few exercises to ascertain their vocal condition that day.

I keep all students' lesson report sheets in a binder in the order in which I see them during the week so that one student's lesson flows into the next. I add sheets of paper for lesson reports as the semester progresses, as needed. Missed lesson policies are decided on a teacher-by-teacher and program-by-program basis. Makeup lessons are indicated as such and receive the same descriptive treatment with a number signifying how many lessons the student has accumulated thus far in the semester. This gives me a running total of lessons given so I can help keep the student on track. In the margin next to each completed lesson is a number grade for that day based on criteria listed clearly in the course syllabus. The lesson log is indispensable for the university teacher as well as independent teachers who wish to track students' progress and repertoire. The log provides an easy way to keep careful notes pertaining to attendance, assignments, material covered, improvements made, new challenges discovered, the teacher's goals for the student, and daily lesson grades.

The Repertoire Sheet

On a separate typed sheet I list the student's name at the top with his or her major and degree program only. Figure 15.2 shows the repertoire sheet used for the student's entire college career or semesters in my studio (usually seven or eight semesters). I list eight category headings from freshman I (fall of freshman year) through senior II (spring of senior year), with semesters and years indicated next to each. Throughout every semester, I list the repertoire assigned and actually studied, especially jury or recital repertoire. I indicate any semesters spent abroad or missed

Student Name   BA Music/Music Ed

<u>Freshman I</u>   (Fa20)   <u>Freshman II</u> (Sp21)
Centerpiece (FM)   Route 66 (FM)
Lost Your Head Blues (BbM)   Blue Bossa (dm)
The Girl from Ipanema (CM)   I Thought About You (EbM)

<u>Sophomore I</u> (Fa21)   <u>Sophomore II</u> (Sp22)
Come Fly with Me (BbM)
Bye Bye Blackbird (CM)
Corcovado (GM)
Up Jumped Springtime (BbM)

<u>Junior I</u> (Fa22)   <u>Junior II</u> (Sp23)

<u>Senior I</u> (Fa23)   <u>Senior II</u> (Sp24)

Figure 15.2. The Repertoire Sheet. Courtesy of Author

due to illnesses or leaves of absence. This record helps me remember
what songs the student has studied; which languages, styles, or eras have
been represented; composers studied; preferred keys; arc of the student's
progress; and other pertinent information. I create a comprehensive repertoire plan tailored to each student's strengths, weaknesses, interests, and
requirements and pay special attention to creating a diverse song list for
each jury or recital. The list reflects a variety of eras, styles, composers,
and languages, and functions as a vital long-term planning tool. I indicate
which pieces will be prepared for juries to make sure the student and I
agree about those required pieces long before the performance day ar-

rives. The repertoire sheet bears no grades or notes—only song titles and source material in parentheses next to the songs, providing an outline sketch of the student's entire college repertoire. Sometimes over summer break I will take out my studio rep sheets and lightly pencil in possible pieces for the following semester. This planning is essential because four years elapses quickly, and we must be responsible to our students, giving careful thought to the repertoire that best suits their voices.

Tailor-made repertoire lists for each singer tend to be much greater resources than across-the-board-identical, required jury repertoire lists. I have had experience with such lists constructed by instrumental jazz faculty at some institutions. Such lists assign the same songs to all jazz majors regardless of instrument, according to the progression of semesters (all first-semester freshmen must prepare the same list of songs for their juries and so forth throughout the students' college careers). Although it is important for jazz singers to be familiar with standard repertoire shown in such lists, some voices may not be technically ready for certain pieces at the same time other voices may be. On the contrary, great care must be taken to assign repertoire for specific technical reasons and not simply because a song is a standard. For instance, "Giant Steps" should not be given to a singer before their ease of singing over two octaves has been attained. As voice pedagogues, part of our responsibility is educating singers about how to continue their own education intelligently and with sensitivity toward their particular vocal needs. Gently and gradually increasing the difficulty level, range, and technical requirements of assigned repertoire should be the decision of the applied teacher and no one else because only that teacher fully knows a student's difficulties, strengths, educational needs, experiences, repertoire, and weaknesses. After teaching thousands of students, no two repertoire sheets have ever been alike in my voice studios.

The Role of the Teacher-Mentor

Because only a small percentage of music majors work in full-time performance careers after graduation, many music pedagogues complete their students' education by instilling some practical vocational skills. Helping singers nurture non-musical strengths in minor fields including business, mathematics, science, languages, graphic design, stage production, arts management, or other disciplines can go a long way toward preparing them for rewarding, sustainable futures. Singers must ascertain how they can contribute their music to the world while earning a living that uses their unique skill set. Wise teachers help students identify not only genres that stand out among their strengths but also ancillary skills. Does your student keep an immaculate, precise journal? Does he or she love to "sit in" at the piano when accompanists skip your studio class? Does he or she ask to observe your other lessons with a genuine desire to learn how to teach voice? Pay attention to the skills and interests your students display and be sure to encourage their development of unique skill sets. Share your encouraging observations with them as often as possible. Those casual remarks complimenting your music theatre major on the outstanding job she did stage managing last week's production may stay with that student forever, paving a way toward a career in the arts she never expected. The modern voice teacher must not only teach but also mentor and guide. Student singers today need much more than vocal technique and repertoire. They need concrete advice from a trusted mentor who can identify strengths and possible career avenues worth exploring. Never underestimate your power as a voice pedagogue. You have more power than you think, so be wary of how you wield it.

The Analogy of Skating

All singers have been influenced by all the voice pedagogues, choir directors, singers, and instrumentalists they have ever encountered. Each of these professionals has contributed to one's understanding of how to sing, or how not to sing, and how to teach, or how not to teach. Further, a singer's influences need not be strictly limited to musical artists alone. Esteemed voice pedagogue Dale Moore once stated in a voice master class that he learned as much about singing by watching Olympic figure skaters as he did by watching professional singers.[1] His statement resonated with me. I, too, marveled at the athleticism, control, smoothness, and beauty of high-level figure skating. He went on to explain that the smoothness of an elite skater's movement on the ice can easily be translated into a singer's legato line. The seemingly effortless muscle tonus, which enables a skater to look relaxed while maintaining speed and strength, relates to a singer's appoggio, which enables the steady, consistent leaning of air against the rib cage to support a tone. A skater moving quickly along the ice with dexterity, precise footwork, and excellent balance could be easily instructive in the art of rhythmic precision and clarity of diction amid brisk tempi. Both skating and singing require the performance of physically challenging stunts, either with the entire body or with the voice, and the acceleration of tempo and physical intensity of a skater's movements mirror the energy variations, tempo changes, and dynamic control that singers must develop for maximum mastery of nuance and musicality. A skater's expressive gestures and face, like a dancer's, express volumes, just as a singer must project their expressive connection to the text toward the audience through facial expressions and thoughtful use of gestures. Both skating and singing require the use of the entire body's network of muscles. Steady growth in balance, coordination, strength, and endurance must be consistently applied throughout a singer's career to maintain one's instrument and keep it limber, flexible, healthy, and strong.

ARTISTRY AS GESTALT

Artistry may be thought of as a fully coordinated, simultaneous gestalt of many aspects of singing. This may be better understood when looking at the great jazz singers of the twentieth century. Each artist comprised a "total package" of mastery across many levels, including intonation, timbre, improvisation, diction, rhythm, expression, phrasing, stage presence, musicianship, and jazz style.

Louis Armstrong's pioneering spirit launched not only virtuosic solo instrumental jazz but also virtuosic scat-singing. Approaching scat-singing as an imitation of instrumental soloing, Armstrong paved the road for every scat improviser that followed. His "hot" style created high-energy performances and recordings that kept him in high demand throughout the world and throughout his lifetime as a superstar performing artist. He played with vocally noisy timbres, chuckles, funny sounds, and swinging motives to create truly memorable works of improvisational art.

Billie Holiday stands as the first major jazz singer whose influence impacted most, if not all, of the singers who followed her in that genre. Holiday's introduction of back-phrasing into the art of singing (thanks to her mentor, saxophonist Lester Young) revolutionized the manner of modern singing in a way that allowed text-based improvisation and individualized interpretation to become part of a singing performer's signature style. Holiday's approach played with vocal noise and drama as an alternative to ubiquitous vocal beauty so common to other singers of the day. Her focus on real-world problems of racism and injustice (vividly portrayed in her recordings and performances of "Strange Fruit") marked Holiday as one of the first artist advocates for social change.

Bing Crosby's innovative closeness to the microphone yielded the first crooner, the first pop singing star, and the progenitor of modern microphone technique. His supremely beautiful tone was enhanced by his flaw-less diction, pitch precision, rhythmic mastery, and directness of textual delivery. Bing's commitment to singing pure vowels teaches a lesson to every observant jazz singer: that vowel purity is the key to maximizing vocal beauty. Crosby embodied the pinnacle of a complete entertainer, excelling in studio recordings, live musical performances, and film musi-cals. His myriad outstanding performances remain worthy studies of how to find one's true north—the natural baseline voice from which all good singing hails.

Pop singer Frank Sinatra's matter-of-fact delivery never missed a consonant, yielding clarity other singers envied. His resonance balancing allowed his relaxed, boy-next-door style to come through without sacrific-ing tonal beauty, and his ability to communicate with his audience shone brightly in every performance. Although principally considered a pop singer, Sinatra must be studied by jazz singers for his outstanding vocal technique, superb ability to communicate, unparalleled number of Great American Songbook recordings, and total package of artistic treasure. He also consistently sang with his baseline, natural vocal timbre, which facilitated a healthy singing approach throughout his long career. Fur-thermore, Sinatra remains relevant to jazz because he was singing swing when swing was popular music. Although Crosby's resonance balance was starkly different from Sinatra's (darker, rounder, and warmer), the two singers combined represented the range of colors a baritone voice could achieve in pop or jazz music. Both artists performed in such relaxed fashion that their senses of humor played important roles in their overall artistry (their duet performances in the film *High Society* are not to be missed!).

Ella Fitzgerald's effortless pitch precision, rhythmic exactitude, and carefree approach to style allowed her artistry to pour through a consistent vocal timbre, whether improvising or not. Fitzgerald's truly exemplary ability to improvise at breakneck speeds using scat improvisation made her a jazz singing force that every singer in this genre must study. Her spell-binding creativity, stunning vocal beauty, and flawless rhythm and pitch gleaned Fitzgerald thirteen Grammy awards and twenty nominations. She remains the female artist with the most recordings in the Grammy Hall of Fame and was the first woman to win the Recording Academy Lifetime Achievement Award in 1967. Accolades aside, Fitzgerald's kindness and likeability accompanied her mind-boggling improvisational prowess and superior vocal technique so that her audiences swelled with love for her by the end of every performance.

Sarah Vaughan's impressively even timbre on every note throughout her massive range never ceased to amaze her audiences. That smooth evenness moving from note to note was only matched by her consistent, effortless vibrato and beautifully pure vowels. She tossed off difficult passages with élan and maintained invariably accurate pitch on nearly every note. Vaughan's beginnings as a jazz pianist informed her theoretical knowledge and harmonic understanding so that her improvisations blended a display of chordal performance (via singing arpeggiated chords) with wide, disjunct leaps. Her matchless singing ranged from baritone to soprano, stunning audiences and providing her artistry with a wide palette of creative options for crafting memorable solos. Furthermore, Vaughan's outstanding achievements as a ballad singer provided historic recordings that drew near perfection with her vocal beauty, phrasing, and well-managed dynamic contrast. These attributes of solid technique were made possible by her outstanding mastery of breath management. Vaughan's baseline voice seems always near to the keen listener. Her stylistic interpretations of jazz and Great American Songbook standards used her natural ability to sing sweetly while connecting musical lines as though smoothly frosting a cake.

Nat "King" Cole's warm, attractive voice contained nuance and tenderness that left audiences breathless. His extemporaneous phrasing style hailed from his experience as a leading jazz pianist whose improvisational abilities revealed fresh, motivic ideas highly worth emulating and transcribing. Cole's syncopated sense of swing was only matched by his uncanny ability to deliver a slow, romantic ballad as if he were wooing a date. Cole's influence on modern singers has remained ever relevant, and his classic recordings constitute required listening for every jazz singer.

Peggy Lee excelled in the art of understatement, influencing an entire generation of cool-style singers. Her impeccable pitch and rhythmic precision allowed her to sing blues, swing, ballads, rock, pop, Latin, and other styles with chameleonic flexibility and stylistic authenticity. Lee strove to find unique ways to interpret her songs, using her own brand of phrasing, ultrasoft dynamics, and a variety of vocal timbres. These and other techniques yielded unpredictable and unexpected arrangements of standards like "Lover" and "My Heart Belongs to Daddy." She led the charge in creating song lists that excited her audiences and kept them engaged. Her experience as a radio show host and a frequent guest on television variety shows (including Sinatra's, Cole's, and Crosby's) added to her stage presence and audience appeal. She actively participated in the process of arranging and composing music, unlike most of her jazz singing peers. Lee represented one of the first major singer-songwriters in American music history, successfully writing several charting hits that both she and her contemporaries (Cole, Vaughan, Mel Tormé, and Dean Martin, among others) eventually recorded. Over a six-decade career, Lee's example revealed a renaissance artist able to do many things well. She capably illustrated the importance of a jazz singer developing other relevant skills (bandleading, show hosting, arranging, and composing) to keep a career afloat and thriving.

Mel Tormé blended a rich, warm, slightly breathy vocal color with rhythmic and pitch precision. His overtly passionate expression revealed a lovely baseline, natural voice that was always present (much like that of Crosby). Tormé's ability to manipulate phrasing and dynamics caused him to stand out among his peers, and his musicianship and rhythmic subtleties reflected his experience as a drummer.

Nancy Wilson's artistry revealed a performer consistently connected to the expression of her text while singing with flawless rhythmic and pitch precision, rich ornamentation, and a heaping portion of style. Wilson's unique combination of breathy and clear tone resulted in artistic delivery with an expressive stamp all her own. Her elegant stage deportment exhibited confidence and class yielding a visual picture onstage as beautiful as the aural pictures she painted with her unequalled vocalism.

All of these artists created their own unique combination of artistry that marked them as both identifiable and outstanding among other performers of their era. All jazz artists must identify aspects of technique or musicianship that make them unique. This uniqueness among one's peers coupled with shared excellence in areas of intonation, rhythmic precision, style, stage presence, improvisational prowess, and phrasing comprise the makings of a great jazz singer.

CONSISTENCY AND PRACTICE

Renowned concert pianist Vladimir Horowitz famously said that if he missed one day of practice, he personally noticed a difference in his performance readiness. He went on to claim that, after two days of missed practice, the critics would notice, and after missing three consecutive days of practice the general public would notice. This piano master built his success around the consistent discipline of daily practice. Many of the greatest talents of our time and of times past were noted to have spent a minimum of four hours practicing their craft on a typical day. Some world-class concert soloists practice for eight hours each day. The human voice generally does not allow for such indulgence because the instrument is comprised of tiny muscles and vulnerable tissues that are easily abused by overuse. How then can a young singer attain "ten thousand hours" of practice or performance to achieve mastery? Creative practicing is the answer. Singing mastery involves much more than simply singing one's songs and vocal exercises over and over for hours on end. Although vocalizing and singing through repertoire are necessary parts of daily practice, experienced professionals recognize that there exist many other ways to hone their craft without placing unnecessary stress on the delicate vocal organ. Studying text; memorizing lyrics; writing out lyrics several times; researching songs, composers, poems, poets, libretti and librettists; researching world history pertaining to the song's setting; and critically listening to a variety of singers' song interpretations and recordings (as well as maintaining a healthy dose of live performance attendance) all play important roles in developing a professional singing career.

Expert jazz singers depend on their ability to imitate instrumental sounds, so their listening diet must not only include other singers but also great jazz instrumentalists of all types. This opens up a world of jazz masters that modern singers can emulate. Watching great musicians performing onstage occupies outstanding singers on a regular basis. With the vast number of digital recordings available at our fingertips in the twenty-first century, there is no end to the worthwhile audio and video recordings we can access to fuel our daily listening regimen. Because listening places virtually no pressure on the voice (although for some, intrinsic muscle flexion can be detected during listening as with singing), listening to great music significantly informs one's own practice. Listening as practice especially benefits a singer during periods of vocal rest.

EVOLVING ARTISTRY THROUGHOUT LIFE

Maintaining vocal conditioning and resiliency as one ages presents unique challenges for the singer. Once again, it may be instructive to notice parallels between singing and skating to illustrate this point. Most singers and skaters eventually discover that their bodies, through the natural process of aging, lose the ability to do certain things that were previously not difficult or at least were possible with hard work. The singers' cartilages begin to ossify (harden) as they come into middle age or late-middle age (fifties through the early sixties). Pitch precision becomes more difficult to execute when singers notice that their ability to fine-tune intonation changes. Voices may begin to sound more brittle and less supple. Some voices take on a more strident tone. These natural transformations can possibly be slowed with dedicated practice, hydration, and a commitment to self-care. Some singers enjoy limber flexibility and youthful timbres well into their advanced years. Unfortunately, there is no proven method to slow down the aging process of the voice. All one can do is take excellent care of the vocal instrument throughout life and understand that certain aspects of singing may change. As one ages, however, research has shown that singers that keep their voices exercised and in shape fare much better than those who do not. Vocal study with an experienced teacher may yield an increase in flexibility; a stable, healthy vibrato; and a restoration of efficient vocal technique.

Just as our aging bodies perform better physically when we adopt an age-appropriate workout regimen into our advanced years, our aging voices also require workouts targeted toward our current needs and challenges. Aging singers who expect to continue singing their best must be willing to work at it even more diligently in their advanced years than they did in younger days. Daily practice, research shows, enhances an older singer's vocal luster, stamina, flexibility, intonation, vibrato rate, and vocal coordination. Plus, singing healthfully tends to enhance mental and emotional health by releasing endorphins, the "feel-good" hormones. Furthermore, singing boosts the immune system, so continuing to sing in community or church choirs provides a generally healthy avenue for former professional singers and singing teachers wanting to continue the enjoyment of making music. Singers having busy performance careers may possess an advantage, keeping the voice in reasonable shape without practicing as much, but care must be taken to treat the voice gently and not drive it too hard. All singers may find lasting success through warming up gently and slowly before each performance, resting the voice (or only engaging in light practice) on the day of and the day after a concert, and practicing consistently on non-concert days.

TRUE ARTISTIC MASTERY

True artists of jazz singing possess several aspects of technique and other skills in masterful proportions. Knowledge of vocal anatomy, ear anatomy, and the science of singing assist the artist in understanding the body as a musical instrument as well as its functional parts and fragilities.

Respect for vocal health, hygiene, and a commitment to proper nutrition, hydration, and protection of the vocal instrument keep the singing artist on a path toward wellness each day. Proper alignment and breath management keep the singer's body in check whether seated, standing, or playing an instrument. Correct phonation creates healthy, beautiful tone for the baseline, natural voice that every singing artist must cultivate. Resonance balancing, manipulated at will (with help from my Mix Continuum), enhances stylistic authenticity and creates a palette of vocal colors available for various songs in many genres. Articulation and dynamics frequently interweave throughout a song's texture, providing interest and variety. Knowledge of jazz ornamentation and stylistic authenticity provide nuances and singing prowess that singing many styles demands. A willingness to learn from other cultures and genres allows the jazz artist to continue to grow and expand in influence, taste, and critical listening skills. Such artistic expansion helps the singer to use many more musical options than mere personal experience can provide. A wide proficiency in improvisational styles (melodic embellishment, scat-singing, text-based improvisation, vocalese, lyric improvisation, free improvisation, and world influences) provides the working jazz singer with important expertise and a variety of options when sharing musical ideas improvisationally. Understanding characteristics of subgenres and historical contexts of jazz enable the singer to approach this art form with confidence and authority. Clean diction and enunciation, both paramount in communicating clearly and artistically with an audience, grace the artist's every song. Mastery of phrasing keeps the jazz artist consistently stretching toward new ways of experiencing and expressing the beauty and art residing within the music. A basic understanding of mic technique teaches singing artists how to properly use the "other half" of their instrument in valuable ways that enhance performance practice. Experience singing jazz in an ensemble setting grows a singer's critical listening skills and hones the ability to self-correct when blending and balancing with other musicians. Experimenting with the Dalcroze method offers both the jazz voice pedagogue and the singer a wealth of creative ways to learn new music, to internalize rhythms, and to grow an expressive palette of musical mastery. Proficiency with relevant jazz scales, modes, and instrumental methods of improvisation allow jazz vocal artists to perform at the level of their instrumental counterparts or higher. The intentional development of mindful singing enhances performance concentration necessary for ongoing artistic success. Mental toughness protects the singer so that work may continue during difficult personal patches in life. Further studies in arranging, jazz theory, jazz piano, jazz history, and other instruments enhance an artist's preparation for a lifetime of enjoyment and self-sufficiency as a competitive jazz musician. Bandleading skills and elegant stage etiquette allow the jazz vocal artist to shine onstage as a professional with whom both fellow musicians and audiences will enjoy interacting. The well-crafted song list, transcriptions of outstanding solos, and thoughtful arrangements provide the jazz singing artist with tools necessary to develop a book of charts that bands will enjoy playing and audiences will return to hear time and again. Consistently cultivating and coordinating all of these aspects of the art form, although perhaps daunting, establish a lifetime of joy and discovery for the professional jazz voice artist.

NOTE

1. Dale Moore, "Singing Master Class with Dale Moore," presented at the Central New York-Finger Lakes NATS workshop, Onondaga Community College, Syracuse, New York, 1998.

APPENDIX:
SAMPLE PRACTICE GUIDE

For a few years I taught a professional crossover singer (mezzo-soprano) who excelled in classical music, oratorio, jazz, and country music and performed frequently as a sacred choral soloist in a major U.S. city. I worked specifically on retraining her abdominal muscles and breathing technique following surgery, which cut several of those muscles. She felt her abdominals did not function the same way they previously did, so she sought me out as a voice pedagogue experienced in rehabilitating professional singers. She was also interested in learning to sing jazz. She felt that, after months of working with me, the lessons and practice guides I provided were enormously successful in restoring her voice technique, breath management, ease of singing, and stylistic prowess. The following represents a transcription of one of many practice guides I gave her in lieu of lessons. It may be a useful study for pedagogues teaching breath management, multigenre singing, vowel purity, voice recovery following a long hiatus from singing, or expression in any genre. It also may be helpful in suggesting ideas for creative exercises singers can use to develop their expressive and improvising abilities.

TEACHING THE CROSSOVER SINGER

For this crossover student I employed the classical book of Italian minisongs, the *Vaccai Vocal Method*. I often use five minutes of this tool after warm-ups for singers that study several styles. The book helps teach many aspects of vocal technique, including appoggio, the concept of leaning the air against the rib cage from the inside. I have found that both classical and jazz singers benefit from this study for a variety of reasons. Classical singers can use the Vaccai book to come to jazz from a place of familiarity. Stylistic indications like jazz smears can be practiced using the same pure-vowel text used to train opera singers. The legato singing achieved through mastering these easy Italian phrases can be modified to teach a jazz legato or smearing note-approach style. The method also helps the opera singer sense how breathing technique can be modified to accomplish the same appoggio for supporting tone. Classical singers then understand better how to move note-to-note in a jazz style without vibrato. This tool can be a great help when teaching opera or classical singers how to quickly change to jazz style and back again.

The Vaccai Method as a Jazz Teaching Tool

From the other end of the stylistic spectrum, jazz singers learn breath management and vowel purity (which the Italian language requires) from correctly singing these minuscule songs. They also learn to gracefully sing larger and larger intervals because the sequence of songs addresses one interval at a time, increasing the distance by one scale tone as the series progresses (Lesson One begins by emphasizing the interval of the second; Lesson Two consists predominantly of thirds; and so on through octave leaps). Each mini-song (most are around sixteen to twenty-four measures in length) can be learned quickly. Principles of diction, breath management, and resonance balancing can be addressed in just a few lessons for each short song as the student moves sequentially through the book.

Vowels and the Mic

Because the purification of vowels lies at the heart of manipulating overtones with a microphone, study of Italian vowels has proven effective in teaching jazz singers. Those who become great at tweaking a vowel's brightness, depth, or roundness, or at creating an array of vowel sounds and colors must start by knowing how to isolate and shape a pure vowel. Further, more and more contemporary jazz involves singing in languages with far purer vowels than American English. Singing well in Portuguese, Italian, Spanish, German, and French requires diction and language study in those languages. Focusing on the purity of vowels, even mixed vowels found in French and other languages, can be a starting point for jazz singers interested in broadening their repertoire of languages performed. The Italian language, having few vowels, allows the singer to master vowel purity in the core vowels: [a], [open and closed e], [i], [open and closed o], and [u].

SAMPLE PRACTICE GUIDE PART I: STRENGTHENING TECHNIQUE

This practice guide served to direct my student's practice sessions over a week or two, until I saw her again. It is presented here as directed practice instructions, as though I am speaking directly to the student.

After reading the introduction to the *Vaccai Vocal Method*, proceed through your gentle, slow warm-up consisting of at least fifteen minutes of stretching, breathing, staccato and legato exercises, easy target exercises (those previously given to address some specific aspect of technique), and finally, the messa di voce (crescendo, decrescendo on one note and one pure vowel).

I would like you to be singing every day—at least a slow, gentle, refreshing warm-up that lasts fifteen to twenty minutes. This regular working out of the voice will be necessary to bring you back into performance condition and will be excellent for your lungs, abdominal muscles, body, and mind. If there's time and stamina, work toward singing one hour per day but no more than that. More is not better at this stage of your recovery and voice building. Daily vocalizing should not be rushed and should feel good! It should be approached much like meditation. This is your time to enjoy and massage your voice.

Once your fifteen-minute warm-up and vocal workout is complete, turn to Vaccai's Lesson One and read the translation aloud, as a dramatic reading. How is your Italian when it comes to translating? If you can, write the exact meaning of each word under the Italian text so that you know each word's meaning as you sing it. Then speak the Italian text with as much expression and dramatic rendering as you did for your English translation, being careful to give proper emphasis to accented syllables and double consonants. Once you are aware of speaking with good emphasis and connected, forward, clear vowels (give yourself several spoken efforts before singing), gently begin to sing the Italian text with as legato a line as possible. Know that when you do this, often the syllabic emphasis disappears. No problem—even native Italians sacrifice linguistic precision for beauty of tone—but do your best to sing with both legato *and* proper syllabic emphasis.

Next, concentrate on spinning all of your vowels from one steady stream of energy, which does not falter, change, or ebb and flow; it is completely consistent from your vocal onset to your release with absolute evenness of energy and consistent vibrato through the whole line. Consistent vibrato is important for jazz singers to know how to do so that they can turn it on and off at will. The Vaccai work is terrific in teaching vibrato consistency throughout the compass of the voice. Vaccai's Lesson One becomes pleasurable to sing in this manner; it should literally feel good to keep your voice spinning as you relax into the sensation of it. As jazz/classical crossover singers, we have to be cognizant of singing this repertoire with vibrato on not only every note but also every part of every note (every corner, nook, beginning and end of each syllable, and even through the consonants). Take some time this week to listen to a favorite opera singer and focus on his or her energy consistency and vibrato. Listen with a critical ear until you find one whose perfectly even vocal energy matches their consistency of vibrato. This discipline builds the jazz singer's vocal technique and will not jeopardize his or her authentic sound—rather, it enhances it with improved breath management, more resonance options, and vowel purity.

As you sing these Vaccai lessons, I have found it helpful to concentrate on having the energy and "spin" spill over from one note into the next—overflowing each note with intensity and round tone so that there is distinct forward motion of the line, *which comes from the air* and not only from adding "twang" or nasality to vowels. This forward motion requires a lot more air than we tend to offer when we sing jazz or commercial music, so find the air around you, inhale it, and use it! Stop here and sing Vaccai's Lesson One again, with this in mind.

We also have to remember to balance our *chiaro* with *scuro* ("light" with "dark" qualities). So, rather than constantly thinking of singing forward in the mask, we need to provide adequate vertical space for all our classically sung vowels. When I say vertical I don't merely mean "up" (a sense of ascending space in the head and imagined space above the head within the room or an elevation of the soft palate) but also space beneath the larynx. Some teachers call this "tracheal resonance," and I have found this to be particularly revolutionary in my own singing. Some singers spend years trying to increase a sense of "space" in the upward direction and stretch their range by forcing the voice up (with the larynx following).

Instead, use the image of the body below the larynx to resonate the tone as well as the space above. If you think about it from the standpoint of a physicist, it makes perfect sense. The tone doesn't simply travel upward and out of the mouth but creates a waveform and consequent sound all around the body. With tracheal resonance (also known to some as "chest resonance"), we are dealing with sympathetic vibrations of the bones in our chest (mostly the sternum and ribs). Concentrating on this vibratory sensation in the chest while we sing high notes actually provides much needed room at the top of our range (mysterious, I know) as well as beautiful balance using our natural "woofers." Our "tweeters" get mighty "chirpy" without the resonance balancing of our chest cavity providing ballast and roundness to the bottom of every tone (refer to my Mix Continuum in chapter 5). Take some time to tap into this deeper quality, especially in the upper-middle and high range. It may feel like you are filling up your chest with head tone, but it is *not* anything like singing with a Broadway belt-style, pressed, chesty tone, so be sure to make that distinction in your sensations. Stop at this point, wrap your mind around this, and sing Vaccai's Lesson One again, focusing on your tracheal resonance. Can you hear or feel a change in tone quality, vibrato, or volume?

The appoggio technique works hand in hand with tracheal resonance to help you find a comfortable singing technique. When your mind is focusing on the horizontal stretch of the rib cage (and likewise outward motion of your external intercostal muscles, which are responsible for inhalation), it is natural to sense the tone spinning in the chest region. Again, it's a mixed head voice tone; it is not pure chest voice. You should have some element of head voice in every note you sing throughout your range (when you are singing in the classical or operatic style especially) and some element of chest voice in every tone as well. This point is of particular relevance as illustrated in my Mix Continuum where you can pinpoint and adjust the amount of head-dominant versus chest-dominant proportions in your singing mix. The element of chest voice that you are developing in this lesson is tracheal resonance, which can be used (through your mix) on even your highest tones in the whistle register. Use of it will give your tone more beauty, roundness, resonance balance, and volume control (since the secret to singing *pianissimo* on a high note lies in the outward stretch of the external intercostal muscles!). We are simply blending the *chiaro* with the *scuro* as needed or desired on different pitches throughout your vocal range.

Now can you sing Vaccai's Lesson One with attention to legato, expression, forward consonants, and dynamics? If so, move on to Lesson

Two and begin the same process, slowly, step by step. Be careful not to get overwhelmed by trying to master and apply everything on the first take. Always translate first, then speak the text, connecting all the vowels in speech until you know it (and feel it) well, and then sing. These Italian lessons, although not musically challenging in terms of notes and rhythms, are meant to grow your appoggio muscles and bel canto technique, so proceed slowly through each interval exercise.

One last note about Vaccai exercises: you should begin each day's study of them (after your warm-up, of course) by starting at Lesson One and singing them one by one through to the lesson you are currently working on. It is time-consuming, perhaps, but the way to an excellent legato is through mastering stepwise motion first, then small intervals, then larger ones. Vaccai designed the book to reflect that natural progression, so it serves even technically proficient singers best when they move through them daily in sequential order. The more you do these in this way, the more you'll value what you're feeling them do in smoothing and strengthening your technique.

SAMPLE PRACTICE GUIDE PART II: EXPRESSION AND COMMUNICATION

Moving on to a different, less technical note, here are some fun exercises that may add a bit more expression to your performances. Try these at home and come ready to explore them with me at your next lesson.

Exercise: Mood Cards

Make flash cards with several index cards. Write one mood, attitude or descriptive adjective on each card (i.e., "bright," "angry," "impatient," "questioning," "sour," "surprised"). Be creative. Sing through your Vaccai exercises while flipping through the cards. Try to make fine distinctions among the different moods. Express the text accordingly. Use a mirror or video camera to watch yourself and determine how expressive you really are. Then repeat this exercise while singing your assigned jazz pieces. See how the moods on the cards change not only your expression but also your tone quality, diction, energy level, articulation, dynamics, vowel shapes, and intentions of your pieces. Journal about your findings.

Exercise: Jazz Moods

Write objectives and moods throughout your jazz piece that reflect how you wish to portray the meaning of the text. How are you going to achieve your character's objectives? Be persuasive about each objective as the song progresses. As your technique improves and your familiarity with your song grows, your focus needs to transition from thoughts of technique to thoughts of the character's expression and meeting stated objectives.

Exercise: Twenty Questions

Ask yourself: Who is singing? Why am I singing this? To whom am I singing? What is my character's environment? What will my actual environment be at the performance? What happened immediately before this that made my character burst into song? What is my character trying to accomplish by singing this? How are the characters influencing each other? What is going to happen in the storyline as a result of my song? Be as specific as possible, create more questions relevant to the song, and if research does not unearth actual answers (if the song is not from a musical or film, for instance), invent the answers to provide "background information" for your character. This exercise provides a powerful set of objectives and settings for your songs.

Exercise: Consistent Energy

Although every word is part of a legato phrase, each is also important in terms of textual expression. Work on singing with an uninterrupted line of energy while using your eyes and face to let your audience know which words are the most important (in your character's opinion). Some words may need more emphasis than others. Find creative ways to bring out those words without disrupting your line. Not every sung line should be legato (connected). Some should be staccato (detached), some marcato (march-like), and some a mixture of these. Always sing with articulatory intention. Know which articulation scheme brings out the message and phrasing most effectively for the style and the text of a given song.

Exercise: The Longest Phrase

Time yourself as you sustain [s] after breathing deeply. Repeat a few times. Then time yourself sustaining [i] ("ee"), [o] ("oh") or [a] "ah" for as long as your breath will allow it. Be sure to maintain a wide intercostal stretch as you inhale and even after you begin to sing, as though your rib cage is continuing to expand through the phrase. This is singing "on the gesture of inhalation." Repeat this exercise for each of your pure vowels. Which vowels are easiest to sustain? Which are hardest? Then take a long inhalation and sing a jazz song for as long as your breath will sustain without a break to breathe. This will mean singing through rests, possibly three or four phrases at a stretch. We are working on establishing a strong breathing mechanism, so that is fine for these purposes. If you can sustain *s* for fifty seconds after breathing deeply, can you continuously sing for that length of time? Practice this daily and you will teach your body to sing longer and longer phrases at will. Obviously, you should always breathe when a breath pause (comma or period) calls for a break in declamation, but this exercise helps produce long, sustained lines when the need arises.

Exercise: Paraphrase

Write your non-English song text's translation in your own (English) words. Modernize it if necessary. Sing the words you've written to the tune of the original. How does the meaning change? What other elements change?

Exercise: Text Improvisation

Improvise alternate lyrics to your song's music. Work to adhere to pitch and rhythm as much as possible. Suggest different scenes, settings, or situations for yourself that will yield completely different storylines, characters, and objectives. This becomes a never-ending exercise with an infinite number of new song outcomes. Work on delivering alternate texts as confidently as you sing the actual lyrics.

Exercise: Music Improvisation

Improvise music to your song's lyrics. Make sure it fits with the meaning of the text and follows the natural flow of the language, including phrases, breaths, pauses, and so on. Use motives, sequences, scales, arpeggios, and anything you like to stretch your improvisational acumen.

Improvisation exercises in jazz, music theatre, or classical music are super for making the performer better equipped when memory slips occur.

Song objectives become extremely well understood through paraphrasing and refashioning text and music. Forgetting a line becomes easily solvable through improvisation. As a jazz singer, you will be equipped to cope with unexpected situations that arise during performances, and your audience will appreciate that you respond confidently in a nonplussed fashion. I encourage you to work on a few of these each day and vary your Part II practice routine to expand your expressive and creative compass.

The Cool-Down

Remember to do a brief (one or two-minute) cool-down after each practice session, lesson, and performance. Descending glides (from your middle voice to low) carry your singing mix down into your speaking voice. This is wise to do before you leave the act of singing and begin speaking again.

The Speaking Voice Takeaway

Learning to speak resonantly with some head mix in your speaking voice will help your voice's longevity and health whenever you need to speak more loudly. It also helps to keep the speaking voice free from noise, bumps, gravel, and inconsistencies that interfere with a smooth singing line or a healthy instrument for both speaking and singing. As you re-build your vocal technique, time and attention devoted to creating healthy speaking habits will be well spent. The healthy speaking voice is resonant, clear, supported with plenty of air for each phrase, and free from vocal fry or physical pain. Developing a resonant speaking voice is necessary for establishing a healthy baseline, natural voice for singing, so spend some time daily checking in with your instrument to make sure you are supporting it properly with clean and ample air, healthy body alignment, nutrition, hydration, gentle exercise, and protective voice habits. Until next time, I wish you blessings as you enjoy the beautiful gift of singing!

SELECTED BIBLIOGRAPHY

Abramson, R. M. "Dalcroze-Based Improvisation." *Music Educators Journal.* 66, no. 5 (1980): 62–68.

Aebersold, Jamey. *Jam Session*, vol. 34. New Albany, IN: Jamey Aebersold Jazz, 1984.

Akkerman, Gregg. *The Last Balladeer: The Johnny Hartman Story.* Lanham, MD: Scarecrow Press, 2012.

Anderson, Doug. *Jazz and Show Choir Handbook II.* Chapel Hill, NC: Hinshaw Music, 1993.

Bachmann, M. *Dalcroze Today: An Education through and into Music.* Oxford: Clarendon Press, 1991.

Berg, Shelton. *Jazz Improvisation: The Goal Note Method.* Delevan, NY: Kendor Music, Inc. 1998.

Bickel, Jan E. *Vocal Technique: A Physiologic Approach*, 2nd ed. San Diego: Plural Publishing, Inc., 2017.

Blackburn, Julia. *With Billie: A New Look at the Unforgettable Billie Holiday.* New York: Vintage Books, 2006.

Bunch, Meribeth. *Dynamics of the Singing Voice*, 3rd ed. Vienna: Springer-Verlag, 1995.

Caldwell, J. T. "A Dalcroze Perspective on Skills for Learning." *Music Educators Journal.* 79. no. 7 (1993): 27–28.

Caldwell, J. Timothy. *Expressive Singing: Dalcroze Eurhythmics for Voice.* Englewood Cliffs, NJ: Prentice-Hall, Inc. 1995.

Caldwell, Robert. *The Performer Prepares.* Dallas, TX: Pst...Inc., 1990.

Campbell, P. S. *Songs in Their Heads: Music and Its Meaning in Children's Lives*. Oxford: Oxford University Press, 1998.

Chapman, Janice L. *Singing and Teaching Singing: A Holistic Approach to Classical Voice*, 2nd ed. San Diego: Plural Publishing, Inc. 2012.

Coffin, Berton. *Historical Vocal Pedagogy Classics*. Lanham, MD: Scarecrow Press, 1989.

Dayme, Meribeth, and Cynthia Vaughn. *The Singing Book*, 3rd ed. New York: W.W. Norton & Company, 2014.

Dayme, Meribeth Bunch. *The Performer's Voice: Realizing Your Vocal Potential*. New York: W.W. Norton & Co., 2005.

Dehning, William. *Chorus Confidential: Decoding the Secrets of the Choral Art*. San Pedro, CA: Pavane Publishing, 2003.

Doscher, Barbara. *The Functional Unity of the Singing Voice*, 2nd ed. Lanham, MD: Scarecrow Press, 1994.

Edwards, Matthew. "Using Audio Enhancement Technology." In *So You Want to Sing CCM: A Guide for Performers*, edited by Matthew Hoch, 72–94. Lanham, MD: Rowman & Littlefield, 2020.

Emmons, Shirlee, and Alma Thomas. *Power Performance for Singers: Transcending the Barriers*. Oxford: Oxford University Press, 1998.

Epstein, Daniel Mark. *Nat King Cole*. New York: Farrar, Straus & Giroux, 1999.

Fleming, Renée. *The Inner Voice: The Making of a Singer*. New York: Penguin Group, 2004.

Garcia, Manuel. *Hints on Singing*. New York: Joseph Patelson Music House Ltd., 1982.

George, Donald, and Lucy Mauro. *Master Singers: Advice from the Stage*. New York: Oxford University Press, 2015.

Gourse, Leslie. *Sassy: The Life of Sarah Vaughan*. Cambridge, MA: Da Capo Press, 1994.

Gray, Henry. *Gray's Anatomy*. London: Belgrave-Square, 1858. Reprint. Seacaucus, NJ: Chartwell Books Inc., 1991.

https://www.musicedted.info/SingingBetter2/Vowels.html. Accessed May 1, 2021.

https://www.musicianonamission.com/types-of-microphones/. Accessed May 23, 2021.

https://www.voicescienceworks.org/resonance.html. Accessed May 13, 2021.

Jahn, Anthony F., ed. *The Singer's Guide to Complete Health*. New York: Oxford University Press, 2013.

Jaques-Dalcroze, É. "The Influence of Eurhythmics upon the Development of Movement in Music." *Proceedings of the Musical Association*, 44th Sess. (1917): 193–98.

———. *Rhythm, Music and Education*. New York: Putnam, 1921.

Johnson, M. D. "Dalcroze Skills for All Teachers." *Music Educators Journal*. 79 no. 8 (1993): 42–45.

Jones, David L. "Self-Supervision and the Singer: The Safety of Intelligent Practice." *Classical Singer*. (October 2004): 32–51.

Kumar, S. Pravin, and Jan G. Svec. "Kinematic Model for Simulating Mucosal Wave Phenomena on Vocal Folds." *Biomedical Signal Processing and Control* 49 (March 2019): 328–37.

Lamperti, Giovanni B. *Vocal Wisdom*. Marlboro, NJ: Taplinger Publishing Co., Inc., 1957.

LeBorgne, Wendy, and Marci Rosenberg. *The Vocal Athlete*, 2nd ed. San Diego: Plural Publishing, Inc., 2021.

———. *The Vocal Athlete: Application and Technique for the Hybrid Singer*, 2nd ed. San Diego: Plural Publishing, Inc., 2021.

Leck, H., and R. J. D. Frego. *Creating Artistry through Movement* [DVD]. Milwaukee, WI: Hal Leonard, 2005.

Levine, Mark. *The Jazz Piano Book*. Petaluma, CA: Sher Music Co., 1989.

Mabry, Sharon. *The Performing Life: A Singer's Guide to Survival*. Lanham, MD: Scarecrow Press, 2012.

Marchesi, Mathilde. *Bel Canto: A Theoretical and Practical Vocal Method*. Toronto: Dover Publications, 1970.

Martinelli, Francesco, ed. *The History of European Jazz: The Music, Musicians, and Audience in Context*. Sheffield, UK: Equinox Publishing, 2019.

McClosky, David Blair, members of the McClosky Institute of Voice. *Your Voice at Its Best: Enhancement of the Healthy Voice, Help for the Troubled Voice*, 5th ed. Long Grove, IL: Waveland Press, Inc., 2011.

McCoy, Scott. "Singing and Voice Science." In *So You Want to Sing Cabaret: A Guide for Performers*, edited by David Sabella and Sue Matsuki, 122–39. Lanham, MD: Rowman & Littlefield, 2019.

McKinney, James C. *The Diagnosis and Correction of Vocal Faults: A Manual for Teachers of Singing and for Choir Directors*. Nashville: Genovox Music Group, 1994.

Mead, V. H. "More than Mere Movement: Dalcroze Eurhythmics." *Music Educators Journal*. 82 no. 4 (1996): 38–41.

Miller, Richard. *On the Art of Singing*. New York: Oxford University Press, 1996.

Miller, Richard. *The Structure of Singing: System and Art in Vocal Technique*. New York: Schirmer Books, 1986.

Oney, Tish. "A Caffeinated Centennial." *JazzTimes* (December 2020): 44–47.

———. "Anatomy of a Standard." *AllAboutJazz.com* (2016–2021).

———. "Know Thy Text!" *Classical Singer Magazine* (September/October 2020): 90–95.

———. "Onward and Upward with Nathan Gunn." *Classical Singer Magazine* (May/June 2021): 28–34.

———. *Peggy Lee: A Century of Song*. Lanham, MD: Rowman & Littlefield, 2020.

———. "The Role of the Understudy." *Classical Singer Magazine* (May/June 2021): 52–55.

Oney, Tricia. "Dalcroze Eurhythmics: An Application to Voice Pedagogy." *Journal of Singing* 74 no. 1 (September/October 2017): 37–43.

Paton, John Glenn, ed. and trans., *Nicola Vaccai: Practical Method of Italian Singing.* New York: G. Schirmer, 1975.

Riposo, Joseph. *Bebop Scales: Jazz Scales and Patterns in All 12 Keys.* New Albany, IN: Jamey Aebersold Jazz, 2008.

———. *Jazz Improvisation: A Whole-Brain Approach*, 4th ed. Liverpool, NY: JR Publishers, 1989.

Roland, Paul, ed. *Jazz Singers: The Great Song Stylists in Their Own Words.* London: Octopus Publishing Group, 1999.

Rutherford, Paris. *The Vocal Jazz Ensemble.* Milwaukee, WI: Hal Leonard Corp., 2008.

Sataloff, Robert Thayer. *Vocal Health and Pedagogy: Science, Assessment, and Treatment*, 3rd ed. San Diego: Plural Publishing, 2017

Scearce, Leda. *Manual of Singing Voice Rehabilitation: A Practical Approach to Vocal Health and Wellness.* San Diego: Plural Publishing, Inc., 2016.

Schmidt, Jan, and Heidi Counsell Schmidt. *Basics of Singing*, 6th ed. Belmont, CA: Thomson Schirmer, 2008.

Sher, Chuck, ed. *The New Real Book, Vols. 1-3.* Petaluma, CA: Sher Music Co., 1988, 1991, 1995.

———. *The Standards Real Book.* Petaluma, CA: Sher Music Co., 2000.

Spector, I. *Rhythm and Life: The Work of Emile Jaques-Dalcroze.* Stuyvesant, NY: Pendragon Press, 1990.

Stoloff, Bob. *Blues Scatitudes: Vocal Improvisations on the Blues.* Brooklyn, NY: Gerard and Sarzin Publishing Co., 2003.

———. *Scat! Vocal Improvisation Techniques.* Brooklyn, NY: Gerard and Sarzin Publishing Co., 1996.

Svec, Jan G., Harm K. Schutte, C. Julian Chen, and Ingo R. Titze. "Integrative Insights into the Myoelastic Aerodynamic Theory and Acoustics of Phonation. Scientific Tribute to Donald G. Miller." *Journal of Voice.* (March 17, 2021). Available at https://www.jvoice.org/article/S0892-1997(21)00055-2/fulltext.

Tharp, Twyla. *The Creative Habit: Learn It and Use It for Life.* New York: Simon & Schuster, 2003.

Titze, Inge. "Major Benefits of Semi-Occluded Vocal Tract Exercises." *Journal of Singing* 74, no. 3 (January/February 2018): 311–12.

Vennard, William. *Singing: The Mechanism and the Technic.* New York: Carl Fischer, 1967.

Wall, Joan, Robert Caldwell, Tracy Gavilanes, and Sheila Allen. *Diction for Singers.* Redmond, WA: Pst...Inc., 1990.

Ware, Clifton. *Adventures in Singing: A Process for Exploring, Discovering, and Developing Vocal Potential.* Boston: McGraw-Hill, 1998.

————. *Basics of Vocal Pedagogy: The Foundations and Process of Singing.* Boston: McGraw-Hill, 1998.

Weir, Michele. *Vocal Improvisation.* Los Angeles: Advance Music, 2001.

Westerlund, H., and M. L. Juntunen. "Music and Knowledge in Bodily Experience." In *Praxial Music Education: Reflections and Dialogues,* edited by D. J. Elliott, 112–22. Oxford: Oxford University Press, Inc., 2005.

Wright, Rayburn. *Inside the Score.* Delevan, NY: Kendor Music, Inc., 1982.

Yanow, Scott. *The Jazz Singers: The Ultimate Guide.* Milwaukee, WI: Backbeat Books, 2008.

Zegree, Stephen. *The Complete Guide to Teaching Vocal Jazz (Including Pop and Other Show Styles).* Dayton, OH: Heritage Music Press, 2002.

Zemach-Bersin, David, Kaethe Zemach-Bersin, and Mark Reese. *Relaxercise: The Easy New Way to Health and Fitness.* San Francisco: Harper-Collins, 1990.

INDEX

Page references for figures are italicized.

entrepreneurship (for singers), 255
epigastrium, 13, 64, 70
epiglottis, 5, *6*, 7, *9*, 78
Eustachian tube, *16, 17*
exercise (physical), 24–25, 32, 37, 47, 60
exhalation, 12–15, 21, 36, 63–65, 70, 225–26
expression, 58, 66, 75, 82, 86, 87, 105, 110, 120, 124, 126, 127, 135, 142, 143, 144–48, 185, 186, 187, 188, 193, 199, 200, 231, 236, 261–62, 265, 271, 273, 276–77
extensions (chord), 212–14
extrinsic muscles (of the larynx), 10, 11, 54, 222

Feldenkrais, 48, 54, 60, 190
"Fine and Mellow," 131
Fitzgerald, Ella, 84, 90, 104, 115, 117, 120–21, 122, 123, 131, 142, 144, 206, 234–35, 263
flow state, 236
"Four Brothers," 129
formants (vowel), 90, 92–94
free improvisation, 132–33
free jazz, 106–7
frequency, 11, 18, 20, 21, 90–91, 93, 150

Gershwin, George, 120, 132, 141, 142
glottis, 8–9, 69, 225–26
Great American Songbook, 66, 120, 142, 143, 159, 160, 240, 263, 264
Gunn, Nathan, 50, 77, 98n1

Hartman, Johnny, 104–5, 143
Hawkins, Coleman, 106, 110–11
head arrangement, 242
hearing:
    aids, 17, 19; loss, *16*, 17–18, 33–34, 254; protection, 18, 19, 34, 153
hemisphericity, 215–16

Hendricks, Jon, 129, 132, 182
Hertz, 20
Hi-Los, 182
High Society, 263
Holiday, Billie, 82, 109, 127, 130, 131, 140, 158, 209, 262
Horowitz, Vladimir, 265
"How High the Moon," 120–21
hydration, 10, 23, 25–26, 267
hyoid bone, 5, *6*, 7, *8*, 10, 59

"I Got Rhythm," 132. *See also* Rhythm Changes
improvisation 107, 119–34, 148, 173, 175, 181, 183, 187, 190, 194–95, 197–98, 202, 210–16, 218, 235, 242, 244, 262, 263, 264, 268; Dalcroze, 189, 197–98, 278–79; lyric, 130–32, 278; scat, 92, 104, 105, 107, 112, 119, 120–27, 128, 129, 159, 176, 178, 197, 206, 219, 262, 263; text-based, 127–28, 140, 158, 262, 278–79
incus, *16*
infrahyoid muscles, 11
inhalation, 9, 12, *14–15*, 21, 48, 50, 63, 64, 65, 70, 71, 198–99, 225, 226, 227, 228, 275; gesture of, 13–14, 65–66, 278
inner ear, *16*, 17, 19, 123, 127, 176, 178, 180, 187, 202, 208, 213
interarytenoids, 7, 8, 11
intercostal muscles, 12, *14*, 64, 65, 66, 67, 69, 225, 227, 278; external, 12, *14*, 21, 65, 275; internal, 12, *14*, 21, 65
intrinsic muscles (of the larynx), 8, 10, 11, 54, 222, 266

jazz language, 99–107, *114*, 115–18, 123, 133
Jobim, Antonio Carlos, 102, 103, 108, 120, 142

ABOUT THE AUTHOR

Dr. Tish Oney began singing jazz professionally as a teenager in Central New York. Since then she has enjoyed an active lifelong career as an international jazz performer, light lyric soprano, recording artist, composer, and professor of jazz and voice. Having released her fifth critically acclaimed jazz album, *The Best Part*, in 2019 on the Blujazz label, Oney has augmented her busy singing career arranging jazz, conducting, and authoring books and articles about music. Earning a doctorate in jazz studies from University of Southern California's Thornton School of Music and a master's degree in voice performance from Ithaca College School of Music, Oney has taught music at eight universities and colleges and has served as artist-in-residence at several more. She has performed as soloist with the Detroit Symphony Orchestra, Williamsburg Symphony, Rochester Philharmonic Orchestra, Symphoria, Spartanburg Philharmonic, the U.S. Army Voices and Army Blues, and the Jazz Ambassadors. Pursuing a dual career in performance and pedagogy, she earns widespread recognition as a headlining jazz singer and master teacher of voice, musicology, and jazz. She presents master classes on multigenre singing for the National Association of Teachers of Singing, as well as choral workshops, musicology and jazz theory lectures, and jazz concerts at professional venues throughout the world.

An avid author, she has contributed articles to the *Journal of Singing*, *Classical Singer Magazine*, and *JazzTimes* and writes a popular jazz column called "Anatomy of a Standard" for *All About Jazz*. She serves on the editorial board for the peer-reviewed journal *Jazz Education in Research and Practice*. Oney's first critically acclaimed book, *Peggy Lee: A Century of Song* was published in 2020. She has been featured as a guest on international media outlets including CBC, NPR, PRI, and Talk Radio Europe as well as the Grammy Museum. In addition to her performance and scholarly work, she has joyfully served churches as a Minister of Music. For more about Oney see tishoney.com.